UNCORRECTED ADVANCE PROOF

Title:	**WHEN EERO MET HIS MATCH:** *Aline Louchheim Saarinen and the Making of an Architect*
Author:	Eva Hagberg
US Publication Date:	September 2022
ISBN:	9780691206677
Pages:	248 pages, 6 1/8 x 9 1/4

D1613404

Agency/Agent info: N/A

For additional information or questions, please contact:

Jodi Price, Senior Publicist
Tel 609-759-8136
jodi_price@press.princeton.edu

PRINCETON UNIVERSITY PRESS
41 William Street, Princeton, NJ 08540
(609) 759-8222 Phone, (609) 258-1335 FAX

In Europe contact:
Kathryn Stevens, Publicity Associate
kathryn_stevens@press.princeton.edu
Princeton University Press
6 Oxford Street
Woodstock, England
OX20 1TR
Tel 609-759-4905

WHEN EERO MET HIS MATCH

Aline Louchheim Saarinen and the Making of an Architect

Eva Hagberg

A uniquely personal biographical account of Louchheim's life and work that takes readers inside the rarified world of architecture media

Aline B. Louchheim (1914–1972) was an art critic on assignment for the *New York Times* in 1953 when she first met the Finnish-American architect Eero Saarinen. She would become his wife and the driving force behind his rise to critical prominence. **WHEN EERO MET HIS MATCH** draws on the couple's personal correspondence to reconstruct the early days of their thrilling courtship and traces Louchheim's gradual takeover of Saarinen's public narrative throughout the 1950s, the decade in which his career soared to unprecedented heights.

Drawing on her own experiences as an architecture journalist on the receiving end of press pitches and then as a secret publicist for high-end architects, Eva Hagberg paints an unforgettable portrait of Louchheim while revealing the inner workings of a media world that has always relied on secrecy, friendship, and the exchange of favors. She describes how Louchheim codified the practices of architectural publicity that have become widely adopted today, and shows how, without Louchheim as his wife and publicist, Saarinen's work would not have been nearly as well known.

Providing a new understanding of postwar architectural history in the United States, **WHEN EERO MET HIS MATCH** is both a poignant love story and a superb biographical study that challenges us to reconsider the relationship between fame and media representation, and the ways the narratives of others can become our own.

Eva Hagberg teaches in the Language and Thinking Program at Bard College and at the Graduate School of Architecture, Planning, and Preservation at Columbia University. Her books include *How to Be Loved: A Memoir of Lifesaving Friendship* and *Nature Framed: At Home in the Landscape*. She lives in Brooklyn.

SEPTEMBER
9780691206677
248 pages. 6 1/8 x 9 1/4.
BIOGRAPHY | ARCHITECTURE

When Eero
Met His Match

Friday, July 17, 1953 and all the next golden days and nights until August 5, 1953 and it was during that most unbelievable and wonderful and beautiful and perfect time that we became "spiritually married", henceforward to be husband and wife...

When Eero Met His Match

Aline
Louchheim
Saarinen
and the Making
of an Architect

Eva Hagberg

PRINCETON UNIVERSITY PRESS
PRINCETON AND OXFORD

Copyright © 2022 by Eva Hagberg

Princeton University Press is committed to the protection of copyright and the intellectual property our authors entrust to us. Copyright promotes the progress and integrity of knowledge. Thank you for supporting free speech and the global exchange of ideas by purchasing an authorized edition of this book. If you wish to reproduce or distribute any part of it in any form, please obtain permission.

Requests for permission to reproduce material from this work should be sent to permissions@press.princeton.edu
Published by Princeton University Press, 41 William Street, Princeton, New Jersey 08540
In the United Kingdom: Princeton University Press, 6 Oxford Street, Woodstock, Oxfordshire OX20 1TR

press.princeton.edu

{~?~Jacket/cover art credit here, for both front and back covers}

All Rights Reserved

ISBN 978-0-691-20667-7
{~?~FULL CIP TO COME}

British Library Cataloging-in-Publication Data is available

Book design by Monograph / Matt Avery

This book has been composed in Lyon and Pilat

1 3 5 7 9 10 8 6 4 2

10 9 8 7 6 5 4 3 2 1{~?~DES: Please delete printings line that's not needed}

FOR PAUL

Contents

Preface

In the summer of the year 2015, I started two projects simultaneously. One was the first chapter of what would become this book, a venture about Aline Saarinen, whom I always identified, to anyone I was speaking to, first as "wife of the Finnish American architect Eero Saarinen" and second as "the first architectural publicist." The second was a five-year career working as a high-stakes, secret, exclusive, and reticent architectural publicist. Both of these projects happened almost by accident. The first I began when I was a master's student in architectural history at UC Berkeley, finishing a master's thesis on an *Architectural Digest* article about Angelo Donghia, an interior designer I had never heard of before somehow writing a ninety-page thesis about him, and I stumbled across a set of letters written from Eero to Aline, and Aline to Eero. The second I began when a friend, a photographer, recommended me to a pair of architects with an office on Lombard Street in San Francisco, who were looking for a website copywriter. We had a phone call, and I agreed to rewrite their text for one thousand dollars. This was a huge amount of money then, considering my graduate school stipend worked out to $1,400 a month, and I knew the work would be fast and easy. What I didn't know is that the one phone call, and finding those set of letters, would change my life for the next six—at least—years.

I had a meeting with the designers, and they asked if perhaps I'd be interested, given my career before grad school as an architectural critic and design writer, in taking on a position closer to marketing. They felt underappreciated and undervalued in their field, and they thought I might be useful in getting them some good publications. I did not disabuse them of this notion; rather, I started name dropping, mentioning my friends at the *New York Times*, my friends at the design website Curbed, my friends at *House Beautiful*. They asked me to write a proposal, and I wrote one in the office, on my laptop, and then emailed it to them, sending my desires across the room and through the air. I asked for $5,000 a month to be their editorial director. I didn't like the term PR rep, even though that's basically what I was, because of the way in which designers, editors, and writers can often still view PR reps: as flacks who don't understand anything about buildings, who send awful and boring press releases about sofas, who can't be trusted. To my somewhat surprise, they agreed, and we signed a contract a few days later. They were my first clients in what would become a three-person business that had revenues of $400,000 a year at one brief and glorious point, a business that I just shut down in order to focus on writing this book, a business that, by the end of it, I mostly couldn't stand doing. It was a business that was based on using all of my narrative and theoretical skills, all of my media contacts, and all of my scholarly acumen in helping to guide and shepherd a number of high-end residential architects' careers through the media. My selling point to them? That I was deep into learning about the very first architectural publicist and was very literally the world expert on the relationship between the visual and the narrative in architectural publishing. The way that I justified it to myself? That I was doing research.

In the summer of 2015, I was also undertaking another project—one to do with my health. After getting married that spring, I'd suddenly become allergic to my home: first just my bedroom, which had pockets of mold growing on almost every surface, then my entire apartment, and then, seemingly, the city of Oakland. A few months after getting married, months I spent living in my in-laws' living room because I was allergic to their basement, I left Oakland for first Palm Springs and then the desert. I landed in a rental house in Sedona, where my then-husband eventually joined me, and from there I launched these two projects. I mention this dislocation because it was relevant; I felt desperate to make money however I could, desperate to pay for medical treatments that would help reduce what felt like an allergy and a sensitivity to the entire world, and so I was willing to do anything. I was also in the odd in-between of comps and dissertation draft. I'd taken my qualifying exams in May 2014, a year after I'd had a major brain surgery, and I'd sort of been a bit of a problem student ever since. I was perennially delaying things, I'd left the architecture department because of forces that felt beyond my control, and I felt intellectually adrift. My solution was to work with my advisor, Margaretta M. Lovell, on coming up with an interdisciplinary topic. So, here I was: majoring in an invented field, Visual and Narrative Culture; living in a tent; trying to figure out how to start writing about Aline Saarinen; and representing these architects' interest in the media, which mostly meant sending Dropbox links to my old friends and asking if they might want to cover this. Some combination of rest, sleeping outside, medical experimentation, and time worked. After six months, I was well enough to go back to the Bay Area, where I started seriously writing, kept teaching, and kept expanding my business.

By the time I wound the business down, I had finished the dissertation, and had represented one of the top architects of the twentieth and twenty-first centuries (by his estimation, but also in some ways the press'). I had dealt with clients who got overly close to me and then suddenly pulled back. I was fired, over email, by a client who had felt like one of my most stable connections. I'd had two of my clients say, to a third friend, that they needed to take me out to dinner to talk about my attitude, until my attitude changed. I briefly had a client who liked to bully me over email and text, who demanded that I come to Napa in the middle of the 2017 fires, and who texted me thread after thread when I didn't respond within ten minutes (even though I'd explained to him that I was still teaching, and busy). I'd worked with a client whose wife disliked me so much that I eventually quit because I couldn't deal with her. I had hired two colleagues, both of whom I'd met at Berkeley, and we had figured out, together, how to work as a team. I incorporated, and put myself and them on actual payroll. I made us SEP IRAs and insisted that they contribute and that I match 3 percent. For a few stunning months, I had enough money to put some of us on health insurance, including my colleague's dependent. When we lost two clients at once, I had to lay her off and hire her as a contractor, until I could eventually hire her back as an employee. It was an odd time. I didn't have a business degree, but I was running a state business, and I kept learning only by totally screwing up.

Once, I sent an image I shouldn't have sent to an editor and it ran in a magazine and I had to take the heat. Another time, I sent an image I shouldn't have sent to an editor and it ran on a website and I had to take the heat. Sometimes, I sent the wrong Dropbox link to the wrong person. "Thanks for offering to send B___'s project, but this is actually E___'s," I would get back. Sometimes, I said that something was exclusive when it actually wasn't. Once, I was so nervous about publishing a project, so afraid that my client would fire me if I didn't place it, that I quickly submitted it to a local magazine after having already submitted it to a national. (The nationals always come first, those are just the rules.) The local magazine editor said she loved it, right when the national one wrote back to say he also loved it. But had anyone else seen it? I had to tell him—yes, a local editor had seen it. "Then it's a pass for us," he said. Even just the act of sharing the image with someone else had been enough to kill the project, even though he liked it. I tried to save face with my clients by saying how great it was that it would be in this local magazine, and how wonderful it was to have gotten it in front of the national editor. I didn't think Aline would have bungled this quite so badly.

Much of my job was to assuage the egos of fragile architects. I worked with mostly men, and mostly men in their fifties and sixties. Many had recently started doing full-scale houses, which most architects don't get to do until their fifties and sixties, and they often exhibited the combination of fear and ego that is rampant in the field. I found that much of my job was as a helpmeet, that I was meant to be someone to reassure them and comfort them and say that it was so unfortunate that this idiot writer didn't really understand what they were doing, but that next time I would try and find a nonidiot writer. (Reader, there were no idiot writers.) I sometimes met these men's wives, and they would look at me first with suspicion, wondering why their husbands spent so much time on the phone with me, why I was invited to the celebratory dinners. I felt often as though I was crossing an invisible boundary, not sure exactly how I was crossing it but still sure that I was. Once, I wrote a wedding speech for a client whose daughter was getting married. Had that been in my contract? No. But I had presented myself as someone who was not only intellectually but also emotionally indispensable. I had built this company, which only I could run, on a cult of personality—the cult being me. I said that I alone could do this. Yes, I had partners, and colleagues, whom I trusted completely, and whom I wanted my clients to trust just as much, but I understood that I was the face. That I was the brand.

I didn't really have someone I could call for advice; the people who did what I did were my competitors, and the one time I'd tried to reach out to an old friend who did this kind of work, she'd balked at giving me any kind of concrete help. But it didn't matter. I had another mentor. Someone whose practices I could copy and someone whose methods I could adopt. She was dead, but that didn't matter to me. She had worked in the 1950s, when email obviously didn't exist, and the architectural community was in some ways different (though in many ways the same), but that also didn't matter to me. What mattered was that I spent years tracking the ways in which she manipulated editors, writers, photographers, and eventually her own client—her husband. What mattered was that every single bit of trouble she got into, she got out of. What mattered was that as I was researching the life and work of Aline B. Louchheim Saarinen, while running an architecture PR company, I started asking myself, at every turn, What Would Aline Do?

My colleagues understood my enthusiasm. They understood my work. They saw the role that she played in my imagination, in my occasional distraction, in my sometimes asking them to handle things because I was trying to finish this project. And they understood that they too needed to ask themselves, whenever we were in trouble, what Aline would do.

This is a book about Aline Louchheim Saarinen, and it's a book about the architectural publishing world of the twenty-first century. It's a book about learning about this extraordinary woman's life for reasons that were about love, and marriage, and partnership, and togetherness—and it's also a book about working in architecture. I have been in the field since 1999, when I started college at Princeton University and realized I wanted to major in architecture. I started writing about architecture professionally in 2003, and published two books about architecture before I went to grad school. The books had pictures, so we aren't sure if they count, but the arguments were sound, the introductions solid. I was a member of an architectural journalism crew in the early 2000s, a group of us who met up at seemingly every lunch for Renzo Piano, every party for a new chair held at the Center for Architecture. We hugged and shook hands in person, we discoursed with each other in print. Briefly, I ran an anonymous architecture gossip blog that remains the most professional fun I've ever had, and then I ran one not anonymously, until it was shut down in the 2008 recession. I have been in the architecture world since I was seventeen, and before then I was the child who read every book about modern architecture I could find, the only twelve-year-old I knew who could differentiate Le Corbusier from Mies van der Rohe. This has been the water I swim in for half my life.

This is a book that aims to explore what about Aline was so compelling, and to trace how what we still do today is in so many ways influenced by her methods. And it's also an academic project, one that aims to revise the way in which many historians have done history. I noticed, in graduate school, that many of the texts I read and the arguments that I encountered were based on the idea of the press as a neutral agent, an actor that indicated the inherent value of an architect. The basic idea seemed to be: x person was written about frequently, therefore x person deserved it. But because I'd worked in journalism, because I'd been on the receiving end of so many carefully crafted invitations and pitches, because since Aline codified a role she originated personally into professional service, because every major architect has had a press representative, it felt like I could see behind the curtain. I understood that images were embargoed, that quotes were given only when fully controlled. It felt like I was reading a history that missed a major actor, and I wanted to correct that oversight.

We will time travel in this book. We will look at how stories are published now, and how things happened in the early 2000s, and in the 1950s, and through it all we will follow a few threads. We will track the relationship between architecture and text, between images and narrative. We will look at how a woman in the 1950s pretended to be goofy and forgetful so as to expertly advocate on behalf of her husband's interests, and we will look at how that performance still echoes today. We will look at my career representing architects, and all that that meant, and I will draw the curtain back on the design media. I will show how it works, and how it worked, and how it works the way it does because of how it did. I will tell a love story, between Aline and Eero, and between myself and the three people I loved while I was working on all the iterations of this project. It is impossible to pretend that I didn't come to this because I was falling in love when I first read their letters, and because I wanted to absorb some of their creativity, and their love, for myself. This will not be a book that pretends towards abstraction, or objectivity. Because, of course, while writing about Aline, while living with her voice in my head for years, I fell in love with her too.

Introduction, or, How to Read This Book

This is not a book of architectural history. Yes, there will be buildings, and yes, there will be architects, but what I seek to do here is an intellectual history slash personal story, and as such I would like to lay out my methodologies, and the reasons behind them.

My primary archives are the Smithsonian Archives of American Art, which holds voluminous correspondence between Aline B. Louchheim and Eero Saarinen, as well as between Louchheim and an assortment of other interlocutors, such as *Architectural Forum* editor Douglas Haskell; editors at Random House; *New York Times* architecture critic Ada Louise Huxtable; and more. I have read every single one of these letters, and from that process have meticulously reconstructed Louchheim and Saarinen's early courtship—following dates to the best of my ability, for they rarely dated their letters—and attempted to follow the threads forward as much as possible. Their correspondence began in February 1953 with their meeting so that she could write about him for the *New York Times*, and continued nearly unabated until their marriage in 1954, when, due to increased physical proximity, their personal letters began to lessen. I also used the Yale collection of office correspondence, which gave me a thorough understanding of the ways in which Louchheim and Saarinen began to enter into a new type of discourse, one based in finding their way through a coherent and collaborative professionalism, and which ended only with his early death of a brain tumor at sixty-one.

I became interested in using letters, as opposed to buildings, as a primary archive for a number of reasons. While I received my master's in architectural history at UC Berkeley, and am therefore trained in the normal science of architectural history, which emphasizes an analysis of buildings, drawings, images, and so forth, my PhD was in an inter-disciplinary field of my own creation called Visual and Narrative Culture. I was drawn to approach my independent work from an interdisciplinary perspective because of my interest in the overlaps between the visual and the narrative, and in the ways in which my own career as an architectural writer had unfolded. I had noticed that I often wrote from and to images, that I was rarely asked to visit a building in person (when I was, it was a special treat); and that when I wrote to and from images I thought about words differently than when I didn't. I also noticed that words had the power to influence how I looked at a building, or an image of a building. I began to wonder if there were perhaps an iterative relationship between the visual and the narrative; if Louchheim had actually influenced the way the shape and form of Saarinen's buildings were perceived through the language that she used. There are models for this in contemporary practice. Caroline Bos, an art historian employed by the firm UNStudio in Rotterdam, is the closest to Louchheim in terms of her role, which is to collaborate with her architect husband Ben Van Berkel and offer a com-pletely different lens and viewpoint than a designer would offer. I myself have been in romantic relationships with artists and found that my ability to tell a story has been something that has shaped not only how they have seen their projects once done, but how they conceptualize their projects while they're happening. I am invested, therefore, in language as a mode of framing and articulating a visual experience, as opposed to relying on more typical historical methods and ideas.

I was asked once if I particularly liked Saarinen's architecture, and I have to confess that I am totally agnostic. This agnosticism comes not from not caring, or not wanting to care, but from the fact that I cannot actually see his buildings clearly—they are visible and legible to me now, having read all of these letters and all of Louchheim's interventions, only through her narrative lens. I cannot imagine seeing the TWA Terminal at JFK, that swooping bird, without thinking instantly of the brochure that Louchheim produced that referred to the building as a bird, and then without thinking almost as instantly of Saarinen's resistance to that met-aphor, and of her insistence that it was a good one. My very first archi-tectural history class gave me a language to understand the visual world that I saw around me, and I remember after a few weeks of class walking around campus and feeling like the world was louder and brighter. Sud-denly I realized that what I had simply thought of as a slab was in fact a pediment; that a line of windows along the top of a building was a clerestory; that an S-shaped arch was an ogee. It felt like the visual world had been suddenly newly activated by this acquired language, and it was that experience that compelled me to keep writing about architecture and to keep thinking about it from a narratively oriented vantage point. Thus this project, and its emphasis on the narrative. I do not want to analyze Saarinen's forms, as others have done that—and so well. I do not want to weigh in on his contributions to the corporate campus, or to college campuses, because my interest here is not in the primary evidence of his buildings, but in this secondary layer—Louchheim's stories and words— that have so far been almost entirely overlooked.

Thus my reliance on the archives that I chose, and the way in which I chose to use them. I also—and this was pointed out to me by my colleague Caroline Riley during a Berkeley Americanist Group meeting— wanted to use these archives as visual documents in and of themselves. It is as though I am following a thread that continues to iterate between the material/visual and the narrative, and I went from the narrative in terms of the language used in the documents to analyzing them visually. I wanted to pay attention to when a letter was typed and when it was handwritten (Louchheim almost invariably typed hers, sometimes on *New York Times* stationary, particularly when, I hypothesize, she wanted to remind Saarinen of her power; Saarinen almost invariably wrote his in scrawling longhand); I wanted to think about the sketches and drawings that Saarinen often added to his; to the use of inside jokes like the "clauses-of-caution" they alluded to frequently as a means of protecting their relationship from outside forces beyond their control, the use of brackets around ideas they were still forming, all of which mix the visual and the narrative. Some might wonder if this approach is perhaps airless, or almost suffocating in its depth and focus. But I found that this was the only way that I could truly make sense of the material: by thinking about the first layer as a way of understanding what had happened when two people got together, and the second layer as a series of visual documents that added depth and weight to the interaction. This is after all the heart of my argument—that in this case, particularly, and also in many other cases, design and language become interstitial to each other. Iterative. I want to argue that the role of language and narrative in architecture and design is not a postgame description of something that exists in some other pure form before it is activated through language, but in fact a constitutive element of design. That even though viewers of Saarinen's buildings might not have known exactly when and where Louchheim wrote that the TWA Terminal was a bird, they thought it was a bird because of the way in which she'd introduced that idea into the press and therefore the popular culture. I argue that their viewing of the building as a bird in fact makes the building a bird. I believe that the way in which we are taught to look at something—that pediment, that clerestory, that ogee—profoundly changes our experience of the visual referent, and that is at the heart of this project.

This book asks us to do a number of things. It asks us to believe that it is worthwhile to understand two people who were in love in the 1950s because it teaches us something about love (always important), and also creative collaboration. It asks us to suspend certain disciplinary boundaries that we may have thought were necessary—that any work that deals with architecture must look at buildings and analyze their value or weight or power. It also asks us to think broadly across time, to wonder how one person can influence another both through time and professionalism, and also more directly. It has consistently asked me to ask myself why Aline Louchheim has had such a hold over me, and it has asked that I continue to return to the source, to the endless letters that she and Saarinen wrote to each other. It has asked me to make intuitive connections that can feel like leaps, and it has asked me to trust that there is an evidentiary needle in a haystack even when it feels like I'll never find the perfect moment. To some readers, this evidence may feel circumstantial. Historians have been trained to look for the smoking gun and in this case, there isn't one. What there is, and what I have found by reading so much, is a series of patterns that have begun to emerge, a gentle and gradual wave of involvement, and a sense that even as this is a story about two people who thought about architecture together, this is also a story about all the ways in which architecture can be thought about. All the ways in which love can be thought about.

It is my hope that in the same way in which their love story compelled me to keep reading the archives, their love story will compel readers now to muscle through whatever doubts and concerns they might have about how this book was put together, and to continue reading so that we may, together, begin to think through what it means to produce architecture, what it means to work together, and what it means to talk about something that we want to talk about.

CHAPTER ONE

Women in the Design World, Then and Now

Many years ago, when I was working as a full-time architecture and design writer, I was in a relationship with a sculptor and art fabricator. We met at an upstate sculpture park, right next to one of his works. It was made out of thousands of pieces of wood, painted black and glued together. It was riveting and fascinating and unusual and I'd never seen anything like it, and while I was staring at it I noticed a tall man, who I thought was handsome, and somehow I thought to ask him if he'd created it, and he said he had, he was the artist, and we chatted for a bit and then he asked if I was staying for the party that night, and I said probably not, and he looked me directly in the eyes and said, "You should stay." That moment became the foundation of our romantic partnership, which lasted a year and a half. I left the person I was living with and moved in with this man, whom I'll call Charles, and, never having heard of Louchheim, never having thought about Saarinen, I appointed myself his publicist.

He had a gallery in Chelsea, but I thought he could have a better gallery. He'd been written about, but I thought he could have been written about more. I was also a food writer for a small New York City magazine, and knew the editors, and figured that if I pitched something about him to them, they would bite. When we met he was preparing for a big solo show, over ten pieces, with a central sculpture that was similar to something he'd made before—but this one, instead of being made just out of white Styrofoam, would be made out of Styrofoam with metallic mirrors glued to every visible surface. I wasn't sure about the aesthetic but he hadn't asked me to weigh in on it, so of course I didn't, wouldn't. I was there, I understood, to help get him published, even though—he would point out later—he had never asked me to. I just thought this was what women who were partnered with artists did; we helped their work get in print. We used our powers for them.

When the show came out, the magazine I was working with did cover it. I remember one day calling him, the hour after I learned that the magazine did want to cover him, and I was telling him that he had to get them a hi-res image, and immediately. "I'm having a hard time hearing you," he said. "You're talking too fast and too loud." I was so excited, so convinced that this was going to be an article that was going to change his life—and therefore mine—forever. I was tied to his career success. I know that Aline didn't have the same need, the same desperation not to be left—she once wrote to Eero that he was in competition was thousands and thousands of lovers—but I felt something of what I would later learn was her drive in me then. I slowed down enough to tell him what needed to happen, got over my own sense of absolute urgency, and the article came out and not much happened. He didn't sell any pieces at the opening, nor did he sell any after. We blamed his gallerist, though I wanted to blame him. I didn't think this new set of projects was as good as the ones he'd made before. Maybe he could return to paper?

A few months later I had an assignment from *T: The New York Times Style Magazine* to write about one of Oregon-based architect Brad Cloepfil's upstate New York houses. I went up with an editor and writer named Pilar Viladas, and we traveled around the property in a golf cart. We talked a little bit, but I was so aware of her power as the design editor at *T*, which was one of the hardest bylines to get, that I had a hard time relaxing. I wasn't even sure how I'd gotten the assignment, it had just happened, and it felt like this was a career maker to me. After I filed the story, the commissioning editor said they'd like to feature me on the contributors page—which was a chance for me to highlight my own accomplishments, talk about future projects I might like to do, and so on. What I chose to do instead was highlight my then-boyfriend's accomplishments. I gave them an image from one of his projects from the show, the central one, which I hadn't thought was that great, and then I wrote something like, "Eva Hagberg lives in Brooklyn with ___, a sculptor."

I think about it now and I'm embarrassed, and ashamed, and horrified, that I gave up this valuable media real estate to support him, but I also don't think that it was just me. I think that the culture had set up an expectation that my power, however limited it was, was meant to be shared with him. That as the supportive girlfriend, the supportive protowife, it was reasonable and understandable for me to use that space to promote his work instead of mine.

There is, of course, a long history of women collaborating with men on projects. I think of Alice T. Friedman's wonderful book, *Women and the Making of the Modern House*, in which she outlines, in careful and deliberate and also nuanced and inspiring prose, exactly how necessary six women were to producing masterpieces of modern architecture.[1] I was an undergrad from 1999–2003; when my mother asked me if I encountered sexism at Princeton, I said of course I didn't, that sexism was something from the '70s, that perhaps she had experienced it but of course I certainly hadn't. In 2019, I gave a quick talk with the *Architectural Record* editor and fellow Aline Louchheim Saarinen biographer Cathleen McGuigan about Aline, and was asked if I thought she'd been a feminist. I'd assumed the entire time I was working on this project, which is on its face an explicit feminist project, that of course she was. But on reflection, and with careful prodding from the questioner, the writer Suzanne Stephens, I came to realize that Louchheim was not particularly feminist. She did not use her position to advance other women, or the general cause of women. She flirted and used her femininity to get what she wanted. Of course she did; that was the option available to her at the time. She became one of those "exceptional" women, like Ada Louise Huxtable. Her role had to be peripheral, just as Friedman shows Edith Farnsworth's had been.

Despina Stratigakos has written probably the best book about women in architecture, called *Where Are the Women Architects?* She illuminates the long history of women being left out of practice, beginning with an account of a 1902 article by the editor of the magazine *British Architect*, who concluded that women should not practice architecture.[2] A swift survey of the twentieth century shows that not much has improved. In 1972, only Robert Venturi was awarded the Pritzker Prize, architecture's highest honor, a choice that overlooked his wife and essential collaborator Denise Scott Brown. As a side note, when I taught at Columbia a few years ago I spent a glorious morning in the archives and was able to see an early version of the book *Learning from Las Vegas*, full of Scott Brown's notes, ephemera, physically cut and pasted sections. It's impossible to see that version of that book and not understand how deeply influential she was. As Stratigakos points out, history did catch up, and in 2013 a Change.org petition was launched, arguing for Scott Brown's retroactive award of the medal.[3] Only five women have won the Pritzker Prize since its introduction in 1979, and of these, two of them have been in partnership with men. There are, in 2022, very few female-led firms that don't involve a male partner. I can think of Zaha Hadid, Jeanne Gang, Galia Solomonoff, and Annabelle Selldorf. Up until now, a majority of female architects have worked paired up with their male spouses, who were often seen as the real architects. Just recently I was talking with a female architect friend of mine, who works with her husband. She said that it was crucial for them that they always design together and then say publicly that they do everything together; otherwise, she said, it was too easy for people to assume that she chooses the colors while he does the real design work. This was in 2020!

Friedman's book, *Women and the Making of the Modern House*, looks at the role of clients. I wonder to myself if maybe in another world some of these women could have been architects—as their involvement was far more gripping and creative than simply signing checks and letting the men do what they wanted to. Rather, Friedman "convincingly argues that these independent women acted as major catalysts in the general development of twentieth-century domestic architecture."[4] I remember when her book came out, and how astonishing it was to those of us who had been taught the canon through the lens only of the architects who'd designed the houses. Yes, we knew that the Vanna Venturi House had been done by Robert Venturi for his mother, but the way we were taught to see that was simply that his aged mother had let him do whatever he wanted. I certainly don't remember being taught that the Farnsworth in Farnsworth was a woman, let alone a single woman who went to medical school when there were still caps on female students, and supported herself as a doctor. Annmarie Adams, in her review of Friedman's book, argues that what Friedman is doing is in a sense "dissolving the field," requiring us to look at these canonical structures with an entirely new lens, whereas the majority of feminist contributions to architectural history have been about including the contributions of women, in a sense expanding what we see through the existing lens.[5] That is what I want to do here: offer the same illumination of the media that Friedman invites us to do with buildings. Where Friedman's focus is on encouraging us to see projects like Farnsworth or the Schröder House entirely differently, so that we can also see the history of modern architecture differently, my aim is to use this analysis of Aline's work with Eero so that historians of both the second half of the twentieth century and today can look at the press differently.

How many stories have we told ourselves about how modern buildings were created in which the woman have an additive or adjunctive role? And to how many male patrons of architecture have we given such tremendous value? It is also important to note examples of women who played similar roles to Louchheim, such as Maria Stone, the second wife of midcentury architect Edward Durell Stone; Olgivanna Lloyd Wright, wife of American modernist Frank; Ise Gropius, wife of Bauhaus architect Walter Gropius; and Ethel Power, partner to Eleanor Raymond.

Mary Anne Hunting has shown how Maria Stone's influence on Durell Stone's career in some ways mirrors what I argue Louchheim did for Saarinen. Similarly to our heroine, Stone "not only understood the power of the image and had an uncanny knack for publicity, but she knew that in the world of celebrity their private life was 'consumable merchandise,' an observation which she 'used to their advantage.'" Hunting offers the example of one of his buildings being named the "Taj Maria," which Hunting argues is a form of "personality advertising."[6] It is clear that Stone's influence was extraordinary, and yet I differentiate what Aline did for a number of reasons. Aline's identity as a writer and *New York Times* reporter and her history writing about architecture and design make her much more of an equal professional colleague than it appears Stone was for Durell Stone. I find a difference between being a wife who has an uncanny knack for getting publicity by selling details of a private life, as Stone did, and what Aline did—which was to leverage her connection with the press and most importantly her understanding of architecture in order to promote Saarinen's *work*. Hunting offers examples of ways in which Stone participated in Durell Stone's design process, but the quote she uses, from a 1959 article in the *Washington Post*, is illuminating. "He wanted the whole house modern, but after they had argued for two weeks, she saved the beautiful, wood paneled Victorian drawing room. Now, he admits, she was right. . . . 'Maria is Italian and likes marble,' explains Stone. 'We have white marble floors, red velvet and crystal chandeliers.'"[7] The feeling here is one of a nonexpert helper, someone who has facility in an entirely different professional world (publicity); whereas the feeling that I will show through the close analysis of the working letters between Eero and Aline is entirely different, one of two colleagues discussing architecture. I want to be careful here in not denigrating Maria Stone, or casting her influence to the side. It is not that. What I am doing is articulating a difference between the roles that they played and the formal expertise that each of them demonstrated.

There is also of course the famous example of Olgivanna Lloyd Wright, who wrote a book about her husband, the architect Frank Lloyd Wright, that was published in 1966 and whose title in some ways mirrors the one that Aline wrote about Eero in 1962.[8] Olgivanna was Wright's third wife, and started the Taliesin Fellowship with him in Wisconsin in 1932.[9] Heavily influenced by spiritualism and her mentor, George Gurdjieff, Olgivanna was instrumental in bringing a sense of cosmic experimentation to Taliesin and her relationship with Wright, as well as his with the Fellows, as the apprentices who came to learn architecture with him came to be called. Her relationship with Wright wasn't as professionally articulated as Aline's was with Eero. The narrative that has generally been shared about her is that she was a young woman from Yugoslavia who fell in with a confusing crowd and brought Wright into a world of orgies and weird sex stuff, often with the Fellows. Her contributions have generally not been taken seriously by scholars or historians; her contributions have, instead, been seen as mostly personal, sometimes managerial (she ran the Foundation from his death in 1959 until hers in 1985), and she has often been subtly or unsubtly criticized. She does not hold the same respectable reputation that Aline Saarinen does; neither when she was alive, nor now. In fact, the salacious book *The Fellowship*, which was published in 2006, finally codified what had been whispered about for years—and shows us the kind of attention that she received.[10] Her obituary, published shortly after her death by the *New York Times* (where it took the top headline over the deaths of a concert pianist, TV actress, ex-state justice, and Nobel Prize Winner), referred to her as "the matriarchal ruler of Taliesin," as well as an "outspoken defender of her husband's work, seeking to protect it from wrecking balls and owners bent on changing his facades and interiors."[11] References to her control over Wright's legacy, particularly at Taliesin and Taliesin West, in Scottsdale, Arizona, show her reputation as an extreme personality: "She presided over a community shuttling between Wisconsin and Arizona like the abbess of a medieval cloister."[12] Here we see a difference in her representation and also how powerful her personality was seen as being—but that all of the attention was about her personality, not what she did for Wright, as well as the control she exerted. While Aline exerted similar levels of control, she was able to manipulate representations and articulations so that she continued to appear helpful—perhaps by being less overtly controlling and pretending to screw things up.

We also have Ise Gropius as a comparison figure. She was the wife of Bauhaus founder and architect Walter Gropius, and a writer and editor in her own right. As Katy Kelleher observes, "Had she lived today, we might view Ise as Walter's equal." However, she "was born at a time when women were expected to stand behind their men, championing their causes, typing their manuscripts, and making their dinners."[13] Kelleher recounts how Ise tried to kickstart her own writing career by submitting an essay to the *Atlantic Monthly* arguing for women's right to work, but was roundly rejected. "From there on, Ise did not seek to publish her own writing, and instead switched her focus to editing Walter's articles."[14] While she remained a crucial supporter of Gropius's work and a necessary contributor to their "New England Bauhaus" home, she never separated herself intellectually from her husband the way that Aline had both before her marriage to Eero, and after. We will see later Aline's displeasure with how much of her work became about Eero, and how hard she worked to dissociate and distance herself, wanting to return to her own intellectual projects. Furthermore, Aline's submissions were, rather than rejected, almost invariably accepted. Ise may have wanted her role to be closer to Aline's, but despite living near parallel lives in many ways, her reputation was both contemporaneously and posthumously much more tied to her husband. The final jab comes in Kelleher's observation about Ise's obituary, which mentions Walter Gropius in every single sentence, bar the last, about who survives her.[15] The implication in Kelleher's analysis is that perhaps Ise could have been less subdued by the *Atlantic* editor's rejection; we may never know what truly led her to stop trying to do her own work. But what matters is that she did.

Perhaps the closest example to Louchheim is Ethel Power, the editor of the design and architecture magazine *House Beautiful* between 1923 and 1934. As Nancy Gruskin writes in her analysis of Power's influence on the architect Eleanor Raymond's life, "at the forefront of Raymond's adult life was Ethel Power."[16] Gruskin acknowledges that "personal relationships are not standard subject matter in most studies of women architects," which speaks to me to the canonical way in which we've been taught to ignore personal lives. Gruskin argues that perhaps this omission is because of the idea that either women architects "had to work too hard to have lives outside the office" or that "their private lives were of no consequence to their career."[17] This is part of the idea that I am attempting to dismantle in this book—that private lives are of no consequence to a career. Of course private lives are of profound consequence; as I have said and will say again, much of my motivation for doing this particular work and thinking about Aline was because of personal drives, personal desires and hopes and dreams that I was mediating through my scholarship. Gruskin dances around the question of whether Power and Raymond's relationship was romantic as well as platonic in the vein of "Boston marriages," where two single women partnered for a companionate life together. Gruskin outlines how Power's "actions revealed her powerful attachment to Raymond." Over the course of her tenure at *House Beautiful*, Power supported Raymond's work, and invited Raymond to write for the magazine from time to time. Gruskin also argues that Power's assumption of "wifely" duties such a household responsibility, arranging travel itineraries, and keeping up with correspondence allowed Raymond to have "the time and the energy for a full-time career in architecture."[18] This model will perhaps most remind us of Aline, though as Guskin points out there is a lack of archival evidence indicating the actual nature of their relationship and whether it was a romantic or platonic partnership. That shouldn't matter that much except that this book is also about the ways in which love and work can intertwine, how partnership can come in multiple forms. We also do not know exactly the extent of Power's interventions into Raymond's career, and whether she did the kind of intense editing and interlocution that Aline did for Eero, or more directly aimed to get Raymond published. Either way, it's important to understand that this kind of helpful partnership has existed in other forms, but that Aline still remains a trailblazer.[19]

Back in New York, living with the sculptor, I was able to come up with a plan for controlling my then-boyfriend's career because by that point, I'd been a freelance architecture and design writer in New York for four years. When I graduated with a degree in architecture that I'd gotten despite being absolutely unable to draw, represent ideas visually, or build models (I was told, later, that I was one of the best critics and talkers and that's how I skated by my otherwise horrific pinups and reviews), I got a job as a research assistant to Philip Nobel, a longtime architecture writer. He was writing a book about the World Trade Center reconstruction process, and needed someone to help sort through press clippings (which were actually physical documents back then), come to press events, and generally think ideas through. He offered me $100 a day, which at the time seemed an astronomical fee, and I enthusiastically moved to Manhattan with a duffel bag full of clothes and a dream in my eyes. I figured that, on the side, I'd start contributing long essays to theory-heavy architectural publications like *Log* or *Any*. I figured that writing about architecture professionally would feel similarly to how writing papers had felt—that I would self-assign thorny intellectual problems and then work them out, submitting them to journals. I didn't really wonder about how I would make money; this $100 a day felt like enough to sustain me for at least a year, and then I'd figure something else out.

That said, I became interested in his magazine writing career. He wrote a column for *Metropolis* magazine called Far Corner, and he also wrote almost monthly for *Architectural Digest*. He was on every press list, invited to every celebratory event and opening. He became my mentor, the person who showed me how it all worked, who got me my first writing assignments, and who read all of my early drafts. He introduced me to his editor at *Metropolis*, Martin Pedersen, who assigned me an almost-unwritable story about a German football stadium's tech-wizard lighting design. Little did Martin know that I spoke German and had a total advantage. The assignment was meant, I found out later, to be a nearly unwinnable test—something that would get Philip to stop telling Martin how much Martin needed to commission me. In the meantime, I'd gone to a party at Storefront for Art and Architecture, where I'd had an internship my junior year, supported financially by a one-time gift from my grandmother in Germany, and had met Cathy Lang Ho, who was then the editor in chief of a brand-new publication called the *Architects' Newspaper*. She asked if I might like to write for them; I said yes, of course. I also met Andrew Yang, a writer and editor who at the time worked for the magazine *Print*, who assigned me a profile on an artist named Anton Ginzburg. An hour before my interview with Ginzburg, I went to a Best Buy in Union Square and bought a tape recorder that held an actual cassette tape. Working on these three assignments, I started to understand how important it was that I go to parties, that I make friends.

Lang Ho assigned me a piece on the unveiling of Reflecting Absence, the young architect Michael Arad's winning submission to the World Trade Center Memorial competition, which had received a tremendous number of entries. I'd been able to attend the unveiling because I'd gone as Philip's research assistant, and I was suffused in the world of the memorial. I drafted a long story, much longer than I'd been assigned, because

I didn't yet know the rules—that writing long was actually offensive, not helpful; that it was my job, not the editor's, to work out what the story was. I submitted it over the weekend, and received some edits that didn't make much sense to me but that Philip helped me navigate, and the story was published on the front page of the *Architect's Newspaper* later that week. I was working as an editorial assistant three days a week for Philip's publisher, Metropolitan Books. The day my article came out, Philip faxed me the front page so I got to see my name in print. It was an extraordinary moment, and I wanted the rush again, and again, and again.

My Ginzburg piece was edited and came out in *Print*, and then my German stadium piece came out in *Metropolis*. I went to the Barnes & Noble in Union Square and saw that there were three publications on the newsstand that had my name in them. I remember thinking that finally I mattered in some profound way—that there was a way in which I was beginning to contribute to the discourse. My professors who I felt had judged me and wondered why I was in architecture school suddenly wanted to take my calls—and I offered to come by for studio visits. Philip introduced me to everyone he knew and told them to commission me; I had a meeting with then House & Home editor Michael Cannell at the old *New York Times* office, before they moved into the massive new Renzo Piano building, and he commissioned an article that ran on the front page of the section, for which I read an entertaining book by Dorothy Draper and tried to throw a dinner party. Soon, he started offering me assignments for Currents, which was a short weekly digest of design news, and it felt, once again, like I had arrived. Reading Aline's letters, so many years later, I felt her thrill of attending garden parties for people like the architect Philip Johnson. While I of course never met Johnson, I attended similar parties—the opening of a garden that Bette Midler was in charge of, which I wrote about for the *New York Times*, an event with the Italian actress Isabella Rossellini. I started getting on press lists, and started understanding exactly how buildings and projects were parceled out to magazines, and most of all I learned about publicists.

That had been the missing piece in college. I remember wondering how the news happened, how it was decided that this person would be in this magazine. I would read *Architectural Record* and *Metropolis* and wonder how it was that editors found these stories. Because until that point my only pieces had been commissions, I'd just assumed that there was some magical repository of information. I realized, too, that a lot of my colleagues and friends had no idea how pieces were selected to be in magazines. I also didn't understand the idea of the exclusive, not yet—but I noticed that, except for rare exceptions for public projects by total starchitects, no two magazines ever featured the same house or project.

The first publicist I met was Elizabeth Kubany. Philip told me to email her because of my piece about the World Trade Center reconstruction; all he told me was that she represented SOM, a massive firm that I'd heard of, who were somehow involved in the project even though Daniel Libeskind had won the competition for the redesign. I sent her a very formal email, addressed to her first and last name, asking her for some information about the project. I mentioned Philip's name, which he'd told me to do. She wrote back to me, generously and helpfully, and I incorporated the information she'd given me into my story. I figured that she was helping me—that it was taking time out of her day to give me a quote from SOM partner David Childs, or a press release. I also, probably also through Philip, met Andrea Schwan, who was similarly helpful. Eventually Liz and I met in person and she asked if I wanted to come on a press trip to Israel, because someone else had dropped out. There were not that many design writers who could take a ten-day trip on two days' notice, but I could.

That first press trip changed everything for me. I had no idea who was sponsoring the trip, or what a press trip was, but I soon found myself on an airplane, headed for Ben-Gurion Airport. I knew that we would be looking at the airport, which SOM had recently redesigned, and that we would also be taking a trip to Yad Vashem, recently designed by the Israeli-Canadian-American architect Moshe Safdie. I don't remember who else was on the trip besides Richard Cook, who was the executive editor of *Wallpaper**, which I'd probably seen on newsstands but didn't know much about. Richard and I hit it off because I'd gone to boarding school in the United Kingdom, and he spent most of the week making fun of me and I spent it making fun of him and by the end of that trip, I had the assignment to cover Yad Vashem for *Wallpaper**. I don't know who sponsored the trip still, but I would guess now that it was a combination of SOM and the Israeli tourism board, whom I believe we met. I do know that I had almost no free time, that there was a sense that I was there to somehow tell everyone I had an assignment.

It's easy to talk about the golden years of something, but those years were truly the golden years of media. Press trips happened almost monthly, and I started being sent all over the country to write more stories for *Wallpaper** and *Metropolis*. Sometimes, all I had to do to get a huge trip, like to Art Basel Miami Beach in 2006, was interview Zaha Hadid for a tiny piece for *Metropolis*. Once again, I was starting to realize that in a way, as a journalist, I was partly the collateral—that I was being asked to show up for parties and dinners, and I started to realize that the PR people weren't just there to be incredibly helpful to me, they were there to make sure that their clients were written about.

2006 and 2007 were the absolute pinnacle of my career. I was friends with lots of publicists, who sent me projects on a near-weekly basis that I learned to pitch to *Metropolis*, the *New York Times*, *Wallpaper**, the *Architect's Newspaper*, and more. I was being invited on national and international press trips to places like Miami, Chicago, Moscow, Switzerland. All I needed to do for those was demonstrate some willingness to pitch a project, though sometimes the publicists asked for confirmed assignments. You weren't supposed to do that, it was understood, and you certainly couldn't do that if you were pitching the story for a place like the *Times*, but even the *Times* understood that freelancers needed to get access to stories somehow, and that we couldn't actually refuse unrelated press trips. That policy has completely changed now, but back then, it was fine. I got on the lists of other publicists, and they would ask me what kinds of stories I was looking for, and it was a constant whirlwind of pitching and paying attention and writing. I remember interviewing Isabella Rossellini in a Mandarin Oriental hotel room. A publicist friend who'd connected me with John Hardy, a jewelry company in Bali, to write about their new bamboo school (which of course I had to see in person, on the company dime), had asked me to come interview her and pitch something to the *New Yorker*. I told him I didn't have any contacts at the *New Yorker*, was unlikely to place anything there, but was happy to try. He gave me a name tag that said "Eva Hagberg, *New Yorker*." I realized only years later that he had been doing his job for his client, the Italian government. That in that case, it was not Rossellini that was the prize, but the *New Yorker*—and that I was close enough.

There's a great scene in the movie *Interview*, where an actress, played by Sienna Miller, meets a reporter assigned to profile her, played by Steve Buscemi. She asks him, "*Newsworld?*" He says, yes, "**from** *Newsworld.*"[20] It's a tiny distinction, but one that resonated with me. Because that's how I started to feel, often. I had these friends, these contacts, who seemed to want to know everything about my life and what was going on with me, but they also really wanted to know what "outlets" I was writing for and if they could pitch me projects that I would then pitch up the ladder. Friendships started to feel transactional, and I participated. Yes, I wanted to know about their lives, but I also wanted quick access to the architects they represented; to be the one with the killer project. I needed to write about buildings to make money to live, and so I needed the publicists as much as they needed me. After a while, it all blurred together so much that I became disoriented; I wasn't sure who was my friend and who was my professional contact, and who was, which was rare, both.

Sometimes, though, I wasn't the prize. Sometimes I had to slowly come to realize that I was being fended off in favor of a better writer, a stronger byline hit.

For example: in 2006, a restaurant named Momofuku Ssäm Bar opened in the East Village. It was David Chang's second restaurant, after Momofuku Noodle Bar, where I'd started going to lunch because it was right around the corner from my downtown Manhattan apartment. I'd also shifted a bit into writing about food, and had a monthly column for *CITY* magazine. Ssäm Bar had been opened with this sort of plan that it would be a Korean burrito place during the day and after ten it would turn into a chef's restaurant, aimed for cooks getting off shifts and other industry types. The menu featured Tennessee ham and veal head terrine and tiny perfect pork buns, adopted from the Noodle Bar. The restaurant was almost always empty, which is unimaginable now, and I started going after ten, sitting alone at the long counter, ordering glass after glass of wine, and getting to know the staff. After a few visits, I noticed that I was starting to be sent comps from the kitchen—whether they knew I was a food writer or not, I don't know. I started going maybe once a week, often staying after closing time, getting to know the chef de cuisine. After a few months the restaurant started picking up, and I realized that I wanted to write about it for my food column. I asked the manager if he'd be amendable to my hanging out for a day and writing a sort of "day in the life." He was friendly, and kind, and said that while he appreciated the interest they were really trying to stay dark on press. They just wanted to focus on running the restaurant the best they could. I was disappointed, of course, but it also made sense to me. Maybe they would want press in a year or so. A few weeks later, the *New Yorker* came out with a huge story about the restaurant, and I realized what the manager had been doing. It wasn't that they wanted to be dark on press. It was that they had to maintain the *New Yorker*'s exclusive, and turn all other press down. It was the first time I really felt the weight of an exclusive, and felt the way in which my value as a writer for *CITY* magazine was less than the value of the writer for the *New Yorker*.

That's what was happening with architecture too. Writers were being positioned. I understood suddenly why, when I went to a group press lunch, people were seated where they were seated. When I was there on assignment for a magazine like *Wallpaper** I was often seated to the architect's right. If I was there with *Metropolis*, depending on who was organizing the lunch, I might be seated a little farther away. There were writers who seemed to play by their own rules on junkets. I recall going Miami Beach one year, and being put up at the Shelborne—as part of Art Basel Miami Beach, or maybe Design/Miami—it all bled together. One editor in our group said that he always stayed at the Standard but would be happy to catch up with us. It was clear he wasn't paying for his room. Was he playing two publicists? I think now, yes. I had also told some hospitality publicists that I was in Miami, and they turned out to be representing a hotel down the street from where I was staying. Did I want a massage, they asked, just to try out the spa? Of course I did! So there I was, in Miami, on a free trip sponsored by someone related to Art Basel Miami Beach, while getting a free massage from another PR company. It was ridiculous. It couldn't last. But it taught me, much later, how to become a publicist. And it taught me what to look for when I was deep in the Saarinen archives.

What does this all have to do with Aline Saarinen? A lot. It's crucial for historians to understand how the media and publication ecosystems work now, so that we can know why it's so important to pay attention to how it used to work. The practice of publishing (and doing!) architecture has shifted from a gentleman's profession where advertising was banned to a well-oiled machine that relies largely on buying writers things—whether that's meals, trips, or thank-you gifts—so that they keep thinking fondly, well, and top-of-mind about the architects that they might later write about. Of course we were supposed to keep our independence. Of course we were never supposed to be swayed by any of this. But after I wrote about the then-young firm AvroKO, who didn't have a publicist and who pitched me themselves, for the *Architect's Newspaper*, I was sent two massive jeroboams of champagne and a lovely thank-you note. I ended up putting two or three of their projects in my design book, *Dark Nostalgia*.[21] Would I have pushed as hard for putting three of their projects in if they hadn't sent me the champagne and the thank-you note?

I want to write about these examples as a way of beginning to frame my analysis of Louchheim's behavior. Later, I'll write about what it was like when I started working as a publicist, though by the time I did that I'd already been reading about her. There's a temporal loop happening here, where I began researching this project because I felt like the way that I'd learned to cover architecture hadn't ever been written about by anyone. Early on in graduate school, on one of my very first days, a group of us were asked to give mini presentations on buildings. One of my colleagues presented a house in India designed by the global firm Perkins&Will. She observed that there was only one rendering that had ever been published, and hypothesized that the reason for this was something theoretical. I realized that I knew exactly why only one rendering had ever been published, which is that the architecture firm was holding on to the exclusive, probably for a magazine like the *New Yorker*, or *T*, and that my colleague just hadn't yet seen that article because it was still embargoed. Embargoing was what happened when we were sent images or information and told we weren't allowed to publish or mention them before a certain date. If we broke the embargo, as writers, it was clear that we would never be given a project again—and that was the publicists' leverage. We'll see later how Aline used leverage like that, icing one editor out while inviting another one even closer. What was shocking to me was that my professors agreed with my colleague's argument—and seemed not to be aware of what had probably actually happened. I don't know that history is ever supposed to be project of figuring out what "actually happened" but it did seem to me astonishing that so many people were in the dark on how this ecosystem worked.

That's when I realized that I wanted to write this book and research this project. In some ways, some of what I argue or have written is a process of retroactive fitting in of an argument. I know that there have been other art publicists, writing publicists, and I will include a brief history of publicity here just to lay the groundwork. But Louchheim was working in a time when architects were just beginning to adopt these sorts of methodologies, and she was truly the first who combined her absolute understanding of how the media worked with an understanding of architecture. That's what sets her apart from the other female partners of architects, whether they be the personality-driven mainly organizational partners like Olgivanna Lloyd Wright, or the editor Ise Gropius, who wasn't able to penetrate the media in the same way. Aline was the precursor for people like Elizabeth Kubany, who studied architecture at the Architectural Association in London and worked at *Architectural Record* before becoming a publicist. She was also the precursor to someone like me, who went from working in the design field to studying this field from a historical and theoretical perspective, to working as a secret publicist. I was so effective because, just like Aline, I'd spent time in the trenches as a writer, I understood the importance of editors and pictures and embargoes, I respected the process. I also had the intellectual backing to charge very high fees.

So, this book emerged from a number of strands of inquiry and interest. When I originally proposed the project, I was in the school of architecture at UC Berkeley, which I left in favor of a more interdisciplinary field, one that I devised. I assembled a team of scholars—an American historian, an Americanist in the History of Art Department, an American Studies professor, an English professor, and a professor from Architecture. In order to justify making my own program, I needed intellectual backing, so I developed this interdisciplinary project, arguing—as I still argue—that only through these multiple lenses could this story be adequately told. I did not want to write a book about buildings, or about architecture. I wanted to write about love, and also self-fashioning through the epistolary, and also life writing. I'd taken a nineteenth-century life-writing seminar with David Henkin, the American historian, and I saw that there were traces of history and theory in what we talked about that would be essential to my project.

   I was used to the rules of academia, the way in which I'd been judged when I first arrived for my history as a journalist. Academics tended to see journalists as lazy, quick thinkers, people who just skated above the surface of things, whereas they, scholars, where the ones who went deep. I adopted this internalized journalism-judgment, which is part of why writing this book feels like such a reclamation of the power of the closely observed first-person narrative. I wanted to be a good and serious scholar, and I also believed, and still believe, in how powerful it can be to write about something intimate so as to expose the grand scale. Still I wasn't sure where this project would land. Was it a work of history disguised as a work of art history? A memoir disguised as a biography? Now, it finds its own form as I write this section on an August morning in a hotel room in Lower Manhattan, where I've come for a five-day self-created artist's residency because hotel rooms are cheap in a pandemic and no one wants to stay by Ground Zero right now. Two days ago, after I'd written four thousand words, I left my room for a break, and walked to the memorial.

   I thought about that first article I wrote about Michael Arad, the process of reporting on the memorial progress—on the selection of Arad, then an unknown architect, and his design for two reflecting pools. Thinking that the way to make a name for myself was by being snarky and critical, I'd critiqued his design and his ideas. I'd made fun of Calatrava's Oculus, which I still think looks like a stegosaurus. But this August morning I walked and just rested at the edge of the North Tower's pool, and I saw what Arad had been doing. What happens with the depression in the center of the fountains, the fact that you can't really see what's going on or where the water is going. The way in which sometimes, when it's windy, the water droplets hang in the air, millions of them. The names of the people who died, each one of them a full life. I realized that I do love architecture and have always loved architecture and that the project of this book was to explain a little bit about how it worked so that maybe we could somehow get back to just loving architecture. I wanted everyone to see that sometimes people became famous because someone handled them really well, that there was no real relationship between merit and fame, that we lived and worked in a world that had so many wild cards.

My professors in the architecture department seemed surprised that this was how things worked. But I didn't want to write a project just about the present, because that would have seemed journalistic, or too diaristic even. So I turned to Aline, because she was in the past, because she historicized it, and also because the more I read, the more I saw how instrumental she'd been both in Eero's career and in working with figures like Douglas Haskell, the *Architectural Forum* editor, to start to develop practices like the exclusive, which I'd fallen into thinking was just how things worked.

After putting that committee together, I passed my qualifying exams and then got sick in that chronic and confusing way that made it impossible to travel. A research assistant and now friend, Athena Scott, flew to Yale on my behalf and read hundreds of letters, taking photographs of them for me to read later. There's something to be said there for the digital humanities. I'm describing how this all worked also partially to undo the myth of the idealized scholar, a myth that I still hold up for myself as an example of how a book should be done, and partially to keep demonstrating how much these small details can matter. In the academic world, we don't talk much about how books actually are written into being, how they begin to announce themselves, first quietly and then loudly, and then how they take over the very interior of one's mind.

I'm showing all of this because that's part of the larger argument of this book. I want to pull back the curtain—as I did on how my own writing career developed, and will on how I shepherded the careers of at least ten architects over the next five years—so that we begin to see what a powerful praxis that can be. The construction of architects' fame has relied on people *not* talking about how it's done; on journalists pretending to editors that they simply came across this tiny house in the desert of Tucson, of editors pretending that they don't know that the journalists are being sent jeroboams of champagne or their equivalent. I don't know if the average reader of *Dwell* magazine will know, for instance, the mechanisms both social and practical behind the publication of a Northern California house or a Southern California one. I don't know if the average reader believes that they need to understand exactly how it happened, but in our world, one in which the media is often accused of being post-fact or even non-fact, it's important to begin to articulate the goalposts. And with that, we need to go to the source.

CHAPTER TWO

When Aline Met Eero

It is time to meet our central actors from the past: the architect Eero Saarinen and the writer Aline Bernstein Louchheim, who was at the time of their meeting the associate art critic for the *New York Times*. Their life together was short, from their first encounter in 1953 to Saarinen's death, from a brain tumor, in 1961. They didn't marry until 1954, and so the formation of their relationship took place in its earliest years, a period documented by a series of what I call "working" letters sent back and forth and now held—and digitized—by the Smithsonian.[1] The letters worked in two ways: one, they work for *us*, as later readers, in offering insight into not only the intimate romantic developments between Louchheim and Saarinen but also the general culture in which they both lived, Louchheim flitting among parties in New York and producing a near-astonishing amount of text for her employer, Saarinen at home in Bloomfield Hills, agonizing equally over whether to leave his wife, the sculptor Lilian (Lily) Swann, and how to become famous (and whether doing the former might lead to the latter). Through her near-daily letters to Saarinen, invariably typed and running two to three pages in length, Louchheim began, along with reporting on her goings-on, asking him what he thought of her drafts, suggesting easy ways to get out of his marriage, to articulate a professional position—later called Head of Information Services—that she would come to occupy; this articulation, in its earliest and most fungible forms, offers us an insight into the way in which their relationship was both reflected and, crucially, constituted in letter form. The letters also worked for *them* in that these documents are not simply representative of what they were thinking and feeling at the time, but also iterative: the letters began to formalize and make coherent a series of plans that ranged from sexual to architectural to logistical. Louchheim and Saarinen's epistolary relationship could be seen as the foundation of, or the precursor to, their real-life relationship, although I find intriguing the idea that their epistolary relationship was actually just as real as the in-person one they built later. In some ways, their epistolary relationship was even more real, being the only one available to us; as a writer who works with the past and with memory, I have thought often about how the past exists and how we trick ourselves into thinking we can engage in processes of resurrection. With this process of reading their love letters and seeing the story of their relationship unfold, it is hard not to feel that this is their undocumented relationship and their in-person relationship might have been, in some way, a shadow of this profound literary and intellectual intimacy. Today, when so much of our communication is mediated through correspondence, whether that be text, email, Facebook message, WhatsApp chat, or otherwise, it is easy to think of non-face-to-face communication as a stand-in for a later, or earlier, more truthful, more real interaction. But social media and texts and emails and long typed and handwritten letters are communication. Their language produces the form of a relationship. And it is lucky for me, for us, that so much of what Saarinen and Louchheim experienced early on in their love relationship has been documented for us in this way. It is in a sense then tragic, for our purposes at least, that, once they began living together, they stopped writing to each other (with the exception of some exasperated memos that we'll get into), for their letters are lively, vibrant, playful, and make their relationship feel as tangible as any photograph of them vacationing on a boat.

A series of letters sent and received between 1953 and 1956 demonstrate the rapid pace of their personal and professional relationship.[2] These letters are useful for a number of reasons, some historical and some conceptual. Historically, they demonstrate the teasing out and working out of a particular role that Louchheim envisioned and came to formalize. Conceptually, they begin to ask us how work is organized and described, how collaboration is negotiated, and how love is developed. Throughout this book, my focus will be primarily on Louchheim's letters and words, not on Eero's. And I want to highlight Louchheim's letters to Saarinen for two reasons: one is pragmatic, which is that there are many more of them in the archives; the other is purposeful: this book is really about Aline, and all the ways in which it was her facility with language, with manipulating the press, with using words to begin to produce entire worlds, that had such a profound influence on Eero's career and, eventually, mine—and so many others'.

Fig. 1. Eero Saarinen and Aline Saarinen vacationing on a boat early in their romance. Box 2, folder 23, Aline and Eero Saarinen Papers, 1906–1977, Archives of American Art, Smithsonian Institution.

A Brief History of Eero

Eero Saarinen set up his office in Bloomfield Hills in 1950. Before that, after being educated at Yale and receiving a degree in architecture in 1934, he returned to Cranbrook in 1936 to rejoin his father's firm and the Cranbrook Academy.[3] In 1939, as his son Eric Saarinen recounts, Saarinen married the sculptor Lily Swann, and had two children—Eric in 1942 and Susan in 1945.[4] In 1950, after Eliel's death, Saarinen founded his own office, called Eero Saarinen & Associates. In the early years, those associates were Joseph Lacy and Kevin Roche.[5]

Saarinen in the 1930s was subject to some press attention, though not much—and I hypothesize that whatever attention he did get was because of his connection to his more famous father. An example of the kind of press Saarinen got before he connected with Aline would be a story that appeared in the October 1937 issue of *Architectural Forum*, then the most respected periodical on architecture and design.[6] The issue was devoted to "Domestic Interiors" (a field Saarinen barely touched), and marked a larger cultural shift from the pure modernism of then-famous architects like Le Corbusier to the more human-centered approach that would come to mark Saarinen's work. "While we have not generally accepted the Le Corbusier house, our kitchens and bathrooms, at least, reflect his idea," an unnamed author of a photo essay focusing on good house design wrote. "Moreover, designers are learning that the small interior is not a large one compressed, and that the open plan cannot be decorated like the closed, formal room." The story was accompanied by a small drawing of Le Corbusier's box-shaped Villa Savoye with a large red X through it, next to a simple gabled-roof New England–style farmhouse, this one without an X. The resistance to Corbusier's famous remark, "The house is a machine for living in," was demonstrated through the confluence of these three narratives—the quotation, running along the top of the page, the text, which disavowed Corbusier, and then the drawing.[7]

This is the context of the Saarinen article, which was a single page that appeared elsewhere in the issue and showed a perspective drawing of "a combined living–dining room–study." The design was done "for the *Architectural Forum*," exemplifying a practice of periodicals commissioning design work, exhibiting the keen interrelationship between publishing and practice. Saarinen, who was profoundly ambitious, would have seen the value of being published in *Forum*, even with this relatively small piece with its focus on the domestic, which wasn't where his ambitions lay. The short description that accompanies Saarinen's design gives us a sense of his developing reputation. "Eero Saarinen is the able son of a famous father," the text reported. The rest is pure resumé, listing dates and locations. "He spent 1929–30 in Paris ... from 1931–34 he studied architecture at Yale, where he won medals on Beaux-Arts projects with almost monotonous regularity." We learn here that Saarinen left Yale before graduating, spending a year of travel in Europe and Egypt sponsored by the Matcham Traveling Fellowship. "He is now back in Cranbrook associated with his father, and is also connected with the Flint Institute of Research and Planning, developing a comprehensive plan for that city."[8]

This document is noteworthy for a few reasons, the most striking of which is that there is almost nothing about his work, or his personality. Yes, we are given biographical data that proves useful in fleshing out an understanding of where he was when, but there is nothing of the sort that we see later—stories of Saarinen looking at a grapefruit and being inspired to construct the TWA Terminal in a similar shape, or loving personal profiles.[9] His work was also not yet as formally developed as it would prove to be. Here, he offered a simple three-part structure for a single rectangular space, which could be divided with the installation of screens and the careful layout of furnishings by Alvar Aalto. The only nod to Saarinen's actual design skills were here: "Of deceptive simplicity, the design is a distinguished, and [an] entirely realistic solution of a common problem."[10]

Between 1937 and 1953, when he met Aline Louchheim and our central story begins, Saarinen appeared in the architectural press thirty-two times.[11] Between 1953 and 1964 (I've extended the years past his death to account for the attention given to the TWA Terminal, which opened in 1962), Saarinen appeared in the architectural press 157 times.[12] It's quite an increase.

A Brief History of Aline

Aline Bernstein was born in 1914, attended the well-regarded Ethical Culture Fieldston School in Riverdale, the Bronx, and graduated with a degree in art history from Vassar in 1935.[13] The daughter of "two amateur painters," Aline was taken on tours of Europe and its art as a young child.[14] As the writer and editor Cathleen McGuigan has pointed out, much of Aline's talent as a writer can be attributed to her training at Vassar with the architect and architectural historian (and later, MoMA curator) John McAndrew.

McAndrew "not only taught the history of art and architecture, he redesigned Vassar's art library and gallery, creating the "first modern interior of an academic building on an American campus."[15] Though Aline had graduated by the time those spaces opened in 1937, she saw a precursor in McAndrew's clean design of the Vassar Cooperative Bookshop, which she reviewed as art editor of the student newspaper, noting its Mies van der Rohe chairs, "adapted from Le Corbusier," and a desk by Marcel Breuer. Vassar had a strong link to MoMA—where McAndrew later became curator of architecture—and Aline likely heard both Philip Johnson and Henry-Russell Hitchcock lecture at the college about their 1932 International Style exhibition at the museum, which she well could have seen herself.[16]

Fig. 2. Aline Saarinen bravely holding a snake. Box 3, folder 13, Eero and Aline Saarinen Papers, 1906–1977, Archives of American Art, Smithsonian Institution.

Before she graduated she married Joseph Louchheim, a public welfare administrator (she would divorce him in 1951).[17] In 1941 she earned a master's degree from New York University's Institute of Fine Art.[18] In 1944, she began writing for *Art News*, a publication that chronicled the American art world, becoming its managing editor shortly thereafter. On December 15, 1947, according to her *New York Times* obituary, she "joined

The Times as associate art editor, a post she held until February, 1954 [the year she married Saarinen].” She remained on staff as an “associate art critic” until 1959.[19] She had two sons, Donald H. and Harry Allen Louchheim, both of whose births were also reported by the *Times*.[20]

Her first major appearance in the *New York Times* was a February 4, 1945, news article reporting on the publication of the *Art News Annual*, a special yearly issue of the magazine that contained an article by Louchheim about “The Great Tradition of French Drawing.”[21] In December 1947, her first bylined article appeared. It was a review of the Miller Collection of Modern Art on view at the Wadsworth Atheneum in Hartford, Connecticut, and the article demonstrates her extraordinary facility with language and art history. “There are instances of abstractions based on rhythmic relationships and unmechanical curves,” she wrote. “Such are the Arp wood-relief with its kidney shape and the improvised color areas which make the pattern of the Helion; [and] the animated, bright cut-outs of Stuart Davis.” Later, she wrote, “This kind of abstraction has less direct relation to architecture than the non-objective geometry does, but it parallels the change in the Thirties when generous sweeping curves appeared in building and in bent plywood furniture.”[22] While Louchheim didn’t explicitly reference Alvar Aalto, it is reasonable to assume that she had the Finnish architect’s style in mind. She closed with a call to belief in modern work. “The spectator who is in agreement with the forthright attitude which motivated the Miller Collection may admit to himself, even in this quite different atmosphere, the fertility of such non-objective painting as a starting point for other more functional art forms as well as a coherent structure for other, more complete contemporary, artistic expressions.”[23] Her work was lyrical, accurate, and sharp-eyed; her statements demonstrate both her belief that art should be for everyone, and her keen understanding of the social mores at play in the art world (then and now). She placed her critiques into a historical context, and was able to see the longer and larger arc of a shape or a color.

In 1966, long after she did all of this, she gave a lecture at Vassar on “style.” We see in a long section hints as to the personality that drove her. “Those who have style have met life head-on,” she wrote, “freshly, as themselves and out of the confrontations have discovered what they are, what their values are and are able to impose their form, their order, their style upon experience. They have reshaped it to their own terms, their own desires, their own necessities. They have made it theirs ... and are in command.”[24] This approach, though written with retrospect and after so

FOR A MODERN MONUMENT: AN AUDACIOUS DESIGN

By ALINE B. LOUCHHEIM

"Gateway to the West," the 590-foot-high, 630-foot-wide arch of stainless steel in the design by Eero Saarinen includes a funicular to lead to an observation corridor at the top.

IN BRIEF: EXHIBITIONS IN GALLERIES

much of what we will read about happened, serves to illuminate her essential character, the creativity and spirit and power with which she addressed and approached her life. It was unusual for someone of her age and her gender, at that time, to begin to have the life that she did.

In the 1940s, while developing her understanding of style, she continued to write nearly weekly articles for the *New York Times*, covering such topics as the new director of California's Modern Institute (noting his lack of secondary school teaching about art), and the word "modern."[25] Her style was idiosyncratic, a combination of loquacious and strident, informed and publicly accessible. In 1948, she and Saarinen crossed paths—though in absentia—in an article she wrote about the St. Louis Arch.[26] In typically informed form, the article opens with a large observation about contemporary monuments—that we don't really have them, and when we do, they tend to be rare. Her facility with architectural history is as complete as her facility with art; she described Mies van der Rohe's "now-destroyed monument in Berlin" as an example of "a transformation of brick masonry into a supremely beautiful abstract arrangement of mass and light and shade."[27]

The Saarinen article was designed around an imposing presentation drawing of the proposed arch. The caption read: "'Gateway to the West,'

Fig. 4. Eero Saarinen's prize-winning Gateway Arch, Jefferson National Expansion Memorial, completed 1965. Location: St. Louis, MO. © Wayne Andrews/ESTO.

the 590-foot-high, 630-foot-wide arch of stainless steel in the design by Eero Saarinen includes a funicular leading to an observation corridor at the top."[28] The straightforwardness of the description is untypical of later coverage. The emphasis on numbers—which are generally meaningless unless one has a keen understanding of what exactly a 590-foot-high structure feels like—is to me an indicator that Saarinen didn't yet have what he would have later: a dedicated press agent ensuring that captions would be far more demonstrative and enticing. The image, however, is appealing: a black-and-white sketch that highlights the sweeping curvature of the form.

Louchheim's writing, as opposed to the caption, is far more meaning-ful. "The plan of the Saarinen Associates has made a real contribution to modern architecture," she wrote. "The arch will stand as a noble symbolic monument. The integration of painting and sculpture is one of the happi-est solutions yet devised."[29] Her use of the word "monument" indicates a familiarity with contemporary architectural discourse, as the term was not neutral at the time. In 1943, the noted Europeans J. L. Sert (an archi-tect and planner), F. Leger (a painter), and Siegfried Giedion—an architec-tural historian who had written *Space, Time, and Architecture*—published "Nine Points on Monumentality."[30] The critique/manifesto indicated a few relevant values: for the use of monument as "a link between the past and the future," and "an expression of man's highest cultural needs."[31] The critique was of modern architecture's abandonment of monuments, and the text was a call to collaborative monument-building, one that in-corporated modern architects' emphasis on improving the human condi-tion (through good school-building, for example) with other disciplines: landscape, painting, sculpture.

For the next years, Louchheim's work for the *New York Times* contin-ued mostly uninterrupted, just as, six hundred miles away, Saarinen's work continued to develop. In 1950, when she had been associate art critic for three years, Eero Saarinen formally became Eero Saarinen & Associates (ES&A). It was a move that caught the eye of a *New York Times* editor, Daniel Schwars. In October 1952, after ES&A had established themselves, the assistant Sunday editor wrote a letter to John McAndrew, Aline's modernist professor at Vassar, asking him to go to Detroit, inter-view Saarinen, and produce a profile that also incorporated an analysis of Saarinen's work. Schwars wanted McAndrew to place Saarinen in the context of his own architecture, as well as the development of Ameri-can architecture at the time. The news hook? Saarinen's General Motors project.[32]

It appears, however, that McAndrew was either unable or unwilling. A historian can dream that perhaps McAndrew, instead, recommended his former protégé Aline Bernstein for the story, though she was already writing for the *Times*. But somehow, the assignment shifted writer, and in November, Schwars wrote a memorandum to his colleague Barbara Dubivsky, who worked as an editor at the *Times*, saying that Aline would do the Saarinen piece, filing in January.[33]

•

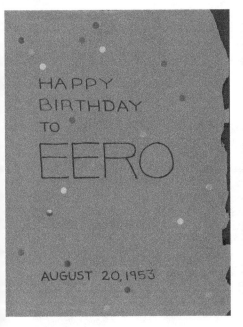
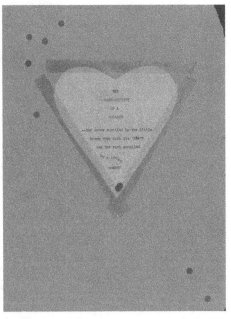

Fig. 5a–b. Front and inside cover of "Case History of a Romance," a birthday card from Aline B. Louchheim to Eero Saarinen, 1953, showing the iterative relationship between images and text the two engaged in. Box 2, folder 22, Eero and Aline Saarinen Papers, 1906–1977, Archives of American Art, Smithsonian Institution.

The love affair between Saarinen and Louchheim is chronicled in a number of historical records. There is a birthday card that she produced for him in 1953, called "The Case History of a Romance," which gives a retroactive accounting of the beginning of their relationship. The card is both textual and visual, giving early hints to the iterative and intertwined ways in which the two of them communicated on multiple levels. There are the scores of letters collected and digitized by the Smithsonian Archives of American Art. In the early twenty-first century, as Saarinen became the renewed subject of architectural focus, a number of popularly accessible articles about their relationship were published. In 2009, the design publication *Design Observer* published "Love & Architecture" by Alexandra Lange, an essay that provides us with a biographical sketch of the beginning of their relationship.[34] The day after Valentine's Day 2015, the architecture website Curbed published a story, "Eero Saarinen's Love Letters to His Wife Are Utterly Adorable," the headline omitting Louchheim's name, demonstrating how even relatively recently, it was Saarinen's identity that took precedence.[35] In February 2016, the popular architecture-related website Archinect published a number of their letters; in 2009,

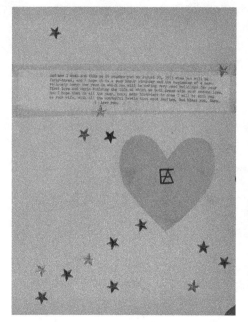

Cathleen McGuigan, writing in *Newsweek*, published a biographical profile of Louchheim.[36] These dates indicate the amount of overlapping attention paid to their relationship. The fact that publications like *Newsweek*, then a serious news magazine; *Curbed*, a now-serious architecture website but then still a publication finding its identity after being founded by the downtown writer and editor (and friend of mine) Lockhart Steele as a way for him to chronicle the goings-on in his Manhattan neighborhood; and *Archinect*, mostly a discussion board aimed at in-school and recently graduated architects, were all devoting time and column inches to the story shows how important their love affair has been in the last decade. However, the stories have been mostly superficial, emphasizing the romance factor and focusing mostly on the visual flair of their cards and correspondence, and missing an analysis of how their relationship functioned professionally and historically.

Their relationship developed at a rapid pace through a series of letters that reveals with great subtlety the melding of work and personal affection. Lest we wonder whether Aline broke up a happy family, it is clear from many letters that Saarinen wrote to his psychologist that he was already considering leaving his marriage to Lily.[37] One letter, written in April 1952, outlines Saarinen's dissatisfaction with his marriage, and his visceral feeling that he should be living a different type of life.

Fig. 6a–c. A selection of pages from a birthday card, "Case History of a Romance," from Aline B. Louchheim to Eero Saarinen, 1953, showing how the placement of text on a page renders a letter a visual as well as textual document. Box 2, folder 22, Eero and Aline Saarinen Papers, 1906–1977, Archives of American Art, Smithsonian Institution.

As he wrote to his doctor, he had dreams that he and his wife could have a cultural connection as well as an emotional one, which had not come to pass with Lily, though she was a talented sculptor.[38] Saarinen seemed to want his wife to be the manager of a sophisticated life. Just as clearly, he wanted more than he had, that is, a cultured wife who would dedicate herself not only to creating and maintaining a fantastically sophisticated and cultured house, but also to being his interlocutor, as he wrote to Dr. Bartelmeier. He had, as he wrote in a later letter, a clear vision of an ideal wife, someone who would understand that his work would come first, and who would remain at all times absolutely bowled over by his talent and his devotion to his architectural success. It is difficult to look completely kindly on these feelings, though we should remember that things communicated to therapists often demonstrate the true worst sides of our human natures; it is important to see, however, how primed Eero was to be swept off his feet, particularly by a woman who would at once provide intense intellectual companionship and always take second place.[39]

Louchheim, meanwhile, was happily divorced, and living it up in New York. She wasn't looking for a husband, having already had one, but rather focused on her career at the *Times*, and keeping up her busy social calendar. It is she who brought an emphasis on the potential professional and artistic possibilities of their connection, and her ability to match what it was he was looking for is almost eerie. We can hypothesize that Saarinen, in the telephone calls that they made reference to, may have openly described what he was looking for; the letters from Saarinen to Louchheim are less direct, while the letters from Louchheim to Saarinen are so direct as to describe themselves as "job descriptions" for the candidate of wife. The relationship between love and work began early for Louchheim and Saarinen, an appropriate mix of personal and professional given the way they met. My account here will be as linear as possible in outlining and demonstrating, from the existing letters, the trajectory of their relationship, but the reader should be warned that the trajectory of their relationship, unsurprisingly for matters of the heart, was not always straightforward.

In early 1953, after they had met but before the publication of the *New York Times* story, Louchheim wrote Saarinen a series of long letters.[40] One particular document itself is undated, but we can place it between January, when they met, and April, when the article was published. They seem to have known each other for just a few short weeks; the letter—which was nominally about some follow-up questions to her article—is full of love and rhetorical flourishes, but it is also about ideas.

"I'm so terribly glad you told me about your work," Louchheim began. "As I told you, I try to imagine what you're working on these various times and how it's going and I hoped you would keep me up to date so that now you can sort of keep me knowing along with you."[41] This idea of "knowing along with you" is epistemologically interesting and pertinent to the questions of this book. The idea that she could—given only narrative/verbal descriptions of his work, through letters—begin to "know" his work (which until this point had been identified only as architecture) opens up questions of what it is to describe, imagine, and know architecture.

Later, she began to pretend not to understand what's being talked about, so as to push her interlocutor. She did it here, as well, in a long passage about his MIT chapel (then under construction):

> The Drake project is indeed very nice, and I like especially the relation of the little chapel to the class-room building.... Of course I know about pure forms, etc. etc., but why not? what's the difference between that and/a facade with a pediment, etc. and a dome behind it? And doesn't this make a kind of culmination out of the relation between the little chapel and the rectangle class-room (which, I am delighted to see, joins the class-room like the dream round-chapels!) Or isn't that true? That's one of the

Fig. 7. Aline Saarinen in a car, presumably on her way to or from a party, undated. Box 3, folder 10, Eero and Aline Saarinen Papers, 1906–1977, Archives of American Art, Smithsonian Institution.

Fig. 8. Envelope sent from Aline B. Louchheim at the *New York Times* to Eero Saarinen at Eero Saarinen & Associates, containing a letter discussing her *New York Times* assignment. Box 2, folder 15, Eero and Aline Saarinen Papers, 1906–1977, Archives of American Art, Smithsonian Institution.

ignorant questions. Will you be patient enough to explain it to me? Also, will you explain more about Milwaukee, which is very intriguing. I think I need a section. It fascinates me. From the Lake I should think it would make a marvelous piling-up mass. Please, more explanation. And what kind of lights on the M.I.T. chapel? That's the most tantalizing remark of all. I could manage to wait until our next weekend to get "fuller explanation department" on the others, but this has aroused my greatest curiosity. So, do write me about that.[42]

This doubling, of performing expertise and then amateurism, could be seen as necessary for a woman of her social and professional stature at the time. Louchheim's career—its breadth and success—was unusual at the time, though perhaps not so unusual as stereotypes of the 1950s imply. Historians have observed that during the 1950s, women "continued to enter the job market and expand their sphere."[43] Louchheim, and her contemporaries like the architecture critic Ada Louise Huxtable and television broadcaster Barbara Walters, were part of this expansion. And yet, despite her professional track record, she still needed to perform this type of nonexpertise in order to, perhaps, assuage Saarinen's ego, as well as to conform herself to gender roles of the time.

On February 11, 1953, Louchheim wrote Saarinen a handwritten letter. She had sent him a draft of her *New York Times* article, and he had responded with twelve editorial suggestions, as well as copious handwritten notes on her typed draft.[44] On the draft itself, he had marked areas he wanted her to cut, and had also made corrections.[45] He also, in the letter, asked her to make changes to specific lines, and then said that he would give her two spanks.[46] The spanks were, of course, a mode of sexual gratification/punishment, and the power dynamic here interests me. She held the reins, as the author. And yet he, by framing his request for her to take out a line (a serious intervention from subject to journalist) this way, and by suggesting sexually charged punishment as opposed to a gentle request, was positioning himself as having ultimately the upper hand. The letter is a seven-page critique of her draft, but Louchheim was gracious in her response: "I am grateful for your comments and they arrived in time, for I will be finishing the piece this weekend," she wrote. "I hope it turns out well—and don't worry about my saying anything that will hurt anyone." The letter quickly turned personal, a shift from her professionalism. "The only part of the article that isn't really honest is the description of you. What it would be if it were honest would hardly be

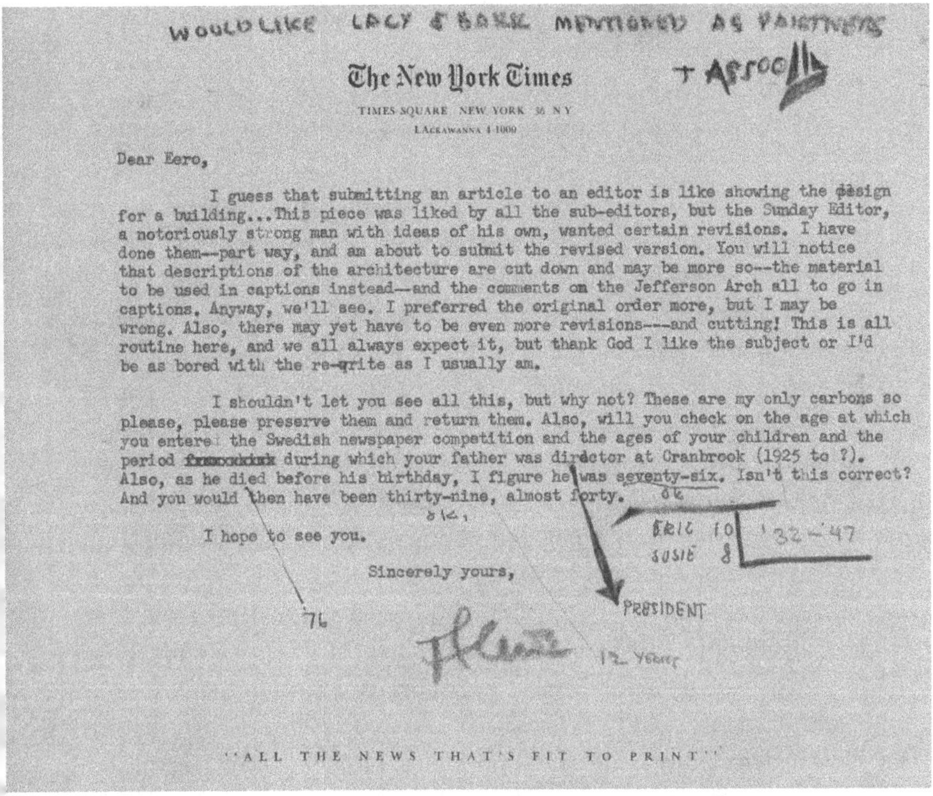

WOULD LIKE LACY & BASIL MENTIONED AS PAINTERS + ASSOC

The New York Times

TIMES SQUARE NEW YORK 36 N Y

LACKAWANNA 4-1000

Dear Eero,

I guess that submitting an article to an editor is like showing the design for a building...This piece was liked by all the sub-editors, but the Sunday Editor, a notoriously strong man with ideas of his own, wanted certain revisions. I have done them--part way, and am about to submit the revised version. You will notice that descriptions of the architecture are cut down and may be more so--the material to be used in captions instead--and the comments on the Jefferson Arch all to go in captions. Anyway, we'll see. I preferred the original order more, but I may be wrong. Also, there may yet have to be even more revisions---and cutting! This is all routine here, and we all always expect it, but thank God I like the subject or I'd be as bored with the re-write as I usually am.

I shouldn't let you see all this, but why not? These are my only carbons so please, please preserve them and return them. Also, will you check on the age at which you entered the Swedish newspaper competition and the ages of your children and the period ~~[illegible]~~ during which your father was director at Cranbrook (1925 to ?). Also, as he died before his birthday, I figure he was seventy-six. Isn't this correct? And you would then have been thirty-nine, almost forty.

I hope to see you.

Sincerely yours,

Fig. 9. Letter from Aline B. Louchheim to Eero Saarinen, discussing her *New York Times* assignment, and showing his handwritten addenda and therefore an early collaboration. Box 2, folder 15, Eero and Aline Saarinen Papers, 1906–1977, Archives of American Art, Smithsonian Institution.

discreet!" She clarified: "I wouldn't have made love with a man who had short legs!"[47]

Publishing the *New York Times* story wasn't enough for her; she already had a plan for what to do next. "I am carefully saving in my files all the business parts of your letters (and the ones from Peter Blake are very helpful) because sometime I do want to do the *New Yorker* article. Yes?"[48] Then, as now, in the hierarchy of cultural publishing, the *New Yorker* is an even more coveted clip than the *New York Times.*

The next letter is on *New York Times* stationery, typed, and only half a page. "I guess that submitting an article to an editor is like showing the design for a building," she began. "This piece was liked by all the sub-editors, but the Sunday Editor, a notoriously strong man with ideas of his own, wants certain revisions." She outlined the material changes to be made, and then wrote, "This is all routine here, and we all always expect it, but thank God I like the subject or I'd be as bored with the re-write as I usually am."[49]

She understood the slippage of journalistic ethics that she was engaging in. "I shouldn't let you see all this, but why not?" she wrote. There are a number of reasons "why not," including journalistic ethics, the perception of source contamination, and general propriety. Her willingness to throw that out with a "why not?" is indicative of the way in which their relationship was already breaking a number of rules. Her signature said only, "I hope to see you. Sincerely yours, Aline," a stark contrast to a previous handwritten note that talked about making love at the St. Regis and mentioned his manliness and broad shoulders. I am interested here in multiple modes of epistolary communication beginning to address different modes of *being*. The historian Thomas Augst, describing diary writing in the nineteenth century, has argued that writing can be a method of beginning to construct the "moral" and also the amoral self, whether in conversation with self (through diaries) or an imagined or real other (through letters).[50] Louchheim's oscillating between the intensely personal—demonstrated by her using pencil on a blank sheet of paper—and the coolly professional are methods of signaling. She may not have had the entire future of her working in Bloomfield Hills worked out (though she began to intimate that as an idea quite shortly), but she had a sense that she needed to represent herself both personally and professionally. The letter is marked with penciled-in responses from Saarinen. At the top, in all capitals, he wrote "WOULD LIKE LACY & BARR MENTIONED AS PARTNERS + ASSOC." At the bottom of the page, in a small and shaky hand are the names and ages of his children—Eric, ten, and Susie, eight. There are hints of this in the tremulousness of the pencil with which Saarinen has written these facts. While, as we know, he was already considering leaving Swann, later letters with Louchheim indicate the level to which he agonized over the breakup of his family.[51] There are hints of that sensitivity in this document.[52]

Many of Louchheim's letters to Saarinen contain accounts of her social life, and demonstrate a social orbit of remarkable complexity and intimacy. "I broke a date with Clifford Odets in order to work on the 'Saarinen' piece," she wrote on an undated Saturday night.[53] She described a concert she attended, establishing herself as an aesthete, and then got down to business. "First, 'the Saarinen piece,' in the journalistic sense, of course," she wrote. The use of quotation marks here presages their later use of "brackets" as a conceptual organizing framework. Her reference to "the Saarinen piece" cleaves its existence into a separate sphere, one that she and Saarinen can occupy parallel to their personal relationship. Louchheim is presenting her performance of professionalism to her editors, and a more personal approach to Saarinen: "[Lester] Markel is adamant that in the revised piece xxxxx [sic] a) there is too much detail about architecture (this should be taken care of in the captions, he says); b) there is not enough emotion, that is, 'the man doesn't seem human enough'; c) the reader would never guess that you had actually talked with the subject. (the 'you' here refers to me—Markel speaking.... It means starting again from the beginning, with a new tone and a new approach and also minimizing the description of the architecture, which I am reluctant to do."[54]

She continued by addressing the strangeness of this double role. "I am in the peculiar position of knowing so much more about him, but having to write as if I knew only what I knew when I boarded the plane late one very pleasant evening."[55] And yet, she admitted, upon rereading, that she understood where Markel was coming from, and planned to rewrite it. "Don't worry, I'll let you see what I've done," she wrote. The letter continued, drifting into a larger professional scope. "Speaking of articles," she wrote, "there is your Yale piece which I read in mss. in your office, but am glad to have. It is splendid. And we must talk of it when next we meet. And there is Miss Gordon speaking up. And I want to listen to you about that."[56]

"Miss Gordon speaking up" must have been a reference to *House Beautiful* editor Elizabeth Gordon's editorial letter, "The Threat to the Next America," which was published in a 1953 issue and which critiqued the presence of International Style architecture in the United States as a style that threatened to move "America toward totalitarianism and communism by way of visual austerity."[57] Louchheim's sensitivity to the issue, shown by her telling Saarinen she wanted to listen to him while also driving the topic of the conversation, was a way of once again demonstrating expertise in this field; she would have understood Gordon's power as editor of one of the top home and architecture magazines, and understood that Saarinen would need to contend with the cultural power someone like Gordon held.

In this exchange we see the earliest glimmers of Louchheim beginning to drop hints that she could become a more permanent professional
interlocutor. Her overtures were subtle, and she continued to perform an
undermining of her own expertise, placing herself in the position of awed
student ready for Saarinen's insight to be bestowed. And yet both of them
knew that her position was one of educated brilliance and professional
high ground. Aware of the power of a confluence of expectations and social performances, on the one hand she was presenting herself as a lesser
supplicant, again consistent with wifely expectations, and then on the
other, reminding him constantly about her professional status—as a *New
York Times* writer, friend of prominent playwrights like Odets.

An undated letter, sent later, continued this inching forward into a professional role.[58] "It occurred to me that among other reasons xxxxx [*sic*,
letters typed and scratched out] that I am lucky is that I met you for the
second and more lasting time at just this period of your life," she wrote.
"I think it's an especially good time for you. It's a sort of beginning time,
really. The beginning to have the chance to do things you want to, to try
ways you want to in your works- enough behind you of real accomplish-
ment to give clients faith in you, and enough ahead of you to allow you to
keep trying whatever you want."[59]

Another letter once again disavowed her professionalism. "I'm not
really happy about 'the Saarinen piece.' It's not really good. You deserve
much better.... I console myself by saying this is just journalism, any way,
and not very important. But YOU are important—and it would be nice if
anything that had to do with you did you justice. I'm better as a woman
than a writer—which, if I have to make a choice—is just as I would want
it. So, even if you get disgusted with A-line the writer, I hope you will continue to like A-line the woman."[60] But then, even with all this emphasis
on how much better she was as a "woman" than as a writer, she reiterated
her professional expertise, "I even find myself worrying about the Boston
contractors and the estimates on the auditorium," a reference to the MIT
building that would be dedicated in 1955.[61]

This process of approach and retreat was repeated throughout her
courtship, both personally and professionally. Louchheim was a consum-
mately sophisticated businesswoman; her sense of networks, timing, and
professional opportunities was, so far as the available archives demonstrate, unmatched. This tension was part of the game, part of the job for
her. A feature, in other words, as opposed to a bug. It is part and parcel of

the same motivating forces that led her to give herself the title "Head of Information Services," a performatively neutral term.

A following letter from the same series, all written early 1953, demonstrated part of her social network, and also her dedication. Describing a party she attended, she wrote about an encounter with "Philip," who must have been the architect and MoMA curator Philip Johnson. "And listened to Philip's description of the chapel he has designed for my alma mater—Vassar. And got secretly VERY angry, because none should be designing chapels now except you, dream chapels any way, and he has a cube and a dome, but obviously no foundation."[62] And then, she started her work. "I talked with Philip about you as an architect ... and Alfred Barr, the angel, started talking about Ottawa and what a nice person you were."[63] The practice of public relations is often overlooked in its simplicity. It is, at its core, the relationship between a person and the public. In this instance, Louchheim was relating to the public—Alfred Barr, the initial director of the Museum of Modern Art in New York and someone who she would have known had tremendous influence over the way in which the contemporary architectural canon was perceived, and Johnson, who was a hub of the social/architectural network in the 1950s in New York, and whose imprimatur would have been valuable. Louchheim understood the importance of name-dropping, the subtle ways in which a person can be "reminded" of another person, which then leads them to want to write about them. Reading these letters, I was reminded of how casually publicists I encountered as a design writer had kept their clients top-of-mind for me, a practice that I later adopted with my writer contacts when I was publicizing architects. Louchheim had already, through this party, begun to take her future job seriously, and her reporting back to Saarinen was a mode of demonstrating value, of reminding him that she was as valuable to him—more valuable—than he was to her. I read some tension in this letter as it closed with her reporting two instances that could have provoked jealousy—"I saw an attractive old beau," and "A writer on the New Yorker brought me home," though she was quick to reassure Saarinen that, respectively, "I didn't act like a debutante," and "I didn't ask him up for a night-cap." Again we see the slippage between personal and professional, between approach and retreat.[64]

Later, she intervened more in his architecture. Describing a project, she wrote, "Your conscious mind is simply an editor. The only thing you changed, as far as I can remember, (for I was in a dreamy half-asleep half-wake mood, too, warm and enclosed and so very much feeling a part of you) was the proportion—for I remember 8 feet, not 12. The 12 is an improvement—that's the disciplined realist."[65] It is the first instance of her directly saying that one architectural decision is an improvement over another, and she immediately countered it by writing "Oh, my dear love——what a very privileged girl I am. This is the way one must have felt when Shakespeare wrote a sonnet to one, or Mozart composed a sonata for one."[66]

Her romanticizing of architecture continued in a later letter, where she began to build upon architectural metaphors. "Darling, it is because I love you in all the many ways, that I say to you, I love you so much. Like good architecture, all the elements are interlocked and interdependent."[67] This mobilizing of architecture as a practice as a way of producing more emotional intimacy speaks to her facility with words and the effortlessness with which she began to seduce Saarinen both personally and professionally.

In a letter stamped "*Received* April 20, 1953," and therefore probably sent a few days earlier, she once again brought up the *New York Times* article:

> When I got the page proof I was furious—for this had been called "Saarinen: Like Father, Like Son" with some equally wrong subhead. I don't usually care about heads, but this time I hit the ceiling and went in to protest to Markel's asst. (The great man is away until Monday). Everyone was surprised at me and one guy said "You usually act like a pro and now you're acting like an amateur" and someone else said "What difference does it make, it's a good head?" But I argued, like a mother hen, I guess, and although it isn't what I really wanted finally settled on "Saarinen: Now the Son" with a subhead reading "A modern architect, following his distinguished father's profession, comes of age in his designs for our industrial era." I hope that's OK with you.[68]

This passage is noteworthy for a few reasons. First, there is the explicit tension between being a "pro" and an "amateur," the implication being that only amateurs have feelings, or "hit the ceiling," or care deeply about headlines. Louchheim's performance of overt and almost theatrical emotionality—using words like "furious" and "hit the ceiling" indicate her signaling of personal vulnerability and "nonprofessionalism" while at the same time she signaled power and professionalism—"I argued … and finally settled on." The title ended up being "Now Saarinen the Son," so we know that there were more edits, but I am more interested in the interpersonal and professional work that this passage does than what ended up happening as a result. Later on, she wrote: "Unless Markel tears everything up, the opening spread is done and I'll finish the run-off page-proofs Monday A.M. and 'put Saarinen to bed' by noon on Monday. Will you still love me?"[69] The "Will you still love me?" feels like a doubling split—a way of referencing their professional connection and the very slim possibility that he was engaging in this love affair in his own public relations effort, but her explicit reference to it in a way disavows its actual possibility. No one would ask that question if they weren't totally confident the answer was "yes."

"I'm terribly anxious to know about the Cleveland speech," she wrote on the next page. "And I wish I had been able to eavesdrop on the office conversation … and then to be in Cleveland and hear you and feel proud of you and watch everyone making a fuss over you."[70] A later paragraph once again explores this tension between personal and professional. In reference to Saarinen's psychologist, Dr. Bartelmeier, Louchheim wrote, "I've begun to think of him as the personnel-manager who has to pass on you before you get the job!"[71] She then imagined "Dr. B's" ideal candidate report. "We find this candidate fitted intellectually, emotionally, and physically to the job. Her background and experience are good and should prove helpful in this situation. … She has a profound respect for the job."[72]

The article was ready to print. "By Thursday I shall have copies—and then, on Friday, you can give me all the additional spankings—for using the picture of you aged nine and for not taking out the ghosts of your father and Matthew Noviski [sic], and my rewards, too, for cutting the sculptors names and the remark about painting and for putting in the 50-year span."[73]

In the lead-up to the article's publication, Louchheim began to plant seeds. "Kimball at M.I.T. was terribly nice and also pleased. He said he hoped I'd come up while it was being built and join the sidewalk superintendents!" she wrote to Saarinen.[74] Here, she has offered herself as a stand-in for Saarinen, placing her own self in between Kimball and the effort of the office, seeing herself as a proxy.

These letters are but a small subset of the hundreds of lines that the two wrote to each other. However, there are a few themes that are repeated: Louchheim's professional and social expertise; her devotion to

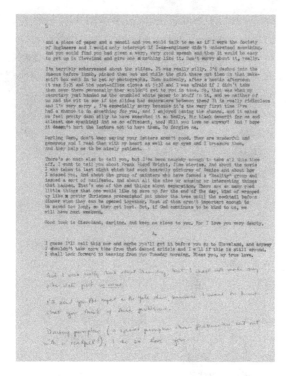

Fig. 10. Letter from Aline B. Louchheim to Eero Saarinen, half-typed, half-handwritten, showing the double layers of epistolary self-fashioning and relating that the couple were engaged in as they navigated a professional and personal relationship. Box 2, folder 15, Eero and Aline Saarinen Papers, 1906–1977, Archives of American Art, Smithsonian Institution.

Saarinen's work; her willingness to understand what his work could be; and her absolute loyalty to Saarinen over even her editors and bylines. It was in these early letters that we can begin to trace her self-fashioning and her beginning to work out what kind of a professional impact she could have on his career.

•

"Now Saarinen the Son" was published in the *New York Times* on April 26, 1953. The byline read "Aline B. Louchheim," and the article appeared in the middle of the Sunday magazine. "First the father, then the son," the article opened. It got quickly to Louchheim's point. "Eero Saarinen is today 42 and is already the most widely known and respected architect of his generation," she wrote, three sentences in. It was a bold claim, but one that she worked to back up.[75]

Saarinen was aware of his peer community. He was also deeply invested in public recognition. "As an architect at the top of his game at 48, Saarinen seemed to pay an inordinate amount of attention to how others perceived him," the historian Pierluigi Serraino has written. "He was indeed independent in his architectural exploration, yet peculiarly dependent on others' approval for his own self-acceptance."[76] On March 16, just over a month before the article was published, Saarinen had written to Louchheim, listing the architects whom he described as part of his subconscious, giving her a sense of the modernist canon in which he wanted to be placed.[77] The list included Saarinen's father, Charles Eames, Philip Johnson, Louis I. Kahn, Harry Weese, Mies van der Rohe, William Wurster, O'Neal Ford, Pietro Belluschi, and Matthew Nowicki. But Saarinen closed the letter by acknowledging that his real list was actually shorter, containing only Mies van der Rohe, Charles Eames, William Wurster, and Philip Johnson.[78]

From a historical vantage point, the omission of Le Corbusier—widely known for not only his modern architecture but his masterful play of the media (as Beatriz Colomina has pointed out)—seems striking, and pointed.[79] The inclusion of Weese, future architect of the Washington, DC, Metro, is surprising only because Weese wasn't yet well known and his work was far more formal and brutalist than that of the others listed, but the rest are all of a piece, though once again geographically spread out, another marker of the relationship between the center that was the East

Fig. 11. Aline B. Louchheim, "Now Saarinen the Son," *New York Times*, April 26, 1953. © 1953, The New York Times Company. All rights reserved. Used under license.

Coast, and the cultural "periphery" that actually occupied much of the geographical center. Of course Saarinen would include his father, with whom he had worked on the First Christian Church in Columbus. The Eameses were old friends of Saarinen and his wife Lily, though Saarinen only referred to one Eames (presumably Charles); Matthew Nowicki's inclusion makes sense given his curved work and recent tragic death, as does Mies van der Rohe's clarity of formal thought—a connection that Louchheim describes in her article as "as strict and classical as Mies in structural clarity, handsome proportions, careful detailing and functional integrity."[80] Philip Johnson was as ambitious as Saarinen, who frequently agonized in letters to his psychologist about how to achieve all that he wanted to achieve.[81] And Kahn's monumentality can be seen in Saarinen's later work, particularly the TWA Terminal.

The point is that Saarinen was not the most widely known and respected architect of his generation, not at the time, and not now. He was known, yes—though mostly, as Louchheim pointed out, for his General Motors Technical Center, and for that he was known mostly in the context of "postwar industrial" American work. And he was respected, yes—that much is clear from his ties to the community and his many commissions. But a public reader would have hypothesized that *New York Times* Associate Art Critic Aline Louchheim was making a valuable and historically accurate pronouncement in the first paragraph of her story, and that this pronouncement should be absolutely taken at face value.

Louchheim took this story as an opportunity to give narrative definition to Saarinen's work. It was an act of creative naming, one that came to influence how his work was seen. "His buildings, which interlock form, honest functional solutions and structural clarity, become an expression of our way of life," she wrote.[82] She would repeat this idea for years.

She returned to the idea of Saarinen's specialness. "He does not serve as his own jury," she wrote. "His respected colleagues—Mies van der Rohe, Charles Eames, Philip Johnson, William Wurster—and the ghosts of both the late Matthew Noviski [*sic*] and his father unwittingly perform that function."[83] If we believe her first paragraph and then this one, Louchheim was openly using the massive muscle of the respected *New York Times* to push Saarinen way ahead of the pack.

Louchheim also signaled professional expertise here, a contrast to the personal disavowal that she expressed to Saarinen in intimate letters. She described the MIT auditorium with compelling architecturally specific description: "The resultant building, a daring modern engineering feat, will be like two clam shells, one above the other. The dome above, of shell-concrete, is exactly one-eighth of a sphere (as thin in relation to its span of 160 feet as one-quarter the thickness of an egg-shell to its area)."[84] The imaginative prowess it took to understand (1) how thin the dome really was and (2) how to go about describing it to a lay reader is a remarkable example of the skill that she had at her command.

Perhaps she could not help herself, or perhaps her editor required it, but the most personally striking moment is her paragraph about Saarinen's wife, Lily, whom we know from her letters she was actively encouraging him to divorce. "Eero Saarinen admires his wife, Lily Swann's, highly original and accomplished terracotta sculpture, especially a fantastic three-toed sloth and a stinging caricature of a friend, which are in their living room.... 'I'm glad Lily has it, too,' he adds," presumably referring to Lily's artistic interests, "'because I'm so little at home.'"[85] It is hard to read this description of Saarinen's home life without thinking of how strenuously Louchheim was pursuing him.

The closing paragraphs can be read as a setup. "Eero Saarinen questions whether he has not let architecture devour too much of his life at the expense of real relaxation, recreation and *domesticity* [emphasis mine]. But one wonders if there could have been any other way for him. He cannot work inspirationally: deliberately, thoughtfully, conscientiously he prods and develops his talent. The drives to prove himself are urgent— and perhaps insatiable—no matter how honored his achievement."[86] Here Louchheim is positioning herself as "the woman who understands," the woman who will not push him into domesticity (even as her personal letters were full of intimations as to their future life together).

This confluence—of press, personal ambitions, and unwritten feeling —is the crux of my argument. Historians have overlooked the personal and often ethically ambiguous relationships that underlay—and continue, as we saw in the first chapter, to underlie—the production of architectural fame and respect, which happens through the media. As historians who often rely on media about the architects we analyze, we have been using a source material that has been influenced, shaped, pushed, prodded, but without a conscious awareness of those influencing forces. Louchheim's proximity to and ambitions for Saarinen may seem like a spectacular example, and I hope that my readers are somewhat shocked to see how intimate this supposedly neutral journalist was with her subject, and also how deeply she has woven her own particular desires, which at times reflect his desires, into documents that could otherwise be taken neutrally as historical evidence. But while their relationship was perhaps more intimate than many of the friendships that spring up now between writers and their subjects, how many articles have we read about architects, on which we based our research, that were written under similar circumstances? How much of our architectural canon, produced by people like Nikolaus Pevsner, Siegfried Giedion, and others, has been brought about through connections formed in garden parties and hashed out over dinners? How much have we been almost tricked, looking into the curtain but not beyond?

It is important to acknowledge here a distinction within journalistic practice between the more cultural approach taken in reviews, profiles, and trend articles than the demands of hard news. Although she would later decline the opportunity to comment on Saarinen's work because of their personal relationship, Louchheim allowed herself to finish this article despite having far too close of a relationship with her subject. The contemporary milieu, however, allowed for that. After the article was published, Saarinen wrote Louchheim a letter, saying how good an article he thought it was, that he was impressed with her work, and that he felt her to be more generous than critical. He also said that she had "made the grade" around the office.[87] Again, despite her having had the actual public power over his career, Saarinen was attempting to reclaim the upper hand, positioning Louchheim as someone who could have either made or not made "the grade." Louchheim wrote back. "Darling, I do love your letters. But don't feel compulsive about having to write to me. I do understand that you're busy and what letters-by-hand mean, and you're supposed to be an architect not a writer."[88] The distinction of his profession versus hers is another subtle approach in the direction of what she could do for him professionally. Louchheim's strategy, both personal and professional, was to continue to highlight Saarinen's dedication and devotion to architecture, to continue to show her fealty to his productive work above all. "As long as it is architecture who is your best girl, I'm quite content to be second-best," she wrote.[89] She was signaling jealousy of other potential paramours, but not of his work.

Then she began dropping more hints. "If I started saying all—or even half—of the things I want to, bracketed things and unbracketed things, serious things and silly things, things about architecture and about your

Fig. 12. Eero and Aline at a party, demonstrating their vigorous social life, undated. Box 3, folder 23, Aline and Eero Saarinen Papers, 1906–1977, Archives of American Art, Smithsonian Institution.

speech in Cleveland (for I had a long talk with Haskell), things about the article, and things about us and love," she wrote, once again dropping her relationship with *Forum* editor Haskell into her correspondence.[90] Louchheim's overt recognition of her conversation with Haskell, particularly in reference to Saarinen's speech in Cleveland, was a mode of work. She continued this strategy on April 29th, three days after the *New York Times* article was published, in a letter that contained a number of name drops:

> The nicest thing about the article is that people talk to me about you so it is all right for me to talk back about you. . . . there was Monday in the office, for instance . . . and lunch at Sardi's with Arthur Lober, where lots of people in the theater mentioned it. . . . Then there was yesterday at the Museum of Modern Art garden opening . . . with ever so many people mentioning you. Doug Haskell was an angel. He described how you won over the engineers, who were first inclined to scoff of any talk about

architecture as an art ... and he mentioned how well you have learned to handle yourself.... And how much he liked what you said. And how he wants to publish it.[91]

The next sentence is where Louchheim truly began her job. "Anyway, for the first time in my life I said 'Yes, let's do have lunch together.' He must have been as surprised as Mr. Zadok! But think of having another talk about you."[92] The letter also mentioned Philip Johnson, Edgar (Kaufmann, her former fiancé), Alfred Frankfurter (who intimated that he knew about the personal relationship behind the professional one), and Philip Goodwin, who "went into ecstacies [sic] about you and said he had been talking with someone on *Progressive Architecture* about how fine you were that morning and how glad he was that the *Times* had taken notice of you! As if you needed the *Times*!"[93] Here she catalogues her connections as a way of reminding Saarinen that she had far more nuanced an understanding of how to manipulate the press than even he could have, while also minimizing her own contributions.

She continued. "The head of something called the Development Office of Rutgers University, New Jersey (Brunswick) called and said they are trying to raise money for a much needed auditorium and wanted to use the MIT model in a brochure saying, look what magnificent thing MIT is doing, why can't we do something wonderful, too."[94] She had taken the reins. "We sent them a photo with strict instruction about identifying caption and credits."[95] This giving of information with "strict instructions" would presage what she did later, managing images and "captions."

It is noteworthy that she provided the image *and* strict instructions about captions and credits. Descriptive captions ran underneath images, and were designed to provide more detailed information than could appear in the longer narrative articles. Louchheim's sensitivity to captions, her desire to give "strict instructions," demonstrates an understanding of the importance of even the few words that accompany a picture—in a sense, an act of textual translation. Her control of the message was beginning, and her airy way of describing how she'd already done it, though disavowing her personal involvement by saying "we," though re-avowing her personal involvement by saying it came with "strict instructions," is repeated in later letters to editors, particularly her correspondence with Thomas Creighton, an editor at *Progressive Architecture*, which came a few years later.

Saarinen wasn't thrilled with the pictures in the article. "You are right about the pictures, but you will remember I've been fussing about that from way back," Louchheim wrote, in response to a complaint. "Next time we'll work on pictures together, too." This wouldn't have been possible for them to do with her as writer, and so once again, Louchheim was hinting at a position that she would soon take. She solidified her reputation by telling a funny story about Lewis Mumford, the social critic and urban historian. "I got a letter from Lewis Mumford telling me he was sure it was the copy-reader's fault but that in two articles recently I had misspelled Matthew Nowiski's [sic] name," she wrote. "I was delighted to discover that Mumford reads me!"[96]

Louchheim was also quick to remind Saarinen that she had connections beyond the New York Times and Forum. Describing an article she authored, she expressed her distress at Markel's heavy-handed editing. "I said I'd rather have the piece killed. The story may have a happy ending as I asked 'Vogue' if they would like a primer on modern sculpture."[97] Vogue was then as now a well-respected women's magazine with the occasional article on art and culture.

On May 2, 1953, Louchheim made her formal professional proposition.[98] She had what sales workers call a "warm lead," Saarinen having written to her the week earlier about the possibility of their collaboration turning more serious. He spoke to the potential of a partnership between them, and the hope that it would fill a gap in her life while at the same time contributing to his own work.[99] He continued by offering the prospect of a writing-intensive career for her, something that would allow the two of them to work together while keeping enough distance between their fields that they would be able, still, to live in relative harmony. He closed by assuring her that he wasn't trying to push her towards anything; that she should approach his idea without concern about any ulterior motives.[100]

Louchheim, however, was undaunted. "Before I write you a letter, I shall write you an essay," she began. She opened with an abstracted series of observations about the difference between art and craft, placing Saarinen's architecture in the former category and her writing in the latter. She continued with a more personal description of herself. "By some grace of God, I seem to be able to be a constructive friend, not as a social-worker, but as someone who xxx [letters typed and crossed out] is, variously, a sounding board, or devil's advocate, or partner-like discussant, or dependent and loving female, or rock-of-gibraltarish voice of conscience, or someone who can be diverting and entertaining." And also: "The more I respect and like and love the person, the happier I am to be some such a good and growing and creative part of their lives."[101] She then, in pencil, edited "their lives" to read "his life," a clear move towards her idea. "I think it is because I feel my own identity as a person and can achieve things outside on my own as a person, that I am able both to give and take so freely and to have the kind of relationships which have closeness and mutual respect without being spoiled by either a voraciousness or demandingness or clinging dependence on my part."[102]

She moved in for the kill. "So, if we may take the brackets off," she wrote. She and Saarinen had developed a language game around the idea of brackets; the conceit was that their professional relationship was mediated entirely within the structure of brackets—a way of controlling and articulating the distinction between personal dreams of marriage and professional conversations about his work. Taking the "brackets off" became a signifier that they would now allow themselves a full exploration into the personal relationship that they wanted, and became yet another epistolary acknowledgement of the multiple roles at play. "We now come to you and me and how all this fits together. And that's what's so absolutely marvelous. It makes a hell of a good design," she wrote. She described more:

> Then, it's wonderful that my "craft" should actually fit so well with your "art." (Our private little Cranbrook—arts and crafts and city-planning, too). But they do fit, because my craft can be used in three ways, all of which appeal to me: a) directly with you in your work, b) in the fields I am now where the subject-matter becomes xxxxx [letters typed and crossed out] some-thing which would interest you, too, in terms of that broadening in the way I mentioned in Pennsylvania, i.e. and c) with occasional forays into separate subjects, such as a short-story or a play—if I can.
>
> I've thought about all this for a long time, (secretly because of brackets and elephant-time-warnings, etc.) but I did dare to mention in my last letter something about the article as a kind of collaboration and hoped it was only the first of many. I don't know how it would divide up-maybe a) 30%, b) 60, c) 10, or maybe a) 45, b) 55, c) 5, or maybe a) 65, b) 30, and c) 5. the nice thing is that there doesn't have to be any set formula. It can adjust itself to the situation—or, be temporarily abandoned, as for nurse's aiding during the war, or when household things become pressing, as when we bought the house in Stamford.

I've even thought about how category (b) would work for me in Bloomfield Hills, rather than in NY which is the center of the material, And I can see how it can work perfectly well. There are dozens of ways. One of them is Dell books (see letter yet to be written about that) or the book that Knopf wants, or the one Simon and Shuster [sic] wants. And articles, even if they mean occasional tax-profitable trips to N.Y. (arranged to suit when you have to go there, or we could be in NY together and share that fun). So B.H. Mich. is even OK for category (b), and for (a) and (c) it is ideal (could be the "best goddamned house" have a pleasant room where I could type and look at the trees, too?) Like everything else that concerns us, it seems to me these questions are easily answerable because the basic things are right. If one sets up a way of life around the central and primary things and these are right, everything else will fall into or can be put into place around them.[103]

What Louchheim was describing was working as a public relations person. "Of course, he couldn't have PR people in those days," Saarinen's associate Kevin Roche recalls, though when asked to describe Louchheim's job he immediately said that she was "the sort of PR person for Eero."[104] This indicates a familiarity with her role, and at the same time a disavowal or almost distaste for being seen to openly support it.

Louchehim's next letter to Saarinen indicates that he hadn't yet decided whether to accept her proposal, but she forged ahead. "Did you ever write the letter you were going to to Huntington Hartford. I wish you'd send me a copy—I'd like to see how you sound when you are 'educating' a client."[105] The guise is that she's merely interested in learning, but the quotation marks around "educating" shows a certain arch distance. And yet she remained committed, despite how strongly she understood that moving to Bloomfield Hills would cause her life to change, dramatically:

It's amusing for me to "make like a newspaper woman," sitting at a press table with the wires service boys and going to our bureau to "file" a story and then being taken by three top reporters for drinks and dinner at the National Press Club and then getting on the plane and arriving in NY and finding the paper xxx with the story already on the newsstands! I'll miss (oh, excuse me, brackets off), I would miss some of this feeling of belonging to a guild (in my craft) of such nice and honest and good-will guys and being treated like a "pro" by them—but I've thought that through, too, and there are many, many compensations.[106]

Louchheim's description of the professional respect she was afforded does contrast with the gendering of the work—the description of the "wire service boys," and of being treated like a "pro" shows that she still observed a tension between typically female and typically male jobs. Louchheim was certainly not the only female reporter or the only female architecture writer around (Ada Louise Huxtable had worked at the Museum of Modern Art, and would start writing about architecture for the *New York Times* in 1958), but this section clearly indicates a modicum of ambivalence about leaving this highly respected and above all independent world of work to becomes Saarinen's helpmeet.

In May, Saarinen began the process of separation from Lily, a decision that brought some amount of tension to his correspondence with Louchheim. On May 4, he wrote to her that he wanted above all to have her as his wife. A few weeks later, he indicated that Louchheim was the right person to fulfill his life's goals and desires. A few weeks later, he returned to architecture, telling her about his upcoming charrette and how much he wanted to make a good impression.[107] She remained as neutral as possible, as supportive as possible, but also as committed to getting married as possible. A letter, written in May from Louchheim to Saarinen, oscillated between the personal and professional in the manner we have now become accustomed to. "Your letter made me a little sad, too. Because I can't help but be aware of what you are going through.... This is a pleasant intermission in the afternoon's work—a stolen time to tell you I love you, to tell you I admire you, to tell you I miss you—more and more.... Dear Eero, it will be good to be with you."[108] The next paragraph is all business. "If you don't have time for Rodolph Schwarz now, don't bother. I'll get Ed Wormley's copy and we'll have it for the weekend."[109]

On Wednesday, May 13, Louchheim wrote Saarinen a long letter, this one on *New York Times* stationery. Three pages into a letter that was mostly declarations of love, she turned professional. "Now that Michigan was postponed from the 7th to the 13th, what about the presentation to the Board of Regents? Is that still for the 11th? And you never told me why Breuer came out. Or what has happened about Milwaukee. And did you hear about the Chicago job yet? And what have you decided about Macy's—the more I think about that the more it seems to me to be simply a question of do you have the time and the staff to be able to handle it."[110] This passage is indicative of Louchheim's unapologetic pragmatism, her way of essentially forcing herself into a role and doing the job before she had the job. Despite her various disavowals that appear so frequently, she was keenly attuned to the ups and downs of Saarinen's career, the possibilities at hand, and, perhaps the importance of keeping him on track.

She became even more boosterish in a later, undated letter. "I do hope with all my heart that you get the job—because I think if it were an opportunity to 'practice architecture as an art' it would be a terrific opportunity and I know you would rise to it. . . . I also believe that if it is the right kind of 'architecture as an art' job you will get it."[111] Her combination of support and also idealism while also defining the kind of work she believed Saarinen could do are evident here.

Though they were not married, she considered them married. "I love you, my very dearest darling Eero, my very good architect and my very good husband."[112] Let's pause to think about her listing, in order, his name, his profession, and his relation to her. Louchheim's approach to the use of Saarinen's name was often artistic—she used it exhortatively, and sometimes imperatively, and always to soften whatever professional indication she might be making. To then follow immediately with "architect" was a rhetorical move that put his profession first before their relationship. Her bourgeoning status as an advisor was being continuously worked out in these letters, and then to close with "husband" indicates a reliance on the personal.

A later letter described an interaction with Edgar Kaufmann Jr., Louchheim's former fiancé. "Why don't you write a joint thank you note to 'Dear Edgar and Dear Edgar,'" she suggested. "And, yes, my love, that will be my department and I will take care of such details happily when we are legally married!"[113] She is writing on two levels here—one, taking care of Saarinen's social life, but two, taking care of professional correspondence. Later, she would write to Kaufmann on Saarinen's behalf; this letter is another preview of the kind of "work"—correspondence with others—that Louchheim was more than willing to take on. She had already set the connection up, writing a long letter to Edgar Kaufmann Sr.

Dear E. J., (Kaufmann, Sr.)

I'm sending you an article on Eero Saarinen of which I spoke not because I am an eager-beaver author who wants to be read, but because I can't help thinking about him in connection with the Pittsburgh opera-auditorium job. Unfortunately, the article is more personality than architecture but even this little bit of illustration and evaluation may help to bring you up to date on his work.

I'm interfering into what is none of my business and treading where angels fear to for three reasons: first, I have a nostalgic and very real affection for Pittsburgh and would like to see it get the best god-damned auditorium, etc. possible; second, I've been interested in this project ever since you first mentioned it years ago and share your pride and enthusiasm in seeing it about to go through; third, I have enormous admiration for Saarinen's work, especially as concerns this kind of structure, and think American architecture would be enriched by what he would do with the challenge.

I want to thank you for your friendliness and your affection and your generous kindness to me. I know that Edgar and I caused you disappointment and hurt. And you've been terribly nice about it. I appreciate it. And I am glad that you and I, who have had so many good times together, as well as Junior and I, shall remain friends.

Always fondly,

On the carbon copy to Eero, she included a handwritten note, in all caps: "TRUE—A REAL BASTARD BUT A NICE GUY. AFTER WE'RE MARRIED (C OF C) I'LL REALLY TELL YOU THE STORY OF THE KAUFMANNS. BUT IT'S A CONFIDENCE I CAN'T BREAK—EXCEPT TO MY HUSBAND (C OF C)." Then she adds, "P.S. I'm probably sticking my neck out and don't care." And then, "Actually, my darling, even if I weren't in love with you, I would have written the same letter. I think it's a job which would be marvelous for you and a job for which you would be marvelous."[114]

By June, Lily Swann had begun to balk at divorcing Saarinen, and asked for money. Louchheim wrote, "I'm not pretending that the news wasn't an awful shock to me, too, nor am I trying to find any rationalization.... She is silly. Because now there will be the long wrangle period. You will make an offer as much too low as hers is too high.... In the meantime you will grow to resent Lily in a way you never have and she will resent you."[115] And then she switched tactics. "Ultimately if you remain firm and strong and remote and calm and convinced, it will get settled. When you feel like blowing your top, blow it to your attorney or to me."[116] Her skill with interpersonal manipulation then begins to shine through. "I've begun to wonder if it really were to matter too much if Lily did find out about us.... I don't see what more she could do." The next few letters stay personal, focusing on the divorce process between Swann and Saarinen, but a few days/weeks later, Louchheim was back to her professional focus.

"And, the Cleveland speech. Your new, more closely defined divisions came in today's letter. Really what you are having to do is to define all modern architecture—and evaluate it—which is a terrific chore. I'm anxious to see the draft."[117] She was once again reminding Saarinen of her ability to tease apart what it was that he was trying to do with his work. She was sympathetic—"a terrific chore"—but also keenly invested, asking to see the draft by way of saying how anxious to see the draft she was. Louchheim frequently used words like "anxious"—again as a way of softening her aggressive interest in participating in Saarinen's career.

A few days later, she prodded him—"I hope the speech comes tomorrow. I'm getting impatient about that. OK?"[118] The next two paragraphs were entirely about architecture. "When you've looked at architecture the way I have—the superficial, esthetic, what-does-it-express approach, you are unaware of the core of thinking that is the exciting part—by that, I mean, the way the limitations of a job can be the exciting things, too."[119] She continued, "It is fun for me to hear about things like the problem of staircases and windows, etc. from the inside—I've only looked at them and thought—that seems awkward, or arbitrary, or meaningless designwise even if I know what has to be there." And then, the explicit disavowal: "I know all this is elementary to you but please, please, please have patience about my big areas of ignorance and naavite [sic]."[120]

Her progression towards taking her professional position increased with the next letter. "On the whole, I think the speech is very good and clear now," she wrote. "I was a little disappointed that you hadn't expanded all of the six sections more, but I assume you had space restrictions. And it all has a good logic and clarity now. I have a few very small, tiny editing kind of suggestions—and two bigger ones, but none very basic. I'm so terribly flattered that you've let me in on it, darling," she wrote. "That is a particularly generous gesture—and it will be wonderful when you do another and maybe by that time you and Bruce and Kevin [Roche] and I can all hash it up together. I won't interfere with your discussions with them—just absorb it and think about it and then you and I can talk later—in the bedroom, with pipe and cigarette and night-cap. And you've done a wonderful job of clearing up some of the very things that did seem confusing in the first draft."[121]

The speech was to be published in *Forum*, and so this is Louchheim's first official performance of her future role. "Won't it be fun to see the speech finally in the Forum? What are you going to do about illustrations?"

She asked so that she could answer. "I should think you'd want to choose one spectacular and very good example for each of your six categories."[122]

"I have sad news," she wrote later. "My agent phoned and told me the *Reader's Digest* had decided against the Saarinen piece."[123] Her referring to the article as "the Saarinen piece" is a direct nod to the way she referred to her *New York Times* article before, when they were, essentially, working on it together. But, she found a spin. "Actually, from your point of view it is probably better. Because the *Digest* has an awful habit of straining articles and taking out whatever pulp there is and leaving only skin. It would probably have ended up without any reference to architecture at all."[124] Louchheim was signaling her own professional expertise here, while also soothing potentially ruffled feathers. Her insider awareness of *Reader's Digest*'s editorial practices is crucial for understanding what she was offering to Saarinen, who was much more focused on abstracted ideas of fame and his desire, as seen through his letters to his psychiatrist, for long-standing fame.[125] This section, once again, marks a mode of self-advertisement.

She continued, in between divorce advice, to bring the conversation back to architecture. Saarinen must have received news about his MIT chapel commission going forward, and shared it with Louchheim. "Oh, darling, I'm so glad," she wrote. "I'm glad, first, because it's a building I just like so much emotionally and esthetically. And I'm glad intellectually, because it's such a good building in terms of modern architectural thinking.... And I'm glad, too, because it's one of your designs in which I've begun to feel privelegedly [*sic*] involved—what with [Harry] Bertoia and the Boston visit."[126]

It appears the *Times* discovered something about Louchheim's relationship with Saarinen. A few days later, she wrote to him:

> I was asked to be on Milwaukee jury but TIMES rules forbid that any more. Then I was asked to come out and see it and I declined. Also, Pepke wrote one of those obsequious letters to Markel about sending "the one important art critic" to Aspen and I told Markel no, I didn't want to go (this is very off the record because I do not wish to antagonize all those design people.) I said no partly because I don't think the conference this year will produce any very significant ideas, partly because I'm tired of hopping around and want to wait now to hop with you.[127]

I believe Louchheim meant "hop with you" in two ways—one, yes, hopping around the world, but two, in a more parallel, forward-facing way.

They'd discussed the difference between his slow-moving "elephant time" and her hyper "rabbit time," and so this reference to hopping is a return to that—to the ways in which she could partner with him, bring her skills to bear to his architectural practice. "Hop with you," then, was written in a professional mode.

Publishing was in a moment of change. Louchheim wrote to Saarinen about a meeting she had with Arthur Hays Sulzberger, then publisher of the *New York Times*. "Sulzberger was curious tonight—nice at certain moments when he talked about ideas and policy and hisbreaction [*sic*] to India and the problems of the paper and acceptability of advertising and so on, nasty when he still wanted to 'make me.'"[128] In the same letter, she continued her pitch for a professional relationship.

> I don't know, and you don't, exactly what outward form it will take, but I think we sense what inward form it will have. Not only won't it be not pseudo-anything, it will be positively something, positively the Eero Saarinen. It will have in it the spirit of Hvittrask, and the spirit of the Eames, but worked out in our own terms, in what is natural and real and right and logical for us. . . . But even more, when it is twenty-five years since you won that St. Louis competition, I hope you have the feeling that the years between have been good and productive and creative years in terms of work and in terms of living.[129]

Her reminding him of a familiarity with the childhood that was so important to him; the professional friendships that informed his work; and the thrill of having won the St. Louis competition are all ways of cementing her status in his inner personal and professional circle.

People in New York were beginning to catch on to there being something going on between Louchheim and Saarinen. Another letter said—"Arthur Drexler at the Museum (Philip's assistant) told Liz he hoped I [would] do an article on the State Dept. architecture but that he hoped I wouldn't 'make it all Saarinen.' We don't know if he said that because of the article or because he's heard of other attachments! Have you had a chance to do any more thinking on that? The Embassy, I mean."[130]

The next letter even more explicitly outlined her pitch:

> Your mother is right that I can never be the kind of direct help-mate that Shu [Florence Knoll] would have been. In many ways I can be less good than Lily, too, in artists response. All I can do is two things—or atleast [*sic*]

I hope I can do—and those are to help you have the kind of life in which you can best realize and fulfill your special talents and gifts and ambitions and ideals and dreams and, a little bit, by "talk" to help you think out and understand your own thoughts and intentions and dreams. Your life won't have to be split in two. It can be whole—and I should think that in itself is a goodness.[131]

Most interesting here is the notion of "talk" as a professional and personal mode. What I believe Louchheim is gesturing towards is the importance of a contiguous narrative mode in the production of architecture and this is the heart of the intellectual interest in this particular relationship. Architecture had long been seen as a visual medium; magazines published first drawings, then photographs, then culled photographs, then renderings. The role of "text" was relegated mostly to historians—contemporaneous writers like Johnson, or Pevsner. Even architects like Corbusier, who also wrote—as Colomina has pointed out—as a means of communicating their architectural ideas, weren't really taken seriously as writers. The role of language was still, at the time, one of afterthought. The drawing, the model-making, then the building—these were all considered to be modes of architectural production. But talk? Talk was not yet on the table.

Louchheim put it there. Both in terms of a presented role as interlocutor—"to help you work out and understand your own thoughts"—but also as a creative process, one of cleaving Saarinen back to himself. "Your life won't have to be split in two" indicates an awareness not only of the unhappy marriage he was in, with Swann, and which seemed not to give him a lot of intellectual fulfillment, but also in the split between architecture and talking about it. "Your life won't have to be split in two" becomes, through our reading now, not only a personal or even historical observation but a conceptual one. What would architectural practice look like if it were not split in two—the visual and the narrative? What if language and narrative could be an integral part of the practice of architecture—of its production? This is what Louchheim was, whether consciously or unconsciously, proposing, and why this moment in this relationship is of such interest.

It's unclear which article she is referencing, but later, Louchheim described working on something for him: "Gene Hayes called just as I was finishing typing your article," and then later in the same letter—"I hope that I was some help on the article. Do let me know."¹³² And then in the next letter—

> The part of the speech is superb—the best part of the whole thing! I'm terribly anxious to read it as a whole. And won't it be fun when it comes out in the Forum? We'll have to celebrate with champagne or aquavit. It was fun to do—although I wish we'd had time both for talk and for my writing—and somehow it tempts me to urge you to say yes to the book. But I guess one of the things we have to be careful about is not to say yes to too many projects. Life is going to be full of all kinds of temptations of things that are fun to do, separately, and together, and somehow we must manage only to do the ones which are going to be the most rewarding and most central. Your primary job is creating—and we ought to hitch the other things around that. Oh, darling, what a wonderful life it can be.¹³³

In July, Louchheim went on a name-dropping spree, reminding Saarinen of her deep ties to New York as a center of media, culture, and architecture. "I have lots of amusing things to tell you about last night's party in New Canaan at Philip's house for Pevsner—with lots of your playmates there including Peter Blake and Haskell and about my talk with Haskell and so on. But later, when I come home. Also, about the article—which I found when I got home last night and which is damn good—but I still wonder if you shouldn't stress Corbu's absolutely magnificent development in India."¹³⁴ Louchheim was demonstrating power here—intimating that she talked to Haskell, then senior editor of *Architectural Forum*, but then also disavowing it by referring to Blake and Pevsner and Johnson as Saarinen's "playmates," when they were obviously hers. Saying "I still wonder" was another way of disavowing what she was doing—correcting Saarinen's article, and couching it in abstracted language. Of course she wasn't actually "wondering," she was explicitly encouraging.

Saarinen came to visit, and she wrote him a letter about the visit after he had left.

> Don't ever tell me you are egocentric. You never mention anything about publications. I saw the University of Michigan xxxx [letters typed and crossed out] in the Forum today—or doesn't anybody tell you about these things? But that presentation was much less good than one you drew for me once on some yellow paper. I am convinced, really darling that we

could do an absolutely marvelous book if you would sort of draw it as you speak and I'd fill in your words. It would be a marvelous thing for people who are interested in architecture but get bored with architectural description, which never does the job anyway. Let's talk about that in California, and then you can speak to your Harper's woman, the Swami-one.[135]

They planned to do the book together, although of course Louchheim would do the book after Saarinen died. Key here is her critique of architectural description, which she says "never does the job anyway." What job should it have done? What job could it do? I hypothesize that Louchheim was describing the practice of captions, which are often solely illustrative, meant to briefly describe factually and on a one-to-one basis what the image is showing. She may also have been subtly critiquing her own field, that of architectural and art criticism, and the limitations of using words to describe buildings. Louchheim's facility with both art and language come through here, even though it is couched, of course, in her pretending that she doesn't really know what's going on or how to understand drawings. She was both flattering Saarinen by intimating that his drawings and visual representations were much more powerful than language but also inserting herself—"I'd fill in your words" has a double meaning as both "writing down his words" but also "filling them in"—addressing gaps that Saarinen, not being a writer, wouldn't even have noticed.

Louchheim understood that being Saarinen's wife would be a job as well. "I also forgot to tell you that when Edgar was talking about 'the public demands' of being your wife, he also was nice enough to say he thought I would answer them very well."[136]

As she continued to apply for a job she was inventing, the idea of "publicity" was in the ether, and it is clear that Louchheim is not inventing publicity as a field. "Second, Eames' toys," she wrote in a later letter. "The publicity girl came in today with them—one is a House of Cards, the other is 'the Little Toy.'"[137] Her mention of "the publicity girl" indicates both that there was a shared understanding about the term "publicity" but also that "publicity" was seen as explicitly women's—or even girl's—work.

The practice of publicity has been studied through a number of fields: history, business, communications. Historians have tried to work out the exact beginnings of the profession, nebulous as it is both in practice and also understanding, and some have tied it to the opening in 1900 of the "Publicity Bureau" in Boston.[138] Others have placed the origins of "public relations" as a practice, as opposed to a field, much earlier—with eighteenth-century reports of American companies like the Trustees of the Georgia Colony writing in blatant attempts to "lure settlers to the colonies."[139] The closest that we can see to Louchheim's practice might be that of Edward Bernays, nephew to Sigmund Freud and probably the most famous twentieth-century publicist. In 1937, Bernays authored an article meant to give a brief overview of the field, arguing that it was largely "confined to trade associations and the larger corporations," and that it was largely a post-Depression cultural landscape that provided the opening for publicists, as opposed to advertisers. The greater public needed to be able to trust large companies again; simple advertisements weren't enough; they needed a personal touch.[140] More recent historians have argued for the understanding of public relations as a two-pronged process, one that "unfolds along two dimensions: market control and social mobility."[141] Louchheim's interventions were in service of both—market control so that Saarinen's work could continue to be built, and a social mobility that she was born into / developed through her previous profession as an art critic.

Louchheim's letter included an essay, which she titled "Let's Forget Love, or Eero Is Perfect for Me No Matter How You Slice It."[142] Section VI is of particular interest to us—and was subtitled "He Makes Me Feel Needed in Good Ways." She wrote: "He allows me the special privelege [sic] of feeling that I can be for him what any dame wants to be for any guy she loves—the sun and air which allows him to grow. Then he makes me feel needed by letting me help him in little ways with his work—like editing the Cleveland speech, which gives him terrific pleasure."[143]

There she was performing submission, and emphasizing his personal strengths and her role as supporter—as the air and water that would help him grow. However, she was also, at times, aggressive in her approach. "I know that whatever happened I would always stick by you, fight for you and believe in you. I will question and argue and still think that Borromini is a great architect even if you don't. . . . But I believe very profoundly in what the Germans would call the Ur-Eero, the basic real Eero both as architect and as person."[144] Her recognizing Saarinen as architect first and person second shows the depth of her willingness to perform this kind of fealty to his profession.

She was a keen observer of the kinds of people who should have been famous, and the ones that actually were. "I spent some time today in the

Museum of Modern Art Library looking up stuff on Charlie," she wrote, referring to their mutual friend Charles Eames. "It's amazing how little has been published about him as a person."[145] Louchheim furthered this distinction here, first introduced by her talking about Saarinen as an architect and a man, by using the words "as a person." And while architects had been subject to glowing stories, the era of the ultrarevealing personal profile was not yet upon us; yes, some architects were famous for their work, and were featured on the cover of *Time* magazine, but this distinction of "as a person" indicates that there was an elision in the culture. What could Louchheim have meant when she wrote "as a person"? This indicates that she had a broader view of the journalistic landscape than most contemporary critics had, and it is a precursor of what she would bring to Saarinen's office.

A section of this letter, which is worth reproducing in full, demonstrates a few notable and important elements of her work life. "I am so bored with the 'Government and Art' thing," she wrote to Saarinen.[146] She had been assigned a long feature on government interventions into the art world.

> The trouble with it is that I have to give all the details of the report in order to show why the opponents are against it. It isn't fair to summarize and get violent and say it is a white-wash and like the men who set out in a row-boat to go upstream, forgot to untie their boat and after rowing two hours saud [sic], "Well, we're holding our own." That would be fun. But the re-write of detail is endless and dull. Moreover, I think it's of too specialized interest for the Magazine and so am recommending running it in two takes on the art page. The silver lining is that if that works I'll have copy ahead for two weeks. But next week I want to run what could be a good, warm story on Ben Shahn's drawing for an off-Broadway production of "The world of Sholem Achleichem," [sic] about whom I just learned today.[147]

By teasing apart these sentences, the breadth of Louchheim's familiarity and facility with the world of art publishing becomes evident. She understood the problems with the art and government exhibition but also the limitations of the *New York Times* and its readers, who would require her to do more than "summarize and get violent." Yet she had the critical facility to know that, essentially, the show served as a summary. Her ability to "recommend" that something run in a particular schedule indicates a level of power that she had with the *New York Times* editorial desk, which is not common to writers, at least not any writers that I have ever encountered or seen in the archives and/or in real life. Her other letters indicated that her editor Markel was pretty controlling; the idea that she could then recommend something indicates a level of respect he must have had for her which is outside the usual realm of editor-writer relationships, in which the editor is the all-seeing eye who determines when a story will run, and the writer must simply wait (as also happened with "the Saarinen piece," which was endlessly tinkered with by Markel and eventually ran much later than Louchheim either anticipated or liked). One of Louchheim's most frequent strategies for getting what she wanted was to pretend to be clueless.

Louchheim valued her career, and was perhaps a little more worried about giving it all up to go to Bloomfield Hills than she often told Saarinen. "Darling, working this weekend I really missed you," she wrote. "It will be fun when we are together. Even when what we are doing is parallel, rather than intertwined (as it sometimes will be), there will be the sense of togetherness and of mutual endeavor." That was the upside. She still had fears. "Sometimes I do worry terribly about not living up to what you think of me … and of no one wanting me to write articles or doing TV or anything. I'm sure I'll find something else to do, if that comes to pass, but I do worry about your becoming disillusioned."[148]

She was very familiar with contemporary architecture, and described a conversation with Edgar Kaufmann, Jr. "I had a fascinating discussion at dinner—me explaining why your generation had been attracted to Mies rather than Wright and he explained how misunderstood Wright is spatially and then from that on to how Mies had really led steel to a dead-end instead of using it as Wright had indicated in his writings (not in his buildings) or as Roebling had, etc. etc. And we must really all talk together sometime, for though Edgar may be prejudiced, he is at least provocative."[149] The distinction Louchheim made between Wright's writings and his buildings is an early way of beginning to tease out a distinction of two modes of production: the written and the designed. Rather than focusing only on Wright's buildings as ways in which he produced architecture, her emphasis on his being able to indicate an architectural *idea* in his writings and then producing an immediate distinction between that and his buildings is a hint at the complex ways in which architecture was beginning to be discussed. The art historian Margaretta M. Lovell has noted that the Kaufmanns came to Wright through his 1932 publishing of his autobiography, indicating a precursor for a textual/personal/architectural mode of designer-client relationship.[150]

Later, Louchheim reminded him of her place in the world. "Congratulations on winning the A.I.A. award," she wrote, referring to his AIA Honor Award, received in 1953 for the General Motors project.[151] "Or didn't you know?"[152] Intimating that he may not have known, even if she was simply performing that he might not have known, was a way of reminding Saarinen that this was just as much her world—that of publications and awards and the production of fame. That his world, yes, was the production of design and drawings and architecture, but that she would and could know of professional advancements before he ever did.

She used a meeting with Wright to again demonstrate her power. "We got in, Wright had been going through Stoller's photos of his work to have slides made (something Aline will do sometimes for Eero) and was exhausted, so I fixed pillows for him and a table for his feet and ordered tea," she wrote.

> Then, suddenly, he switched to how there aren't any architects ... for some reason he began on you (prompted by me). And began again about you were the one hope, but you are a thief and how could any one that young have had that sense of detail, section, etc. in the St. Louis arch, etc. etc. again. I really got furious and that gave me courage—and I interrupted and said god damn it, I was sick of that talk. And then I went on and said that you were perhaps the one really good architect and that what is more you had just as much integrity and just as many ideals and just as much as sincerity as he, Mr. Wright. Then he interrupted me said, "He has taste but he doesn't know" and then launched a big discussion of "taste" and how it ~~differing~~ differs [sic] from knowing.[153]

"WHAT HAPPENED ABOUT LUTHERAN UNIVERSITY MEETING?" she asked in a following letter. "Oh, darling, I hope they decided to go ahead. It sounds like such a perfect job for you."[154] Later in the same letter she wrote, "I'm also dying of curiosity about Doug Haskell's reaction to your article. I read it again—and darling, it is good."[155] She then public relation-ed him. "Magazine proposal at *Times* that I do a spread on contemporary religious architecture in America," she wrote. "What do you think? Will you have the new chapel ready?"[156] Again anyone familiar with how the news should work may be surprised here, and this is part of why she still had to keep the relationship as secret as possible, though she hypothesized that Markel had some sense of what might be going on. "In a sense he's one of our godfathers," she wrote of her long-term editor.

She continued to weave the personal into the professional. A following letter opened with "I have been thinking about you very, very much and wondering how all the various things are working out for you—from the form of Milwaukee to the business of telling the children, from the connecting link of the Drake chapel to the separation agreement."[157]

She thought a lot about the chapel: "I've thought quite a bit about the chapel and its crown and when I get the energy will write an essay about it.... I'm anxious to know what Bruce and the others thought about the 'company models' and the Bertoia ones."[158] She continued on:

Random thoughts for your speech—in case you get to thinking about it—I think there is a strategic paragraph on page 8 of Scott—the one beginning obviously there is room for confusion. The "condition of delight" in architecture—its value as an art—may conceivable be found to consist in its firmness, or in its commodity or both; or it may consist in something else different from yet dependent upon these; or it may be independent of them altogether.... There is no reason to suppose that there exists between them a "pre-established harmony." Then you might discuss who xxx [*sic*, letters typed and crossed out] emphasis has shifted in different periods—and how in our esthetic the quality of delight does seem strongly to spin in large measure from expression of "firmness" or "structure"—and then that could lead you to the different kinds of expression of structure—the difference between "expression of structure" and "exposure of structure"—the difference between what Scott calls "constructive integrity in fact" and "constructive vividness in appearance."

Then maybe you might go on and talk in an indirect anti-Liz Gordon way about the confusion of the quality of "delight" or "spiritual quality" with undisciplined romanticism.... I wish I were giving the talk—because then I could end it with a fine summarizing section on General Motors as an example of where commodity firmness and delight all work together.... Or are you going to concentrate on concept and precept?

Hi darling what fun it would be to talk about these things with pictures and examples to test what we said as we went along.... It's especially interested in architecture—as you pointed out—because you "perceive" in stages as you experience each building. And yet, as you also pointed out, a "pure Renaissance building" makes its point by being static and self-contained and imposing a single perception upon you.[159]

Louchheim's use of the word "delight" was no doubt conscious, and one that the architectural historian Andrew Shanken has hypothesized is related to the architect Minoru Yamasaki's reintroduction of the ancient Vitruvian term (as in "commodity, firmness, and delight" being the three requirements for successful architecture).[160] "I still owe you the essay on MIT [*sic*]," she wrote a bit later, "but maybe we can look at the model and talk about it instead."[161] This idea of owing him essays is intriguing—she basically had taken it upon herself to start writing essays that went along with his work. Frequently, her "essays" appeared in the form of letters.

She formalized an agreement in a later letter. "Resolved: That Eero and Aline will spend time on Eero's speech and any other problem which he would like to discuss with Aline, including M.I.T. chapel, if he wishes. Also, sculptors for styling. Also, maybe talk about Drake so she can then constructively assemble photos for that."[162] This idea of "constructively assembling photos" goes to the heart of much of what is novel here—in the assembly of certain photographs to tell a certain story, of the idea of photography being a construction of the building as much as the building itself is. In the same letter, she discussed having "dinner with Creighton on Thursday and lunch or drinks with Haskell,"—Creighton being her friend Thomas Creighton who was then editor at *Progressive Architecture*, and Haskell at *Forum*. She was beginning to come to what she described as "being at your side in a permanent organized way."[163] Saarinen, meanwhile, valued her contributions, though saw how different they were. He described the difference between writing and architecture as one of individuality versus teamwork, lamenting that he often sat down to draw one line and immediately heard the telephone ring.[164]

"I'm afraid we didn't do very much about your work this weekend," she wrote to him.[165] "But we will make up for that in the nice, long future."[166] The future wasn't that far way. In a letter from late 1953, she wrote, "I'm dying to know about the Lutheran site—I hope it's nice, because it's such a good project. I'm also especially anxious, after all this viewing of concrete, to see what you do with it. The problem is terribly different here, of course, due to cheapness of labor in making wooden forms. Too bad you don't need brise-soleil in Indiana—they are really wonderful for plastic and dramatic architectural effects."[167]

She began solving a problem with her social network. "As for your Milwaukee museum problem" she wrote in a letter close to Christmas-time:

> I really believe Porter McCray is the head-and-shoulders above anyone else best god-damned possible person. He has had architectural training enough to have helped him understand installation and practical problems; he has had art training enough to understand quality and significances of styles etc.; he has had enormous experience, through his job as head of Circulating Exhibitions, not only in creating exhibitions, but in knowing the special problems, needs and desires of small museums and galleries throughout America: and he has the tact, charm, patience and intelligence to get on well with all kinds of people—from city fathers to women on boards.... He would be perfect—and the only question is whether he has the time to act as a consultant. I would make every effort to get him, if I were you, and perhaps the best way would be for you to speak first to him to see if he were interested and then to get Rene in on the act in the sense of Rene allowing him to do it. This is really a good suggestion....
>
> My feeling is that Alfred Barr will be on much too remote and esoteric a level for this job—not aware enough of human and community problems. Another possibility, although I don't really know what's happened to him and his personality is against him, is Bill Friedman, who was really the brains behind front-man Defenbacher at the Walker Art Center. But Porter is really best and worth making an effort to get. He could probably use the extra dough, too, as the Museum pays such lousy salary.[168]

She also advocated for Saarinen to have more private commissions. "Edgar's father had told him he had spoken to Heinz and Edgar said he thought the way was open for much more than a wing on the house. That would really be nice, wouldn't it? I think it was Heinz who was in favor of the local boys doing the auditorium and so now it would be nice if he advocated you for one of the other big jobs."[169]

They agonized over going public and about whether they would consider themselves secretly or publicly married. Saarinen was also aware that marriage might change their relationship: "The ideal way to be married to you would be to have you live in a different city—then I would continue to get these absolutely marvelous letters—if we were living together—I would miss these too much—," he wrote.[170] Whether that was a way of expressing some actual hesitation, or simply a way of deeply complimenting her epistolary self, they did decide to marry, and cohabitate in the same city. Louchheim wrote a letter to her *New York Times* editors sometime in the end of 1953. "This memorandum, which for important personal reasons I earnestly hope you will treat as confidential, has two purposes," she wrote to Lester Markel.

> The first is to tell you that I am planning to marry Eero Saarinen around the middle of February. I would like, therefore, to stop working on the basis I have, on January 31. I will be moving to Bloomfield Hills, Mich., where Eero has his office. But we are planning to keep a New York residence and I will be here for one week out of every month. The second is to present a proposed plan for the art page to which I hope you will both agree and which might be tried on an experimental basis for the remainder of this art season i.e. into June. At that time we could all re-examine its merits and failures. This plan is attached.[171]

The memo outlined what she perceived as the successes and challenges of the existing art page, and suggested that she continue to write two stories a month on "subjects with which I have been supposed to deal."[172] She then recommended some European authors who could contribute international material.

The two married in February 1954. Louchheim moved to Bloomfield Hills. On February 9, 1954, the *New York Times* ran a wedding announcement.[173] The dek (the subheadline) read: "*Times*' Associate Art Critic Married to Eero Saarinen, Who Heads Own Concern," a mode of professional acknowledgment for both. Their short biographies were impressive. "She has been associate art editor and critic of the *New York Times* for the last six years. She will continue as associate art critic," which means that her proposal memo to Markel was accepted. "Mr. Saarinen, a fellow of the American Institute of Architects, was graduated from the Yale School of Architecture in 1934 and heads his own architectural concern in Bloomfield Hills. He designed the General Motors Technical Research Center at Warren, Mich., and the auditorium and chapel under construction at the Massachusetts Institute of Technology."[174]

Later that year, she wrote Saarinen a note. It was a combination of typed text and handwriting, and she wrote, "Because he deserves a wife who proves herself an individual and never a parasite and one who

Fig. 13. Eero and Aline shortly after getting secretly married, early 1954. Box 3, folder 23, Aline and Eero Saarinen Papers, 1906–1977, Archives of American Art, Smithsonian Institution.

accomplishes something in her own right which earns his respect."[175] A few pages later, she wrote by hand—"And please let Eero always have a chance to pursue architecture as an art."[176] We see here the continued braiding together of the personal and the professional. Yes, she was promising not to be a personal parasite, but also not a professional one either. It is surprising to me now how hard she had to convince him that she wasn't going to detract from his skills or his projects, and it is also heartbreaking to imagine her promising not to be a parasite when she had done nothing but significantly orient her work and life around supporting his. It reminds me of the way in which female partners of male architects were often seen—particularly Louchheim's contemporary Olgivanna Lloyd Wright, who received nothing but contemporaneous and posthumous judgment for the way in which she had been seen to co-opt Wright's genius and poorly influence his (often literal) affairs. It is possible that Louchheim was aware of how a male architect partnering with

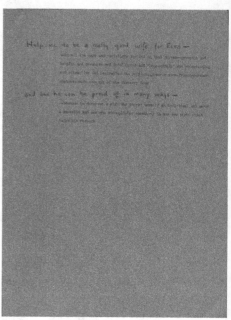

Fig. 14a–b. Birthday card from Aline Saarinen to Eero Saarinen once again demonstrating the relationship between typed text and handwritten addenda, 1954. Aline and Eero Saarinen Papers, 1906–1977, Archives of American Art, Smithsonian Institution.

a wife could look—and the ways in which other partnerships had been judged; the women often being seen as predators who simply lived off the genius of their partners while perhaps throwing them a dinner party or two. Her assertion that she wouldn't be a parasite speaks far more to social and cultural expectations about the role of women and the capacity for women to be seen as parasites than it does to anything truly present between them.

CHAPTER THREE

On Becoming a Publicist

While I was writing much of this book, I was also deep into a career as an architectural publicist. I started by accident, as many careers can happen, because in the summer of 2015, a year after I'd passed my qualifying exams in my PhD program but spent most of my days recovering from a number of surgeries and medical procedures, a friend of a friend, who was an architectural photographer who'd sought me out for coffee and friendship and work connections when I moved to the Bay Area, emailed to ask if I might be available to write some copy for his firm's website, which he and his partner were redesigning. I had a quick phone call with the two partners and quoted them the price of $1,000 to write about one thousand words of copy. These were grad school prices, quick and dirty prices, and they must have been expecting something much higher because they immediately agreed. A few days after we agreed, they invited me in for a work meeting. We talked about my research about publicity and Aline, and we also talked about my history as a writer. They asked, at the end of the meeting, if I might be interested in taking on a bigger role, something in the marketing and public relations world. They asked me to write up a proposal. Never being one to wait for anything, I settled into one of their desks, opened my laptop, and wrote a proposal. I listed all the publications that I had connections to, and all the ones I could get connections to, and mapped out what I would do for them. I said that I would send targeted pitches and work on getting specific residential projects published; I said that I would handle holiday letters and quarterly news reports. I said that I would manage all incoming press requests, and ensure that only the best stories about them were published. I asked for a monthly retainer. They agreed.

This firm, Garcia Tamjidi Architecture Design, remained my longest-running client. They had a few projects that were coming up, and they knew what they wanted to do in the future: a ground-up house. I advised that we focus on publishing their residential work, even as they were most known for doing sleek offices for venture capitalists and commercial clients in the Bay Area and beyond, and we understood that they had an extraordinary twelfth-floor residential apartment that would soon be ready to shoot. I involved myself in much of what they were doing almost immediately, even as I got sick and had to leave the Bay Area. They provided me financial support so that I could continue to stay alive and pay for medical treatments and experiments, and I worked on sending their projects to outlets like *Dezeen* and *Wallpaper**. Some of their projects had already appeared online, and so I had to explain to them the absolute importance of maintaining exclusives. In working with them, I came to realize how much I had learned by being a writer that made it incredibly easy to work on this side of things. I'd understood as a writer what happened when I hadn't checked the exclusivity—an editor would ask me, I'd have to ask the PR, and the PR would have to tell me that actually it had been promised to someone else. So I knew to pre-empt, to tell them to protect. Sometimes, Farid Tamjidi would post projects on his Facebook and I would text him immediately, telling him to take them down. "The image is your collateral," I would write. "Without it we have nothing."

If I had been asked to write a PR manual at that time, I wouldn't have been able to. The work all felt intuitive and reactive; we had a project and I would think about how to photograph it, what to emphasize, and then where to take it. I would think about which writer would want to hear about it six months ahead of time, and how to tease that, and tease the firm's work and identity, so that when it came time to pitch the project, they were primed. That jewel-box apartment, with sweeping views over the Bay Bridge, was photographed to articulate its relationship between solid and void, the incredible geometry at play. Tamjidi and Garcia were geniuses with minimalist space, and hated trends. Sometimes, Tamjidi and I would talk about how goofy the latest trend was, and how much they hated seeing architecture firms that were poppy and playful and put guitar studios into offices spaces get covered by the press. They preferred to stay outside of the design world, which sometimes made my job hard but also made it really clear. I never had to wonder if they were going to suddenly change in any way, if their identity would suddenly change, changing my job with it. I knew what kinds of triggers they had and what topics not to talk about. Sometimes Tamjidi would send me an article without the slightest context, and I would try and figure out if he liked what it said or hated it. Eventually, we understood each other's language. I also, through conversations with them, began to think that I might be able to influence how they spoke to reporters—to influence, in other words, not only how the writers felt about the work but about how the designers talked about it. My fingerprints, I figured, would be everywhere—even if no one ever knew.

We had one big conflict early on. They wanted to post a number of photographs of other peoples' work on their website, under the heading Inspiration. I said that they needed to include photo credits; they disagreed, wanting the grid of images to stand on their own. I was driving my then-in-laws' van around Oakland, almost yelling at them about how wrong they were. Finally, I told them that they could do what they wanted, but not to call me to protect them if they got in trouble. I didn't think they would necessarily take legal hits, but I was concerned about their reputation. It was the first time I realized that protecting their reputation was something that I felt was part of my job as their publicist. They agreed that they wouldn't ask me to speak on their behalf if anyone did criticize, and I agreed to let them do this.

If this sounds like an abrasive style on my part, it was—which is something that I heard again, and again, from client after client. Sometimes Farid would tell me that he could feel me rolling my eyes. I was a thirty-three-year-old professional. I didn't want him to hear me roll my eyes. But that early relationship, and the ways in which my behavior felt monitored and coded, taught me to be attuned to issues of gender and power in the workplace, and primed me to see Aline's behavior under certain lights. I was just starting to become deeply familiar with her and Eero's correspondence, just starting to get into the archives that covered their working lives. And here I was, feeling policed for the strength of my opinions and convictions, and the way in which I delivered them.

Garcia Tamjidi, despite my eye-rolling, liked my work enough to recommend me to some friends of theirs, a husband-and-wife team. I went into a meeting with them and bonded with the wife instantly, and liked the husband on sight. I described what I did for Garcia Tamjidi; we went to lunch and then the husband and I talked about the specifics—and he said they'd love to hire me to do for them what I'd seemingly done for GT. By this point I'd come up with a day rate, based on a longtime architecture friend who also worked in editorial telling me that that's what I needed, so I offered him a day or two days at $1,500/day. He felt this was a good fee, and I wrote up a basic contract that probably didn't cover half of what I needed to cover, and I had my second client. It was still just me and my personal Gmail address, and I could handle remembering the needs and wants of two clients. They also shared the photographer, Joe Fletcher, with Garcia Tamjidi, and so Joe and I started spending more time in conversation. Every so often we'd have a taco lunch and talk about designers, actually rolling our eyes at how they never seemed to understand how important things like exclusives were. "That's just not how it works!" we often said to each other, reminding each other that we did know the rules, that they didn't. Sometimes when I wasn't totally sure about something I'd ask Joe and he'd remind me that yes, of course, photo editors didn't want to see images of a project that someone else had even seen. Even if a magazine hadn't accepted, the project editors needed a total visual exclusive.

A few months into working with this second firm, their flagship project was finished and photographed. I sent it to a friend who worked at *Departures*, who said he liked the project and wanted to think about it. Then the husband sent me an email saying they didn't want to wait anymore, so in a panic, I sent it to another friend, then editor in chief of *San Francisco Cottages & Gardens*. She wrote back two minutes later to say that she definitely wanted to publish it, right after which the *Departures* editor emailed to say he was interested and to ask if anyone else had seen it. I had to tell him the truth. By this point I had read enough of Aline's correspondence to know that the best move was to play a little bit dumb. He asked if there was an exclusive, and I said it had been shown to *San Francisco Cottages & Gardens*. I figured if *Departures* took it, I would withdraw it from *SFC&G*, although that would have cooled our relationship for some time. Still, in the math, getting it published in *Departures* would have been far more valuable than getting it published in *SFC&G*, unless of course you were thinking of the value of the local market. He said that, either way, if someone else had seen it, he wouldn't take it. I tried to write back as though I hadn't really known the rules or hadn't remembered them. I don't think he bought it. It took a while to repair the relationship, and I realized then that I could never play with this. The house ended up being published in the last-ever issue of *San Francisco Cottages & Gardens*, which was shut down by its parent company for seemingly no reason.

That moment taught me everything I needed to know about how seriously I really had to take these rules. Moving forward, I realized I had to have my files completely in order, but that if they ever weren't in order, the next best move would be to just copy what Aline had done and pretend to be totally overwhelmed. I realized that I needed to have all of my Dropbox links set up, and make sure that no one saw images they weren't supposed to. The rules seemed so set in stone, so shared, and that's part of why researching this project about Aline Saarinen was so compelling. I could see the traces of the development of exclusivity in those conversations she had—as we will see later—with editors like Douglas Haskell of *Architectural Forum*. That meant: it hadn't always been like this! Did that mean it was possible it might not always be?

I signed another client, and then another. Most of my clients were middle-aged men, who had started their firms a decade or two earlier, and who had been used to a certain level of acclaim. One of them in particular, whom I'll call Frank, I hit it off with. He was my third client so I didn't yet really have my sales pitch down. I was still just a person with a Gmail address and a PhD in progress, and he liked that I charged by the day, and he said he'd pay for two days a month. He had a house that was going to be published in *Dwell* magazine, so I went to see it, and then because the piece had already been assigned to a writer, I didn't have a lot of inroads. But I wanted to make myself useful, and so I told him that we should prepare for her interview. I also looked up the writer, read the things she had written, and saw that she was smart, and a great writer. I wrote a project description for him to send to her, which was unusual for him, but it was my way of starting to mold the conversation they would eventually have. Then he and I talked on the phone, and I asked him questions and pretended I was the journalist running the interview, and when he answered I said things like, good start, but maybe say this instead, and it reminded me so much of Aline writing to Eero about what to say in his speeches. Once again I was behind the scenes, slowly pushing what I saw in the building, what I thought was most fascinating about it. Frank wanted to open by talking about the gray water reclamation system. Remembering how I read Aline had encouraged Eero to talk about being inspired by a grapefruit, I told Frank to talk about the massive tree that he had ended up organizing the house around. "Talk about yourself, your own memories," I told him. "That always plays well."

The interview went well and the story, which ended up on the cover, was a hit. I sent the writer a fan mail thank-you note, and asked Frank to do the same, and then when another client of mine had another project, I took it to her. "You were so amazing with that last story," I wrote, "and

I thought you'd be the perfect person for this one." Suddenly I felt like I was rereading all the emails that publicists had sent me when I'd been on the receiving end of pitches. How many times had someone told me I was the perfect person for something? How many times had I totally believed it? Except in my case, with this writer, I did believe it; just as I think, in many ways, the publicists who were pitching me did too. That was kind of the trick of the thing—it wasn't just a trick, it was real. I did the same process with this writer and the new project and my other clients, where I interviewed them ahead of time and we practiced and I sent them talking points. My business grew and I paid a research assistant to help me out a few hours a week, and then I contracted to another friend, and then I realized I really needed to hire them and I incorporated and put them on payroll and suddenly we were a three-person company. We had a company retreat and talked about our five-year growth plans, plans that would never come to fruition because of personal reasons and also professional ones, but it felt, in that moment, like we were onto something.

Our favorite element of the work, we realized, was the feeling that we were secretly contributing to a discourse. Two of us had a lot of experience with publications and bylines, with seeing our names in print, and so the thrill of that had worn off a bit; one of us didn't seem to register seeing her name as a thrill, but found deep satisfaction in knowing that a story in *Wallpaper**, for instance, used her *ideas*. We started tracking the number of projects that were published that used our ideas, our particular outlook and historical and theoretical vantage point. We thrilled to realize that what we thought was most interesting about a building was what we could ultimately ensure got published, by drafting a project description a certain way, by pitching a project using certain language, by preparing our clients to stay completely on message. We practiced with our clients, sometimes asking them boring questions and then training them to redirect to theoretical ideas that we'd convinced them were the most interesting ones, and were maybe even their own. We felt like we were everywhere and nowhere. Almost no one knew I had this job; it was the same for them.

I noticed that we were all women and that our clients were overwhelmingly men. I also noticed the way in which I started to create a certain intimacy with my male clients, an intimacy that never crossed the line into the sexual, but that became nevertheless a form of the erotic. Much has been made of the erotics of the classroom, of the particular rush and thrill of intellectual intimacy, and that happened here too. I was married to someone who was in such a state of what I imagine was profound depression that he could not communicate with me, someone who did not understand my world and seemed to have zero interest in it. Instead of feeling inspired at home, then, I felt inspired by my hour-long phone calls with men who spent most of their days telling other people what to do, who ran companies. More than once, Frank told me that my intellect was intimidating. It made me play the exact same types of disavowals that we have seen Aline do. I pretended to be less organized than I was; I told unrelated personal stories in meetings so that they would feel my relative youth. I exclaimed, excitedly, whenever I saw a project of theirs, particularly if I got to see it in person. I understood that I could not be solely intimidating, but that I had to always, just as Aline had, temper it with femininity. With enthusiasm.

After growing and solidifying what we did and how we did it, I decided that I wanted to work for a particular famous architect, and spent a year making my case, similarly to how Aline had made hers. Except that my photographer friend made most of the case—as did my client Frank. I did a long slow burn of a sell to him, never letting him know that I was selling myself. Finally, while he was on deadline for a book, he emailed me from New England, where he was trying to write. He asked for my help, and I agreed, and I knew that the rule of the game was that I had to fly to the city in which he lived. So I booked myself a flight out, and three nights in a hotel, and went for a meeting. He said he maybe also needed someone who could do PR, as well as help write this book, and I said that's exactly what I did, and then he asked how much I charged, and I asked how big his studio was—I decided in that moment to say that I charged by size of studio, as opposed to number of days—and because he currently had thirty-five people I asked for $5,000 a month.

"I could hire a junior designer for that," he said. "You could!" I said. Then we stared at each other. Everything in me, everything that has coded itself into being unobtrusive and helpful and not asking for high salaries wanted to say, "Of course it's flexible!" or "I can do it for less!" But I forced myself to just sit there silently. We looked at each other. Would Aline have balked? Would Aline have said something like, of course it's flexible? I didn't think she would have. Finally, a phrase came to me. "Are you worried about being able to pay that much?" I said. It was the most emasculating way I could have come at this, and it worked. "Oh no," he said. We can afford it," he said. "Good," I said. We shook hands. I now had a major client.

Working with this person was difficult for me. The first project that I worked on for him was an essay for the book he was writing. He'd shown me a lecture, which I'd transcribed, and I'd turned the transcription into an essay that followed the contours of his lecture. "This is a convoluted mess," he wrote to me after reading it. I'd forgotten, after so many years out of architecture school, the ways in which architects talked to each other—and to their employees. I'd forgotten that I wasn't the only abrasive person in the industry. I'd heard rumors about what a difficult person he was, but I'd wanted to work for him because of the fame I would get by being the person who was making him even more famous. Eventually, I wrote the essay, with the help of one of his associates, and the book was finished. He had a few projects that were also finishing, and I worked on placing those, and for two years he appeared in the press so many more times than he had before. The work was good; I was good at my job.

Again, I felt that thrill—this time of name-dropping that I worked with him without ever actually naming him. I realized that if I told my clients that I never told anyone who my clients were, that I could start to build a sense of mystique around me. Other publicists that I knew would list their clients on their websites; it made me immediately devalue whatever publicity I'd seen their clients get, knowing that they had, in a sense, paid for it. It made me think of how subtle Aline was, and how naming herself the Head of Information Services was a way of keeping herself out of things as much as possible, in a way. I told prospective collaborators that I only took clients on referral, that I purposefully didn't have a website, that I purposefully never let anyone know that I did this kind of work. "I can be most effective when no one knows you're working with me," I said. I believed it then; and still believe it now.

Almost all of my clients were happy with our work; they were delighted to be on the covers of magazines, were happy with the way the stories turned out. They said that they felt like the writers they talked to had really gotten the projects we had sent them, had really understood. I didn't point out that this was all part of a consistency of a narrative that I had actually produced—from the very first project description, through the pitch, through the interview prep. I wanted my clients to feel like their ideas, their work, were just miraculously being brought into the world. But sometimes, it just didn't work out.

For example: Frank, my other client, finished a house in a vacation town. Frank really wanted it to win a Record House, an accolade that almost every architect I worked with was obsessed with. I couldn't understand why they all wanted a Record House, but it is seen as a watershed acknowledgement for almost every single architect I've ever encountered. Frank felt to me like someone who really wanted his peers' approval, even as I felt his work was so strong that he didn't need it. Many of our conversations devolved into me saying, "You're better than that person!" and him sort of laughing. It was intimate.

Joe and I flew to the house to do a shoot. That was the other part that I'd learned to do from Aline: be involved in the shoot, in the very earliest ways the house was beginning to be pictorially imagined. It was important for us, I said, to understand a sense of where a project could be published before we shot it; *Elle Decor* wanted different images than *Architectural Digest* wanted different images than the *Times*. I also thought of writers ahead of time, about who I thought might become fascinated by a house, and the photography often was oriented towards those writers. For a Record House, then, we knew we needed to emphasize the volumes; the formal moves; the exterior. But in case we didn't get a Record House, I wanted to have backups—like *Architectural Digest*, which wanted celebrities and interior decor. Joe's job was tough. My job was also tough. I had to assess how likely I thought it was that the house would get a Record House (I thought moderately likely) but then also gently shape the types of pictures Joe took so that, if we didn't get it, another magazine would still bite.

We finished the shoot over two days, and went to an uproariously celebratory dinner. I sent the images, along with a project description that Frank and I had worked on together, to *Architectural Record*. And then we waited.

A few months later, he fired me. The house hadn't been selected—though it felt to him like it was he who hadn't been selected. I had other ideas for where to publish the house, and kept trying to get a hold of Frank, but he kept dodging my calls. Then I got the email saying his associate would be in touch to close down business, and I never spoke to either of them again. At the time, it was disorienting and upsetting. I was disoriented and upset. But I came to realize, maybe too late, that I had been subject to my own failures. I had overinvested in the relationship—written a speech for his daughter's wedding, picked up his phone calls whenever he called. I had referred to myself as his friend, had pumped him up when he felt insecure, had laughed coyly when he said how intellectually intimidating I was. I had failed to keep a professional boundary—and so then, when he'd gotten mad at me both personally and professionally and had ended the relationship, I found it hard to handle. It reminded me of how Aline had said that she would always see Eero as an architect first and a person second. I had forgotten, however briefly, that our relationship was fundamentally one based on business, had seen Frank as a person first and an architect second. I still miss our conversations. I believe that we will never speak again.

I also had successes, moments that made me think Aline would have been proud. There was a residential house that I placed in *Wallpaper** that went on to be nominated as one of the top four private houses of the year. There was the way in which I built relationships with writers that I truly liked and respected, and who I believe truly liked and respected me. There was the thrill of getting a project accepted, and the thrill of a long long chase. For one story, for a client in Palo Alto, I sought out the editor in chief of *Dwell* magazine, invited him to lunch, had lunch, casually mentioned the firm, and then a few months later sent him their project. It was finally published, with a story direction influenced by my employee, who had understood the work of this Palo Alto firm better than I could, who had shaped the narratives and also the interviews, and so as we read the issue of the magazine, we knew that both of our intellectual ideas were all over the piece, even as no one else ever would. I loved the game of thinking that far ahead, of being strategic. I was being strategic with people, with human emotions, but I had learned from my experiences as a writer to also only ever be genuine. I didn't want to pretend that I wanted to be friends with someone I didn't actually want to be friends with, and so I focused on contacting only people that I really respected. I had lunch with a German journalist and we spoke German the entire time. She told me how once she'd changed jobs, people had stopped contacting her. I stayed in touch with another friend, who had been the editor of a cool downtown New York magazine when I was a young writer and gone on to become editor in chief of one of the major shelter magazines before she was fired in what we would see later amounted to a coup. I heard later that so many of her contacts, her friends, had stopped calling once she no longer held the job. What a transactional world we all lived in.

After a while, I started burning out. I thought that I was burning out on architecture, that I hated seeing pictures of house after house after house. In November of 2019, during a family Thanksgiving, I started crying. "I just can't do it anymore," I said. I felt that my clients had started to see me as more than their publicist. Some of them, it seemed to me, were trying to work out their personal issues through me. There was the famous architect, whose behavior and way of doing business caused me extraordinary anxiety and stress. There was Frank, of course, whose rejection still stung. There were the Palo Alto clients, with whom I couldn't quite connect anymore. I burned out on what I perceived as their needs, needs that I couldn't address. I found myself becoming more and more crass with what I asked, more and more direct. I didn't have the patience to talk to every client before pitching a project. I wanted to be left alone with my photographs and my magazines, and I couldn't be, because there was so much desire and so much need.

Aline worked for only one client, her husband. And that relationship had within itself a clarity that mine lacked. I was almost a wife for some of my clients; for others a daughter. There was one set of clients, the only ones I would consider working with again, who just deferred to me and let me do my job. Joe used to say that the best advice he could give people was to just "let Eva get on with it."

That Thanksgiving, my mother said I might be working too hard. She took me on a vacation to Curaçao, where I didn't work for three days, and then I returned home. I developed a loathing for my email so strong that I had to set a twenty-minute timer every morning to force myself to go through it. I was still making a lot of money, but was also trying to get divorced, having realized that my marriage was no longer safe harbor from this professional storm, and so the money that I was making was being funneled to lawyers. Or to my debts, from furniture that I'd bought in an attempt to make ourselves a home. But even the money didn't make it worthwhile, at all. It was so overwhelming and I hated it so much, and then all at once and in the same week almost all of my clients let me go. COVID-19 had come to the United States, and with it a near-total shutdown of all architecture and construction work. In a month, I went from running a business with revenues of almost half a million dollars a year to filing for pandemic unemployment.

I took the summer off. I didn't do anything for anyone else, and having those months not to deal with clients, and to write this book, helped me see so much about the work I'd been doing. I'd made mistakes because I'd modeled myself off of Aline, had thought that emotional intimacy was part of what I needed to be exhibiting. I got too close to my clients partly because that was the way in which service-oriented work needed to work for me, and I got too close to them partly because, as a codependent person, I'm bad at boundaries. But I also realized that I'd used as my model someone who was married to the person that she worked with. All of the articles and essays that Aline had pushed she had done because she loved Eero, and wanted him to succeed. She had worked the way that she had worked because she'd been equally invested in his success as in hers. I had too, with my clients. Their hits were my hits. Their fame was my (secret) fame. But they weren't my spouses. My model had failed.

That was another thing. Part of why I kept the work secret was strategic. But part of it was shame. I had fear and worry that if people would know that I were a publicist, they wouldn't respect me. As writers, we were taught to judge publicists as people who weren't as smart as we were—and yet, the publicists were the ones who made the money, who had the steady salaries and got to engage with what we got to engage with. They got more access to architects and designers than we did. I told some of my writer contacts but always played it as vague as possible. But why?

Why was I so afraid to have anyone know that I did PR? It made me think of Andy Shanken's essay, "Breaking the Taboo," about the AIA's stance against advertising, and how I still thought there was a taboo, that I still had to somehow keep myself economically pure, that to do PR work was somehow not as noble as teaching for $12 an hour at UC Berkeley. It was doing the PR that gave me financial freedom, I kept arguing to myself, but that's not how it ended up feeling. Once I made money, it cost more money to keep that money. The shame was entirely mine, and that's why, sometimes, I wonder if that's why I took to Aline. I wanted to resurrect publicity because I felt so ashamed of my own career, and I thought that if I talked about how smart she was, how good she was, that I would feel better about the career path that I'd chosen, this complicated mix of architectural history and photograph management and interpersonal skill and manipulation that I was, despite myself, so extraordinarily good at.

CHAPTER FOUR

Kresge
and Ingalls:
A Comparison

In 2014, ArchDaily, an architecture-focused website launched in 2008 and which now describes itself as "the world's most visited architecture website," and which features a range of content—from video uploads of Dutch architect Rem Koolhaas's lectures to news breaks about Instagram's new zoom ability and how it relates to architecture—revisited Eero Saarinen's Kresge Auditorium at MIT, finished in 1955. The post described the auditorium, a thin-shelled concrete swoop, each point of which gracefully and almost ballerina-like touches the ground, as a "feat of sculptural engineering," and as "one of Saarinen's numerous daring, egalitarian designs that captured the optimistic zeitgeist of post-war America."[1]

This chapter considers three of Saarinen's projects through the lens of publications. Kresge Auditorium, Ingalls Rink, and the TWA Terminal are useful case studies for a number of reasons. Kresge Auditorium, a campus project built for MIT and dedicated in 1955, is a project that Saarinen had begun before he met Louchheim, and discussions of the auditorium made up some of their earliest epistolary interchanges. Because Louchheim was not involved in its publication efforts, the press about the auditorium lacks the kind of metaphorical and narrative flair that we see her subsequently bringing to all correspondence about TWA, focusing rather on a "facts and figures" approach. The Ingalls Rink was a project Saarinen began in 1953, the same year he met Louchheim, and completed in 1958, well into their professional and personal partnership. TWA was a major project for which Louchheim played a large role.

Tracing the ways in which the press covered these projects demonstrates how the press about Saarinen became more narratively sophisticated the more Louchheim became involved.

Fig. 15. A straight-on view of MIT's Kresge Auditorium, showing the modern clarity of the Cartesian gridded windows and what would become Saarinen's signature swooping form for the roof. Location: Cambridge, MA. © Ezra Stoller/Esto.

Kresge

The Kresge project was conceived in multiple parts: (1) a small non-denominational chapel, (2) an auditorium, (3) a student union, and (4) a connecting plaza. Only the chapel and the auditorium were ultimately completed. The student union building was never built, and the plaza—something that Eero discussed extensively with his then-brand-new interlocutor Aline B. Louchheim—was also "rejected in favor of a simple lawn."[2]

It is the third paragraph in the recent ArchDaily post revisiting Kresge that will open our investigation:

Although the technology had arrived from Europe beginning in the 1920s, Kresge Auditorium was one of the United States' first large scale thin-shell concrete buildings. The elegant reinforced concrete dome comprises one

eighth of the surface of a sphere and is primarily supported by three pen-
dentives. The truncated dome encloses a triangular space approximately
a half acre in area that then reaches a height of fifty feet. With the primary structural roof varying between only 3 and 7 inches thick, the span is
113 feet. Thickened edge-stiffening beams along the perimeter define the
roof and bound large transparent facades. A second 2 1/2" thick nonstruc-
tural layer of lightweight concrete was applied as a substrate for roofing.[3]

Close your eyes for a moment, and try and picture what it is this paragraph is describing. It should work, right? There are enough details here
—materiality, numbers, discussions of a truncated dome and a triangular
space, a span of 113 feet, a perimeter, a substrate—and yet these words,
so technically descriptive for one type of person (probably the engineer),
give us almost no sense of the image of the building itself. A reader might
wonder how an article published in 2016 is relevant to our discussion
of Louchheim's interventions in the 1950s. I contend that the available
source material about Kresge from which the ArchDaily author drew was
so limited that she was drawn to repeat a dryly factual series of numbers
in the absence of anything else. Compared to architectural historian and
author Alastair Gordon's opening of his airport monograph *Naked Airport*
by comparing the TWA Terminal to a bird, we can see how the lack of a
consistent narrative in the 1950s has remained, leading to a lack of consistent narrative in 2014.[4]

The post gives us a cursory history, stating that most periodicals "followed the planning process, most with great enthusiasm."[5] Yet "the completed project faced strong detractors who criticized it for failing to relate
to context, having structural shortcomings, and being an inappropri-
ate form for an auditorium."[6] The author, Michelle Miller, explains that
in 1955, *Architectural Record* was critical; in 1956 *Record* listed it as "the
15th most significant building from the preceding hundred years"; and in
2008 listed it as one of Boston's top ten buildings.[7]

Miller's accounting of the development of the building's reputation
tracks with our interest in Louchheim's interventions. For Kresge, because the majority of publishing happened before Louchheim began her
work, the only consistent thread lies in a recounting of construction details. Eero was already deep into the project by the time he and Louchheim met, and while it is one of the first topics of their correspondence, in
a sense the train—both design and narrative—has already left the station
by the time she set up her desk.

There were contributing factors beyond the shrewd efforts of Aline Louchheim that could explain Saarinen's increasing fame: an orientation in popular culture towards celebrity in the 1950s and 1960s; a strong cultural interest in architecture; the rise of publicity and PR as a practice. And because archives are, as ever, withholding on some potentially useful evidence, much of this discussion is based on pattern recognition, on beginning to see a relationship between an increase in Louchheim's professional correspondence from the office and an increase in publications that skewed towards praising Saarinen, from which to draw inferences. There are some ideal moments, but there are many more suggestions, threads to follow, traces to make. And yet to overlook Louchheim—as every Saarinen historian has done so far—as an essential piece of the puzzle is to overlook both an important contributor to the Saarinen myth, and how architectural practice and press relations are conducted today.

The Kresge Auditorium project provides an ideal case study because it was underway when Eero and Louchheim began to correspond, and it was finished a year after they formally married. How the two spoke about Kresge to each other (the conversation was limited), and how the contemporary architectural press attempted to make sense of this spectacularly engineered building both serve to illuminate the behind-the-scenes process and its public effects.

From very early on, Louchheim understood what Eero's relationship to his practice could be about, and began to write it into being in her earliest letters to the architect. She saw far beyond what had been written about him before she interviewed him for the *New York Times*, and we read in an early letter, sent in 1953, her dedication to his brilliance being recognized: "For the obvious thing—so obvious that only the most superficial of journalists, like a certain writer on *The New York Times*, would fail to bring it out in an article—is that your devotion to architecture has little to do with 'competitions with self' or 'competitions with father,'" she wrote, a few months after they met and shortly after the publication of her 1953 *New York Times* profile (to which she is alluding), "but with a very real and very honest and very whole-hearted enjoyment and respect for and sympathy with—in short, love for architecture. It's in your heart as well as in your brain; it really is your means of expression—and you must never, never, never get sidetracked."[8] Her assurances that she understood how important architecture was to him speaks to a vision for his career both in line with what he wanted, and far more ambitious.

Fig. 16. A view of the sweeping corner of Kresge Auditorium, showing Saarinen's use of curves and angular grids to create a then-novel architecture and contained sense of interior space. Location: Cambridge, MA. © Ezra Stoller/Esto

While Louchheim was writing her *New York Times* profile, Saarinen mentioned the Kresge project, but almost always in passing. "If you need any more background information to plough through on the M.I.T. job I wrote a couple of long letters to Peter Blake and you could ask him to lend you those," he wrote.[9] The fact that he referred to his letters for "background information" indicates that his work for Kresge was internally neither well documented nor well-articulated. He was, in a sense, offering the dregs of his professional archive.

The Kresge Auditorium operates at multiple scales and ranges, and for this reason the idea of looking at it as a series of numbers is, while a fascinating exercise in imagination, impossible to do as an attempt to see the totality. Saarinen was deeply invested in addressing the totality of the whole, both in terms of his own location—remember the list of architects he wanted to place himself with, which did include the canonically accepted modernist masters Mies, Kahn, and even Johnson—but also in terms of what he thought about while he sat at the drafting table and the model shop. Saarinen's self-mythology, produced, as I have argued earlier, in conversation with Louchheim rather than in isolation, relied on a

Fig. 17a–b. Interior view of the chapel at MIT, completed in 1955, a project that Aline B. Louchheim and Eero Saarinen discussed extensively in their early letters and that he completed in collaboration with Harry Bertoia, who designed the altarpiece screen. Location: Cambridge, MA. © Ezra Stoller/Esto.

sense of his own deep psychological interests as other, novel, and valuable to the exploration of the built form. However, the publications about Kresge missed much of what made later articles so compelling. A close analysis of a few will show how they miss the interpretive mark.

In January 1956, a year after the chapel and auditorium were completed, *Architectural Forum* published an article on the project. The dek read: "MIT completes two of today's most talked about buildings—a cylindrical chapel and a domed auditorium."[10] The "most talked about" seems to be an editorial intervention, a way of writing into being that this would become a subject of discussion.[11] The self-reflexiveness becomes explicit in the article—"Ever since Eero Saarinen's designs for the MIT chapel and auditorium were previewed three years ago (*AF*, Jan '53), fellow architects and other critics have been talking about the merits and demerits of this daring project," the article, which does not have an author, opens. Remember that in January 1953, Eero and Louchheim were just about to meet—and so her interventions would not have begun. Kresge is important for our purposes because it was a project born before Louchheim and completed shortly after she moved to Bloomfield Hills and was not yet fully integrated into the practice. This particular article "inspects the buildings pictorially," with the note that "a subsequent issue will present the judgment of a group of noted architectural critics."[12]

The text is reminiscent of the kind of school paper that addresses "one school of thought" versus "another school of thought." The article makes reference to "fellow architects and other critics" but without naming them or saying where these conversations appeared, aside from an earlier preview version of Kresge itself, in this publication. The plans for a subsequent issue are equally undetailed—who will this "group of noted architectural critics" be? The emphasis here on showing images, on "inspecting" the building pictorially is interesting for our ekphrastic purposes. First, this implies that buildings can be inspected through pictures—not only through experience. Second, it implies that there is a purity of observation that is possible—that it is not the combination of images + words + models + pictures + plans + elevations that need to be viewed, but that images in and of themselves are inspectable. This is interesting to us because so much of Saarinen's later work required a phenomenological approach, and the writing was an attempt to embody what was a completely ethereal experience on the part of the physical viewer—but that work found its linchpin here, with Kresge. Pre-Kresge were projects like the corporate campus for GM, or the Crow Island School, projects that were more angular, less surprising to a popular audience. Kresge marked the first example of what would be explored later in the Ingalls Rink at Yale and then in Saarinen's capstone achievement, the TWA Terminal in New York City.

Interestingly, the 1953 *Architectural Forum* preview contained far more text than the later publication. There are multiple images, beginning with a photograph of a model of the entire plaza, and the text is visually broken up. The left side of the first page contains a series of six questions, based in the headline which reads "Saarinen Challenges the Rectangle, designs a domed auditorium and a cylindrical chapel for MIT's laboratory campus, raises these six questions about the accepted shape of buildings."[13] I will not duplicate the questions here, but I will point out the main thrust of the questions, which are all questioning conventions, as the headline intimated they would. The questions begin with "Is there any reason why ..." or "Does a chapel have to be ..." or "Is there really a fixed relationship between ... ?" I see in the use of words like "reason," "have to be" and "fixed relationship" vestiges of the International Style of modernism, which relied on angular forms to exert suggestive control

Fig. 18. View of TWA Terminal, opened 1962, taken from the side and showing a bit of the bird-like structure; the building appears crouched for takeoff. Of particular note are the then-unusual curved concrete forms. Location: New York, NY. © Ezra Stoller/Esto.

over buildings' inhabitants. Here we see a break with the Saarinen who listed Mies and Johnson as his influences. He is beginning to break out on his own, and these questions—which appear, crucially, in *language* that in the magazine precedes the images—are part of a new architecture. The text of the article agrees. "Eero Saarinen and his associates ... have challenged current thinking and started some basic rethinking about architecture and building."[14]

Here are the early beginnings of not only a formal turning point but also a narrative one, in which the editorial questions—seen adjacent to and in concert with a photograph of a model of Kresge—are part of what brings to light this next phase of his architectural career. "The auditorium is a wide departure," the text continues, and then lists the engineers that have made this possible. The next paragraph discusses the brick cylinder

Fig. 19. View of the exterior corner of Kresge Auditorium, showing clearly Saarinen's facility with marrying modern grids and novel swoops. Location: Cambridge, MA. © Ezra Stoller/Esto.

chapel, which the author argues is an example of how "Saarinen and his associates have out-traditionalized today's traditionalists just as conclusively as they out-modernized today's modernists in using a dome instead of the familiar wedge shape for the auditorium." And then, a break in the text for an italics section: *"Before getting into such details most readers will want to know how Saarinen came to these remarkable solutions. Was this simply an effort to be original or was there something deeper behind it?"*[15]

This idea of curiosity about there being something deeper than "simply an effort to be original" does not resonate with the contemporary modernism of the time. Think of Saarinen's General Motors project, or Mies's Seagram Building (1958). These did not raise questions about there being "something deeper." The architecture "followed function"; the modernists were supposed to be interested in orthogonal lines and the ability for well-proportioned structures to be able to change and augment the human experience. The color photograph of a model showing different triangular shapes on the plaza overtly addresses this issue. "The two buildings on their platform represent an overhaul of Louis Sullivan's credo ... that 'form follows function.'"[16] The next section is philosophical. "His dome is, on the contrary, a generalized kind of structural shape—the universal kind of shape which would span that kind of space with greatest economy of material regardless of whether the space were an auditorium, an exhibition building or even a supermarket."[17] The author then describes Saarinen as a matchmaker. "In all marriages, the success depends upon two things: first how well the partners were suited to one another, and second, how well they can adapt themselves to one another."[18] This, then, is more of a marriage than a formalist or modernist line in the sand or stake in the conceptual / art historical ground. The observation about the messiness and above all partnership that goes into producing the Kresge Auditorium links directly back to this book's argument that it was not only how Saarinen's architecture looked that changed the course of architectural history, but how it was discussed. Kresge is like the amuse-bouche of our architectural meal, to throw multiple metaphors together; it is a tantalizing example of what we are to see later, once Louchheim's operation was in full effect.

The next spread goes into details, particularly cost, and shows pictures of models, the same selection that is shown in the 1956 follow-up, but this time mirrored—an unintentional reference to Saarinen's practice of writing in mirror writing and then transforming his text through carbon copy.[19] In the mid-1950s, with architectural photography being published in black and white, floor plans and elevations and sections were a common sight in magazines. The first page emphasizes the chapel, and then gives a site plan which shows two circles, one of which has been turned into the curved triangular canopy of the auditorium, the other of which has become the "windowless" cylindrical chapel.[20]

The next two pages are devoted to the chapel, and then we come to a spread featuring the auditorium. The text is mostly an extended statement from Saarinen. "A dome seemed right for many reasons: 1) that shape is a recurrent motif of the existing MIT campus; 2) it gives expression to the idea of sheltering a large space." The text goes on but doesn't illuminate much—the emphasis is on the structure, and also on "a pleasant interior space." As a reader, I find myself glossing over the text, looking for something to hang on to. What exactly is the auditorium about? It seems to be very much about a "thin-shell concrete" form, something with acoustical "floating clouds" and a "sweep of the dome," but a consistent message does not come through (in contrast with the sense of the TWA Terminal's being the "bones of the bird," as we read in the introduction and will read more about later, and the relentless emphasis on the magic of flight that the terminal created in its visitors and passengers). And yet the text is accurate, as Kresge is hard to encapsulate in words and in drawings. Photographs—like the one in *Record*—tend to show some version of a sweeping vista, an expanse of glass and a thin-shelled concrete roof, and yet the interior of the auditorium, the programmatic part itself, seems utterly disconnected from that swoop. A picture on the top right of the page shows this interior, and it looks much like one hundred other anodyne auditoriums might look: rows of seats, a slightly detailed ceiling presumably for acoustic effect, a stage. And yet a section, a visual form that almost never appears in publications today, shows a much more kinetic structure. We see the swooping dome collect the elements within its singular shape. Two lobbies, the theater, the stage, are all specifically and purposefully detailed within this encapsulated space, and it is the section that gives the viewer something closer to a phenomenological experience than any of the photographs, which are too glossy, too external, too split apart to give much of an actual sense of experiencing the building.

In 1955, *Architectural Record* published an op-ed about the building written by Edward Weeks, then editor of *The Atlantic Monthly*, then as now a general-interest publication. Why Weeks, whose *New York Times* obituary described him as the first person to publish Ernest Hemingway in a national magazine?[21] Two years later, Weeks would talk with Mike Wallace about "'bigness,' mass culture, tastemakers, advertising and media," and so he was perhaps perfectly positioned—though ironically so—as someone to take on this new project, poised as it was on the cusp between Saarinen pre-Louchheim and Saarinen benefiting from Louchheim's skills.[22]

Weeks's article placed the building into a larger cultural context, opening with a description of MIT, "to whom one looks for the latest word in science" and observing that it "has just unveiled the latest novelty in the field of the humanities."[23] Weeks described the auditorium as "a festival hall," and then placed it within the context of university performing arts spaces, describing how Harvard (where he studied) had attracted "budding playwrights like . . . Eugene O'Neil." His allusion to Harvard was, however, in contrast with MIT—"If you detect envy in these remarks, it is there all right, for speaking as a Harvard man this is only one of several instances where I had admired and envied the initiative of M.I.T."[24] The article moves to architecture, and the description of Kresge is technical, and will be familiar to us from the ArchDaily paragraph that opened this chapter: "The dome is one eighth of a sphere, pinned down, anchored at three points on heavy sunken abutments and then the dome cut way between these points ... the building covers about half an acre."[25] After a brief-sentence interlude describing other things that auditorium has been compared to (a diaper, for instance), he returns to the technical details. We learn that it seats 1,250; that the doors are of "solid oak"; that the "little theater" seats 250 and lies directly below the main auditorium. Weeks then writes about his own experience as a lecturer, then talks about other performances he has seen in various places. The article meanders into a memory-lane trip about places Weeks has been and people he has heard speak; it seems impossible for him to both see the architecture at hand and to have compelling interpretive thoughts about it. The article oscillates between rote physical descriptions, and these kinds of discursive asides that, though interesting, do not tell the reader anything more about the building. He talks about fresh air and a sense of "serenity," and the only truly critical point is that "the architect has made no concessions as yet to the rigors of the New England climate."[26] This transitions him to more critical thoughts. "This is an impersonal igloo," Weeks writes, though this is only in comparison to the Little Theatre, designed by Winthrop Ames.[27] He does not quote Saarinen, though he did, reminiscent of presidential press secretaries, speak with "one who had had to do with the auditorium," who said that the philosophy of the building was "to enclose space at the least possible cost."[28] Emphasizing cost rather than his interest in space, or innovative form, or the human concerns that we saw he was so interested in discussing with Louchheim shows how, without Louchheim's guidance, Saarinen did not intuitively offer the most exciting remarks.

Saarinen had already claimed that the issue of cost was not the driving force behind Kresge's design, and while it fits into Weeks's editorial desires, it does not fit into any consistent narrative about the auditorium. And so what to make of this article, which took up six pages in the vaunted July issue of *Architectural Record*? Was this a play at bringing architecture to the greater public, by hiring a nonarchitecture critic to write this article? Possibly—architecture was beginning to enter a larger public consciousness in this decade. What this article demonstrates is that there is as yet no publicly accessible and narratively consistent way to look at architecture without either telling stories about it that are only very tangentially related to the project at hand, or to recount a series of factual details. There was no reportorial or critical consistency in this article, no developed explication of how this building could be understood in a wider context—not as it was being practiced by contemporaries like Vincent Scully or Nikolaus Pevsner or Siegfried Giedion.

The Weeks article is followed, in the same issue, by one by N. Keith Scott, and is a reprint of the February issue of the *Journal of the Royal Institute of British Architects*. Scott is an architecture critic—he calls the building "one of the most controversial buildings of our time."[29] Scott appears to be directly responding to Weeks—or perhaps to the cadre of writers Weeks fits into—in saying that "there has been a tendency among those who should know better to cover their embarrassment in some premature and ill-informed criticism." Scott enters the conversation started earlier, about Saarinen's nonadoption of Sullivan's "form follows function" credo, and begins to tell the story but then slips back into the technical speak—describing how it is one eighth of a sphere and sits on three abutments. The majority of the article is then about acoustics.

A year later, in the November 1956 issue of *Architectural Record*, Eliot Noyes, an architect and industrial designer and a noted modernist, described the auditorium, which was tied for fifteenth place in the "top 100 buildings of the century" with Matthew Nowicki's State Fair Arena in Raleigh.[30] Noyes wrote, "The interior form of the large auditorium expresses clearly, convincingly, and somewhat surprisingly its relationship to the exterior form of the great structural shell, and this major interior-exterior relationship is strong enough to make the design convincing."[31] The approximately one-hundred-word article is short and to the point, though Noyes ended with an overt reference to "the nearby Aalto dormitory," a project by Alvar Aalto that was part of what Merkel referred to as MIT's architectural adventures.[32] The image of the auditorium, which appeared on the preceding page, is a study in planes—in the perfectly gridded Cartesian glass front wall which appears to disappear into an overhanging concrete swoop. A set of double doors outlined in bright white make clear that this is a building to go into (rather than a folly designed to be seen only from afar), and yet the auditorium is photographed from far enough away as to lose all sense of human scale. How big are those glass windows? How big are those doors? How far does the swoop actually go?

The media ecosystem in which Louchheim was working was based on the independence of critics; writers like Lewis Mumford and Henry-Russell Hitchcock decided which buildings to write about, and how to write about them. There weren't yet embedded publicists who would gently encourage a writer in a certain direction, casually suggest that they think about a project in a certain light or with a certain philosophical background in mind; Louchheim had not yet fully codified her practice into the career choice it would become for so many architecturally oriented publicists decades later. And so we see in these articles about Kresge a repetition of the same observations—the spectacular engineering; describing the auditorium as the eighth of a dome—but without a clear narrative of the kind that would begin to appear with Ingalls Rink and the TWA Terminal. Kresge is a complex building, one that fits into the canonical narrative of Saarinen and his work, and yet it is one that is often overlooked when people are idly thinking of Saarinen's greatest hits. It is easier to think of the St. Louis Arch, with its singular—and singularly spectacular—swooping parabolic move, or of the great corporate campus that he did for GM, which has been so well explored by historians like Alexandra Lange, or of the colleges for Yale. These have begun to fit into neat categories—the Ultimate Saarinen (the Arch), Corporate Saarinen (the GM campus), Mind-Blowing Saarinen (TWA). Kresge was still misunderstood by its contemporary interlocutors.

While there was interest in Saarinen, the way in which his projects were being written about lacked a narrative flair that we will see later. While he was a good interviewee even without Louchheim's ministrations, what this short case study about the way the Kresge Auditorium was discussed has shown is how disparate, seemingly random, and inconsistent the press can be. It has proven important to show what the press looked like before, so that we may fully see how profoundly Louchheim's presence and interventions changed it. These articles clarify how poorly managed the press was before Louchheim's arrival. The Yale Ingalls Rink (1953-1958) more thoroughly represented progress both in Saarinen's architecture and in its representation.

Ingalls

Turning to the Ingalls Ice Rink project, completed in 1958, we will see the development of an increasingly coherent narrative. Richard Knight's memoir, *Saarinen's Quest* (2008), Pierluigi Serraino's biography (2005), and Jayne Merkel's biography (2005) all undertake analyses of the project.[33] Knight was a photographer who worked in the Saarinen office, and his retrospective observations are aphoristic and impressionistic rather

Fig. 20. Oblique view of Ingalls Rink (a.k.a. the Yale Whale), completed in 1959, showing the catenary curve that makes up the "spine" of this building. Location: New Haven, CT. © Wayne Andrews/Esto.

than scholarly. However, they are useful, as he was an on-the-ground observer. Serraino is an architect and the author of a culturally influential popular biography on Saarinen; and Merkel is a working critic and freelance architecture writer. That Saarinen can sustain such a varied level of authorial and audience curiosity speaks to the enduring interest in his work, and to the way in which architectural styles can wax and wane.

Saarinen's emphasis on using study models enabled his office to generate narratives before buildings were completed, thus offering Louchheim a chance to start working with editors, critics, and writers from a vantage point much closer to Day 1 of an architectural project's life. Richard Knight, who wrote extensively about Ingalls Rink and whose biographical observations about its design will provide a way of introducing the project, points out that "in the late 1950s, Saarinen upended the architectural profession and revolutionized the way buildings were designed by using large models to investigate the forms and functions of his intended work."[34] While the available archive does not directly address whether this choice had anything to do with Louchheim, she was in the office, sitting at a desk facing Eero's, during the late 1950s, and it is reasonable to infer from her detailed letters asking about specific design moves, as discussed in chapter 2, that she would have supported anything that promoted an extensive dialogue about design. As context, Knight reminds us that "not since the Renaissance were models used as extensively as in Saarinen's designs."[35] He gives us a short history of the design process, arguing that, up to the mid-twentieth century, architects would "design buildings by drawing plans, sections and elevations," and only with "the client's authorization" build a "small, precisely crafted model."[36]

Knight and I are in agreement that "the way buildings and complexes were designed in Eero's architecture practice changed dramatically beginning in 1956 when he designed the Ingalls Hockey Rink," the Yale University campus building which is our next object of study. "A year later," Knight writes, "his use of large three-dimensional studies literally took off when the office designed the T.W.A. passenger terminal at Kennedy International Airport."[37] Knight is right that Saarinen's form-making changed, and yet he overlooks another important element contributing to this shift: Louchheim. It has been agreed—by Knight, Merkel, and others—that there *was* a shift in Saarinen's work in the mid-1950s and while he of course had his own creative ideas and exploration, this is also the period in which Louchheim fully mobilized herself. Knight reported that "the structure of his firm would change dramatically, too," from "an atelier" to "a more formal organization."[38] Knight mentions the three partners, Kevin Roche, John Dinkeloo, and Joe Lacy, as well as Warren Platner, but does not mention Louchheim, who of course brought a more formal organization to the way in which the firm communicated its architecture to the outside. Knight's focus on the restructuring is correct; but, he has missed an essential actor. His omission of Louchheim, despite his presence in the office, speaks to a gendered invisibility; perhaps her self-described role as "helpmeet" and the intimacy with which she interacted with Saarinen in their neighboring desks clouded Knight's perception of the professional aspect of her assistance.

"David S. Ingalls Hockey Rink, Yale University, aka The Yale Whale is like none other," Knight continues. The rest of his memoir is comprised of a series of photographs showing various types of models and group portraits of Eero and partners. Louchheim is completely absent from these images. The Saarinen biographer Serraino offers an afterword to Knight's book. As with so many predecessors, he evaluates Saarinen against Mies: "While Mies van der Rohe was doing research in architecture with the mindset of the physicist—reaching back to general principles of universal applicability—Saarinen took on the challenges to test those principles with [a] rare urban design sensibility," he says.[39] He also gives us another insight into Eero's seemingly quiet (though of course we know overt) obsession with his place in the canon, with his ambition. "In every building, Eero would measure himself against architectural history," Serraino says. Serraino also offers a new observation—that Eero's dyslexia, plus being "able to draw and write with both hands with equal dexterity," "made him develop drawing skills as a way to communicate over words and reading."[40] Serraino also says that Eero was "keenly responsive to the power of the media in crafting an image that could appeal to the masses." Serraino here is missing how Louchheim was an essential translator between these drawings that could appeal to the masses, and the editors who could publish them. Yes, Eero was responsive to the power of the media, but he himself, with only his drawings and his dyslexia, would not have been able to negotiate coverage and publication, nor handle the influx of interest that came with projects like the Yale Whale or TWA on his own.

There are fleeting shadows of Louchheim everywhere—her presence is palpable in these various biographical texts, but she is never directly named, and when she is, it is only to be described as his wife, as an orchestrator, as an art critic. It is as if the historians of Saarinen are unable to see *her* as contributor/collaborator, while very clearly seeing her contributions. This is reminiscent of the other examples discussed above: Ise Gropius, the women clients whom Friedman outlines, and figures like Molly Weed Noyes, wife of famous modernist architect Eliot Noyes, whose contributions were utterly overlooked while at the same time being subtly understood. Yes, Saarinen was interested in fame. Yes, Saarinen was very good at thinking about how images and models could represent his ideas. Yes, Saarinen's career exploded in 1956 and he experienced a new level of interest in his work. And yet all of these patterns have been seen as self-reflexive, as simply part of the work that he did, as the next obvious thing, and not as the result of a new kind of partnership. A few pages later, Serraino does mention Louchheim, but he still gives the power itself to Saarinen. "Eero's comfort level in navigating the politics of the media was as developed as his design talent," Serraino writes. "Magazine editors, museum curators, academics, corporate leaders, photographers, and master architects," he says, "were the nodes of a vast social network that Saarinen cultivated, especially since his second wife Aline, Associate Art Critic of the *New York Times*, orchestrated his publicity campaigns around his buildings."[41] The structure of this sentence takes power away from Louchheim, and it also misidentifies her. She was associate art critic when they met, and she would continue to hold the position in name only until her resignation in 1959, but her work in Saaarinen's firm was as Head of Information Services (from 1954), a title that Serraino completely overlooks. And this is how it happens over and over and over again—she is elided altogether or identified (or misidentified) and then not fully acknowledged.

"The competence of his collaborators explains why the office could run practically on autopilot for years to complete the projects that he had left unfinished at the time of his premature death," Serraino says.[42] Yes, architects like Roche and Dinkeloo—who finished Saarinen's projects before opening their own firm—were essential to keeping the office's extant projects going until completion. As, however, was Louchheim.

On December 17, 1956, the *Yale Daily News* published an article about the rink. The writer, Scott Sullivan, quoted the noted art historian Vincent J. Scully as calling the rink "at once the most logical and the most imaginative building of its kind yet designed."[43] Sullivan continued. "Mr. Saarinen's design looks from above like a cross between a flounder and a turtle."[44] Clearly, the whale comparison had not yet been made. The flounder/turtle idea continued in a later article. "It might be interesting to watch the progress of this Eero Saarinen structure to see if it really will look like a flounder from the top and a turtle shell from in front."[45] A year later, the flounder reference was still going strong. "First attempts to make ice in Eero Saarinen's flounder-shaped rink . . . will be undertaking within the next two weeks," reporter Albert S. Pergam wrote.[46] Intriguingly, a caption underneath a photograph of the rink alluded to "considerable controversy in architectural circles," a sign that the shape was, perhaps, not so embraced as student reporters had anticipated just two years

Fig. 21. Side view of Ingalls Rink, showing how it could also be seen as a "turtle." Location: New Haven, CT. © Wayne Andrews/Esto.

prior. In October 1958 a headline referred to the structure as "the controversial 'turtle.'"[47] However, the text of the article itself made reference to "the gaping whale-mouth entrance."[48] It may not have been an appealing phrase, but it was a step in the right direction. The *Yale Daily News* continued to cover the project and Saarinen, profiling the architect in late 1958; it is clear that the campus community was both invested in the rink, and also enthusiastic about its designer, whether he had produced a turtle, a flounder, or a whale.

It is worth looking at how Ingalls was written about decades later in order to track some of the development of its descriptions. The art historian and architecture critic Jayne Merkel groups the MIT project together with the Yale Whale because of their formal similarities. After Saarinen conducted "dogged research," Merkel says that he "sketched until he arrived at a form specifically suitable for hockey—raw and rugged but also graceful," and argues that he was influenced by Matthew Nowicki's Livestock Judging Pavilion in Raleigh. Merkel then immediately turns to the structure's "huge, wide parabolic arch for a central spine held in place by a grid of cables running both parallel and perpendicular to it, and hung

Fig. 22. Interior of the Ingalls Rink, showing the extraordinary curve in some ways reminiscent of the form of the St. Louis Arch in Missouri. Location: New Haven, CT. © Wayne Andrews/Esto.

it in a saddle shape to form a tension web." Merkel describes the "forty-foot canopy over the entrances" and says that it "resembles a gigantic, humped, slithering beast or, some say, an overturned Viking ship." That may not sound very appealing. But from inside—from the interior, where, some would say, buildings are meant to be experienced (although we know, of course, that they can be experienced in so many forms, from sentence to drawing to building)—Merkel says that "it sweeps you up in a skating movement," an observation supported by an image of the extraordinarily soaring interior. Here, Merkel observes, the architect "operated as a sculptor as well as an architect." Merkel tells us how the donor's wife initially hated the project, and was swayed only by the Yale president's interventions, and Eero's own, but "after the building was finished, the Ingallses were delighted."[49]

In terms of press, the usual suspects appear: *Architectural Forum*, *Architectural Record*, *Architectural Review*, *L'architecture d'aujourd'hui*, *Baukunst und Werkform*, *Zodiac*, and *Casabella*.[50] The range of publications and countries from which they were produced coincides with Saarinen's general increase in celebrity, which also coincides with Louchheim's arrival, indicating that her presence dramatically increased his public profile.

The international press praised the project, and the articles were much more dynamic and breathless than any of the Kresge coverage had been. The architecture critic Walter McQuade, who would write about the TWA project and was therefore a repeat assessor, wrote an extended review of the building in *Architectural Forum*.[51] The first paragraph places Ingalls Rink into the pantheon: "The David S. Ingalls Hockey Rink is even more notable as Architect Eero Saarinen's most successful attempt to mix visual flavor into the recipe of modern architecture," McQuade writes. No modern architect respecting his (unfortunately it was always *his*) salt would have considered their glass panes or extended meditations on the rhythmic use of steel (as in Mies's Illinois Institute of Technology Crown Hall) to have been "visual flavor." And yet McQuade embraces this metaphor on behalf of Eero. Compare the poetic way McQuade wrote about the Whale with the relentlessly factual way critics—writing in these same publications!—wrote about the MIT project: "The lawns and parking spaces slide away like the trough of a long slow wave, leaving the building riding the crest, a graceful exciting, almost baroque structure," McQuade writes. "Saarinen . . . has shaped a structure loaded with personality." He continues, "For the spectator, the over-all impression indoors is of concrete bulk and heaviness under him, and exhilarating lightness above." And then—the building "has already spawned a number of affectionate nicknames; its users liken it to everything from a great whale to an oriental barn." He then plays devil's advocate. "Should a building curve so freely? Is this not too rash and undignified to be a serious modern design?" He returned to his culinary motif. "The design has so much flavor that some critics refuse to swallow it." In short, they think it looks "clumsy," or that it includes "insecure afterthoughts" by the engineers, or aspects of the design look "awkward." McQuade then says that "laymen develop affection for buildings slowly," something that I don't agree with, and that I don't think Saarinen would have agreed with either. The Yale Whale is not a study in forms that is meant to be interesting or legible only to experts within his architectural community. In fact it is the very opposite—a building so evocative and so powerful that even laymen would be able to get it immediately. McQuade finds fault with these criticisms. "Architectural expression has been narrowing for years," he writes, "decreasing tamely into a series of techniques, such as the jewel-like detailing of the exquisite curtain walls." Usually, "it is only the vulgar American buildings that are spectacular." The Yale rink is different, McQuade contends. It is "both spectacular and fine. Great sensitivity and daring are combined in this building." He ends with, "It is done to please the architect [himself], and this is what eventually pleases everyone, even if it surprises them at first."[52] The *Record* article was illustrated first with a swooping photograph that took up a page and a half; another swooping photograph showed the back of the roof; then an obliquely angled photograph, and three images—plan, section, transverse section—and then two interior details. The editorial interventions of placing the photographs in this order gives the reader the sense that McQuade is trying to produce a specific response in readers with his words—that this is a building whose phenomenology must be experienced. Louchheim was also by this point involved in choosing which photographs to send to which editors, and would have been just as involved in the Ingalls project as she was later with publicity for the TWA project.

An August 1957 article in *Architectural Record* shows a photograph of a model of the Ingalls Rink in a brief one-page article. The text again opens with interpretation—saying that the rink "marks another significant and firm step towards a more fluid, sculptural design vocabulary."[53] It is only at the end that the text goes into details, another departure from the way the MIT auditorium was discussed, even though it is objectively as thrillingly designed as this building, and another sign that this time, there was a clearer message being forcefully delivered by the Saarinen office as a whole. In 1962, *Architectural Record* revisited Ingalls as part of a broad look at Yale's campus architecture.[54] "If the [Kahn] gallery is uncompromising," the text proclaimed, "the hockey rink is completely uninhibited," describing the "Whale" as having "exuberant form," a phrase that could well have appeared in one of Louchheim's previous *New York Times* articles, and whose word choice I attribute to her. The text further distinguished Saarinen from the existing canon: "The Yale rink provides an unusual spatial experience, unclassifiable by ordinary architectural canon."[55] Relevant to our tracking of Louchheim's interventions, *Architectural Record*'s campus issue was first discussed in 1960. On June 30, 1960, Senior Editor James S. Hornbeck wrote to Louchheim. "I realize that Eero is extremely busy, and harassed by all sorts of things, but I do feel that our proposed piece on campus planning—which we will be happy to develop from his dictated notes—will be worth the time he spends on it," he wrote. "An article by a person of Eero's authority would make a real contribution to the architectural literature of a live issue."[56] He wrote later that they had tentatively scheduled the article for late fall, "but ultimately we must have the final article and accompanying illustrative material by the end of August, at the very latest."[57] It is no surprise that the article did not come out until 1962—delays are almost standard for magazine publication schedules—so what this letter shows is that the press was starting to solicit direction from Eero, and this approach is made by way of an appeal to Louchheim. The style of the letter is extremely complimentary of Eero—"extremely busy" ... "but I do feel that our piece"—and we see that Hornbeck is eager to convince Louchheim to convince Eero. And why not write directly to Eero himself if, as those like Serraino have suggested, Eero was so in pocket with the press, so good at media handling? A handwritten note on the top solidifies Louchheim's place. "PAT FILE/I spoke to Eero about this."[58] The relationship of note here is between Hornbeck and Louchheim—Hornbeck's letter opens with "I greatly enjoyed seeing you the other day when I was in Detroit; my only regret was that our visit was so short," introducing a sense of the personal, of locating both of them in time and space. . Hornbeck, by calling back to the last time he saw Louchheim, was reconstituting their personal relationship before moving to this professional request—and it was presented as a *request*—and thereby exhibiting her power. A month after this letter, Pat Burley, Louchheim's assistant, wrote to Hornbeck, updating him on the progress, and reporting that Eero had begun to dictate some notes that would be sent as soon as possible. Lest Hornbeck worry that Louchheim was absent or uninformed about this, she opened with a direct reference to Louchheim, reporting that she'd spoken with her about his potential trip to the office, and advising him, via Aline, to phone only a few days ahead of when he wanted to come.[59] Aline is here directly positioned as an authoritative gatekeeper, and also as someone who is ultimately on Hornbeck's side in soliciting Eero's attention. She is disclosing Eero's schedule and also suggesting exactly how Hornbeck can work around Eero's busy-ness. Hornbeck certainly appreciated Louchheim's interventions, and wrote later: "I wrote Eero telling him how grateful we were for all the time and work he had put into the article and I wanted this note to add our thanks to you in the part you played in the project.

Although it is not apparent on the surface, I am sure your contribution was a very important one and we at the RECORD are all grateful to you for your efforts."[60] We see here his recognition of her interventions.

Louchheim sent word of the Ingalls project to her friends and professional contacts. Wayne Andrews, an architecture and art writer who worked as an editor at the book publishing company Charles Scribner's Sons, wrote to Aline on October 30, 1958, thanking her for the news of the finished Yale rink, and informing her that he and his wife were on their way to MIT to take some photographs of Eero's buildings but that perhaps they might also head to New Haven.[61] The letter ends with this simple sentence—"The thought of something even finer than the GM center is tantalizing."[62] While we do not have Aline's letter to which he was responding, the shortness and specificity of this response imply that much of her letter was setting this up—that Yale was worth seeing even more than MIT; and that it was even finer than the GM Center. The idea of the Yale project as absolutely important continued after Saarinen's death. In a condolence note written on September 30, 1961, Irwin Miller, the Indiana-based industrialist and architectural magnate, brought up the Yale work: "I suppose you know how much resistance to good architecture there was at first at Yale," he wrote. And yes, "The influence of Eero on the [Yale] Corporation has been very great, and all by himself he will have changed the face of the University, not alone with his own buildings but also with the quality of all that are to follow."[63]

Decades after these publications, Merkel's book about Saarinen was published. It is worth looking closely at how one of Saarinen's most astute and dedicated biographers interpreted Ingalls, as even with the distance of time, Louchheim's interventions ring clear. Merkel starts with four sketches placed against each other—each showing the basic form but still unrecognizable as its evolved finished form. We see cross-hatching, single pen sketches, curves. We see one shape that looks like a banana and another that looks much more like a butterflied anchovy fillet than it does a majestic whale. In these images we can see Eero's design process, and it is not necessarily as transparent as Serraino has argued his work was. Instead, we can see images that need to be translated into not only study models but also words. Why did viewers think it was a whale instead of an anchovy fillet? Why do we focus so much on that curve and how it bends? There is the implication of movement in some of these drawings, and there is even more the record of a creative person working something out through drawing—of exploring iterative modalities and images that would ultimately end up with this perfectly engineered design. The next page shows a longitudinal section and a transverse section, as well as a plan, and none of these images are particularly inspiring or moving. Rather, they are minimal, descriptive without being evocative. In the plan there is a slightly more evocative sense of movement in the curves of the exterior walls, but the rink looks like a standard rectangular rink. We see rows and rows of seats, and an opening. In both section drawings, we see lines and stairs, with only gentle swoops to the side. This is not the magnificent project that we are seeing historians and critics universally agree began to change Saarinen's career, Yale's campus, and architectural design in the United States.

The photographs, however, made the status of this building clear. A full-spread photograph shows two children in motion, ice skates swinging from their hands, as they run towards the door. We see the overhang, described by Merkel, and here it is a swooping shape jutting out over the plaza. And then, the wonder, which comes from seeing that this singular spike overhang originates not from the overhang but from the central spine of the building itself. The ribs in the roof that looked like receptive lines in the section here become almost kinetic. It is hard to look at this photograph and not think of smoothing something out in model, of not wanting to touch these lines because they are so deeply phenomenologically moving. This is a project that needed to be photographed, and from the outside. Merkel's book includes one interior shot and it is busy with hockey team flags and the motion of hockey players. Motion is a repeated idea; people are either running towards the building or skating quickly inside the building, and yet the interior photographs miss what the exterior does so well. The last photograph looks like a giant bird spreading its wings, an idea that is fully developed in the TWA project and its publicity.

Why Fame?

CHAPTER FIVE

I realized, once I got to this section, that nowhere in this book so far have I paused to question why someone would want to be famous. As we saw in chapter 3, Saarinen himself knew simply that he wanted to be dean at Yale; was open to the help of Aline because he saw how publications would help him get there. We saw in chapter 1, about my own writing career, that I wanted to be famous and bylined so that I would know that I existed, so that I could feel some sort of adjacent power. The architects and designers that I wrote about wanted to be famous because ... well, I never asked them. I never asked why designers hired the publicists who pitched me and, for a long time, I didn't ask my own clients.

We have an aversion in the design field, in many fields besides entertainment, really, to saying explicitly that we want to be famous. When I published a memoir, *How to Be Loved*, in 2019, I wrote about how I'd wanted, as a child, to be famous—to feel like I existed, to feel like the work that I did mattered. As a child, I'd felt like the majority of my value came from my work, from the potential for future achievements and accomplishments. I'd often felt like if I weren't producing something or writing something that mattered, I myself didn't matter. So of course I sought bylines; of course I craved the belief that the words that I wrote were important. When I wasn't brave enough to write my own essays about the topics that I wanted to, then, I hid behind writing about other peoples' work. I remember learning early on from my first mentor that I should use other peoples' words to say what I wanted to say. That I could begin to construct arguments through the work that I did, but that until I had some kind of bona fides—an advanced degree, a body of work—I should let more established people do the talking for me.

Fame, then, for me, was something on the way towards a sense of purpose and a sense of drive. I'd never asked the people that I wrote about what was in it for them, because I understood how important it was to keep up the facade of not caring about any of this. Maybe they hired publicists because otherwise they simply couldn't keep up with the volume of inquiries; that was often what they said. But I knew that many architects hired publicists because they wanted to be famous. And they wanted to be famous because they wanted more work.

Remember that California father and son team in Palo Alto? I started working with them early in my publicity career. I'd written about them once before, a big profile for *Metropolis* magazine, and then I reconnected with them when an editor I knew assigned me a piece about a house they'd done for *San Francisco Cottages & Gardens*. The son, whom I'll call James, and I had an interview about the house. He hadn't been prepped, I could tell; I didn't think the photographs were extraordinary. But I'd remembered them from ten years earlier, was happy to be back in touch. Over the course of the call, I slowly revealed that I did the kind of publicity work that he'd mentioned being interested in having someone help him with. I wrote up a short proposal, and sent it in. They became a client.

Working with them was a challenge because of a disconnect between what they said they wanted and what I believed they needed. What they said they wanted was an intellectual connection, someone to have conversations with about architecture, and also to help them with a book that they'd started writing the year before and, I realized years later, kept postponing so as to be able to add the latest project. They seemed to me constitutionally incapable of ever feeling finished with something. As soon as they finished one project, or came close to finishing it, they wanted to look to the next one. They were always very excited about what was coming down the line, and totally over what they'd just done. It made it hard to publicize their work because projects have such long life-spans; it takes years to go from initiation to sketches to renderings to models to construction drawings to completion to photography to publication. By the time we had photography ready for publication, the designers almost invariably thought the project was old news. I also had a pragmatic approach. I wanted them to say that they wanted to be published to get more clients; they wanted to say they wanted to get published so that they could contribute to the discourse.

A few years ago, my colleague Marianela D'Aprile and I gave a joint presentation at Yale University. I'd been invited to give a talk about fame, and about its productions, and the ways in which it all came down to money. I wasn't able to actually give the talk, and so she gave it in my stead, but added her own critiques. Ultimately, we were there to question the role that money had in the design world, to draw attention to the ways in which discourse was just used as a vehicle for fame, which was in turn used for material security. I often found myself deeply frustrated when talking to my clients because it seemed like they wanted security but never wanted to actually admit it.

Together, my firm published a number of their projects, each one in better and better publications. I'd pitched to them the idea of doing a "director's cut" of some of their projects—taking a story written by someone else and then adding our own spin. That had worked when I'd pitched it for the story I'd written, but once we had a piece by a writer I really respected, who was someone I'd met and cultivated a relationship with after she'd done a tremendous job on a story about one of Frank's houses, I found that I didn't want to do a "director's cut" for her. One, it would have insulted her. Two, it wouldn't have added anything—because we'd so thoroughly coached the architects from the get go. I found a book editor who wanted to work with them and brought her out to Palo Alto, where the three of us had a meeting around a long work table and talked about the kinds of essays we could do. By that point, I'd written multiple drafts of essays for the book, and my team had written thousands of words of project description. We were starting to home in on a sense of what the firm could begin to articulate.

From our perspective, they were a tremendously land-oriented firm. My other colleague was a tremendously gifted landscape thinker, and she began taking over the intellectual heavy lifting. By this point, I was starting to burn out, and didn't have as much enthusiasm as I'd had when I started. I wanted to, but after a while the disconnect between what they said they wanted and what I thought they needed became too much. I stepped away, and my colleagues, working together, began to develop the identity for them. We carried that identity through in every project description we sent out, every time we prepped the architects for an interview.

The last publication before I stopped working with them was the *Dwell* feature. It was a moving story, beautifully rendered and wonderfully photographed. It felt like the capstone of our years working together, and it felt like I had done my job. Their work had been described in a way that they were delighted with, and I knew that we had had a profound influence on how they made it legible. I thought of all the other stories that we'd placed for them, in magazines like *Luxe*, and *Wallpaper**, and how popular I hoped we'd made them. But I never had a sense of the kind of work that they had coming down the line, just that they had work.

I stopped working with them; I ended up dissolving my firm, and so I referred them to my colleague whom I'd worked with, whom they'd also worked with. They wanted the same thing they'd wanted from me: someone to discourse with, someone to produce a sense of an architectural and literary identity. She also told me that they had reached what they'd wanted to reach when I'd started working with them years earlier: the luxury of being able to say no to work.

I always told my clients that publicity was a long game. That they could not expect to hire me, and have a few publications, and suddenly be inundated with the kind of work that they longed for. I told them that this kind of reputation-building took years, took patience, was a long slow burn of just making a legible identity. That was always the word I used, legible. It's because of how clearly I saw Aline's influence in making Eero's work legible—with the whale at Ingalls, or, as we will see, the bird at TWA. I understood the need for consistency, and for every piece of press to work in concert with every other. When I talked to clients, I told them that what we were doing together was outlining a plot of land, and that there might be a super theoretical goalpost on one side, and a super user-friendly design-happy one on the other. My job was to figure out what kinds of stories needed to be placed and published so that, over years, that entire plot was filled in. With this firm, we had outlined the plot. They were friendly, smart, able to do soft interiors and work with interior designers; they were also intensely historical, deeply affected by the landscape, and emotive. We saw every piece that came out as a potential additive or corrective to the one that had come before. We were filling in the plot.

I had told them that it would take four years for them to cement their reputation, and it did. I stopped being able to engage with them in the way that they wanted to be engaged, but as a team, my colleagues and I did our jobs. They paid my firm $3,000 a month for around four years—a total of around a $150,000. And for that, for years, they wondered where the money was going. Weren't sure if it was paying off. It was hard, some months, I knew, for them to justify the fee that they were sending and seeing no publications in return, no increase in inquiries. But what they have now is exactly what they wanted. The luxury of being able to say no to work, of doing the kinds of projects that only they can do.

It is a truism that the reward for doing a good job is getting to do more

work. And that's all our clients wanted, and all Eero wanted. He wanted
to do more projects, which is why so many of his letters to Aline and from
Aline were about potential jobs, future jobs, jobs that she was going to
help him get and jobs that he thought if he just got, he'd finally be happy.
So much of our culture is based on the next thing, on the next project
being the one that will finally bring security, or joy, or fulfillment. So many
of my clients paid me not so that they would be published in the moment
at hand but so that, in some future world, they would get the kind of clients that they thought they deserved, so that they would get to do more
work because they had done such a good job at their job.

Eero planned to do so many more projects before he died. I wonder
sometimes how close my former clients believe they are to death. In so
many ways, architecture is a project of immortality; we build so that we
may imagine a future for ourselves, or for our children. A later client of
mine once built a house for someone that could stand for a thousand
years. Would we still have California in a thousand years? The house was
fire-resistant. But even so, I wanted to ask, would we still have California
in a thousand years? I saw how many people that I worked with wanted
to think about this field because of a fear of death, a fear of everything
coming to an end. Architecture felt, for many, like a way of making a line
in the sand, of saying that they existed. It wasn't so different from why I
wrote, from why I write. We all just want to know that we're real. We all
just want to be reflected, and want to be seen. Paying someone to get us
out there, and help others see us, that's just one more method.

"Bones for a 'Bird'": Publishing TWA

A 1956 *Time* cover story about Saarinen offers a sense of Louchheim's contributions during the early days of her time working with Saarinen and can provide a transition into an exploration of the process of publishing the TWA Terminal, to outline more deeply Louchheim's specific contributions to this moment in Eero's career, and the practice of architecture.

On July 2, 1956, *Time* magazine featured Eero Saarinen on its cover. He was not the first architect to be featured—in fact, *Time* was engaging in an ongoing practice of featuring architects, and had already presented Frank Lloyd Wright in 1938, Richard Neutra in 1949, and would go on to feature Le Corbusier in 1961 and Minoru Yamaski in 1963. By 1956 Saarinen was well known enough (thanks in part, of course, to Aline's glowing 1953 *New York Times* profile) to join this august peer group.[1]

The *Time* article is a remarkable encapsulation of the myth of the great man that pervaded both Saarinen's career and much of the representation of architectural practice throughout the twentieth and twenty-first centuries. The article's first mention of Louchheim was as follows: "Last week, as his wife watched with fascination, he casually turned over his breakfast grapefruit, began carving out elliptical parabolic arches which he then carried off to the office to see if they might do as an idea for the office model of T.W.A.'s new terminal at Idlewild."[2] Not only was Louchheim not named, but she was presented as someone there simply to raptly observe Saarinen—unrecognized in the far more involved role we now understand she was playing. I would contend that Louchheim was probably responsible for coming up with the idea to casually turn over his breakfast grapefruit and begin carving out parabolic arches; as a journalist, she would have intuitively understood the value of a scoop—which

Fig. 23. Cover of the *Time* magazine 1956 issue, which contained a long profile demonstrating Aline Saarinen's narrative interventions. © 1956 TIME USA LLC. All rights reserved. Used under license.

watching Eero make architecture out of breakfast fruits would certainly have been.

The utterly unveiled sexism was ubiquitous. Describing Saarinen's famous Womb Chair of 1948, the *Time* writer described its genesis as follows: "The wife of a furniture designer urged Eero to design a chair that women can curl up on."[3] That "wife" was Florence Knoll, certainly more than a "wife" and one of the driving forces behind the development of midcentury modernist furniture through her company, Knoll, and who has already appeared in Eero's life as one of Eero's most beloved (and financially supportive) correspondents, known affectionately as "Shu."

Louchheim's complex participation became even more apparent as the article shifted to the personal: "As Saarinen's G.M. began going up, his marriage was washing out. The marital problem was discussed sympathetically in a story written by the *New York Times*'s Associate Art Editor Aline B. Louchheim."[4] I have already discussed the way that Louchheim wrote Eero's existing marriage into her *New York Times* profile as a way of positioning herself as a counterpoint to the effusive yet troubled sculp-

Fig. 24. Aline Saarinen and Eero Saarinen at a party, Aline sitting in Eero's famous 1946 Womb Chair produced by their friend Florence "Shu" Knoll, undated. Box 3, folder 23, Aline and Eero Saarinen Papers, 1906–1977, Archives of American Art, Smithsonian Institution.

tor Lilian Swann, and this is an insider's way of introducing the ultimate subject of their marriage. I read the word "sympathetically" sarcastically. Louchheim's discussion of the marital problem occurred while she was trying to work out with Saarinen how he was going to get divorced. Knowing that Louchheim would be his wife and that the *Time* article was about to illuminate that, this is a tiny piece of sardonic foreshadowing and the currency of architectural gossip.

The article then described their joint study, "where Eero, working over his drafting table at night, glances up frequently to see Louchheim chewing up pencils over her writing."[5] It is here that we see a tiny reported clue as to the depth of their collaboration. Saarinen drawing, working over his drafting table, looked to Louchheim for reassurance, for collaboration. And she, "chewing up pencils over her writing" indicates both a nervousness and a physically embodied presence, as well as one that is slightly infantilized—one imagines very young children chewing pencils. Saarinen was described as distanced from his body—there is no mention of him being "hunched over" or "scraping across his table." But Louchheim has a body that we as readers are immediately given visceral access to through the writer's description of her "chewing up pencils," something that minimizes her professionalism while maximizing intimations of her unprofessionalism and anxiety.[6]

Another line in the *Time* essay gives an even deeper indication of the disjunction between what we know was going on behind the scenes and what was represented in the profile: "After he was divorced, Eero Saarinen and the author of those understanding lines (herself a divorcee) were married. He told his new wife frankly: 'I think you will be able to be married to me, because you understand that my first love is architecture.'"[7] What is represented was Saarinen unilaterally telling Louchheim how their relationship was going to be; what we know from having read her early letters closely is that part of her selling point and a narrative that she developed, was that he would always be an architect first. Louchheim's willingness to have this version on the record indicates her understanding of how to consistently articulate to readers that Saarinen was a brilliant architect whose "first love is architecture." What the article does not touch on—but what we now know—is the way in which Louchheim herself negotiated their marriage to be centered around his architecture, and the ways in which she could help him. And so the *Time* representation of their relationship is a profound example of contemporary reigning thoughts about architecture, that it must be created by great men who would necessarily love architecture more than they loved women, and that she loved him for his love for architecture. The line is also intriguing for the way in which it is positioned: "He told his new wife frankly," when in fact they discussed his love for architecture while they were negotiating her becoming his new wife. Furthermore, she is described simply as "new wife," rather than given her own, quite well-recognized name. Also, the representation is of a grand mythic pronouncement rather than a negotiation. What is so fascinating about it is that Louchheim was somewhat involved in the conceptualization of this article (because it was edited by Cranston Jones, with whom Louchheim had an ongoing professional correspondence). It is likely that she pushed for Saarinen's representation as a genius, but was not yet embedded enough to produce a crystal-clear message.

The *Time* article placed Saarinen on a contemporary architectural map and in direct counterpoint to another star modernist, the German émigré Mies van der Rohe, who was becoming recognized with projects like Crown Hall at Illinois Institute of Technology and the Lakeshore Apartments in Chicago. There are sprinkled references to other modernisms—as worked out by Mies, as well as by Le Corbusier and the Bauhausian Walter Gropius—throughout the essay: "Rejecting the cult of the cube as the answer to every problem," addressed the way in which Saarinen's organic and swooping forms were a remarkable formal and conceptual critique of the reigning solutions of the day.[8] However, there is also evidence in this essay of the role of Mies among Saarinen's list of important architects that he wrote to Louchheim early in their courtship.[9] "Saarinen readily admits Mies's crystallizing influence on his work," the author writes. After a description of the GM structure—which Louchheim mobilized in her 1953 *New York Times* article as an example of Saarinen's breadth and also trustworthiness with large (and therefore lucrative) corporate projects—this nod to Mies feels like a way of reassuring the reader that Saarinen is not only going to do dramatic arches—he will also do proper buildings with "glistening expanses of aluminum, greenish glass and grey porcelain façades, interchangeable office paneling and windows 'zippered in' with neoprene gaskets."[10]

It is clear from the *Time* article that the Saarinen office hadn't yet fully decided how to be represented. Was Saarinen a modernist after Mies? Maybe! Was he a dramatic and genius architect who was so bewitched by the parabolic powers of a grapefruit that even his wife becomes nothing more than an adoring set of eyes? Possibly! Compared to the later publications, in which Louchheim has exerted far more editorial control and intervention, this particular article is emblematic of just how confusing the message could be without Louchheim's public relations directives. She was in charge of images, yes, but the singular clarity of message present in later articles is absent here.

The architectural historian Alice T. Friedman has offered a reading of this article—and of the rest of Saarinen's work—and found Saarinen's words, as quoted by *Time*, "both reassuring and encouraging."[11] "If anyone was going to put U.S. architecture on the map, it would be Eero Saarinen, with his renowned father, his Ivy League education, his professorial pipe, and his Finnish accent."[12] Friedman names three themes to have emerged from her review of Saarinen's projects—first, "the exploration of new building technologies and materials"; second, the treatment of "every architectural commission as a separate artistic problem"; and third, the clear imagination of "his buildings as inhabited and animated spaces."[13] Friedman quotes Saarinen as having "come to the conviction that once one embarks on a concept for a building, this concept has to be exaggerated and overstated and repeated in every part of its interior so that wherever you are, inside or outside, the building sings with the same message."[14] This is a restatement of a standard modernist idea: the *Gesamtkunstwerk*, or the idea that a work of art is made up of the totality of materials and processes of which it is incorporated.

This last statement about the message the building sings comes from the book *Eero Saarinen: On His Work*, a book written and edited by Aline, and a book which we shall investigate in the final chapter. And so not only did contemporary writers fall into the trap of using Louchheim's words as Saarinen's, but so too do historians. Now that we understand how deeply Louchheim worked with Eero to massage his message, we can see that even the most careful history has actually been shaped by Aline's interventions.

One of the clearest examples of a singular message beginning to be controlled—and expressed—through the life-span of a building is in the management of and publications surrounding the TWA Terminal at what was then called Idlewild Airport (now known as John F. Kennedy), in the New York City borough of Queens. I will analyze some publications about the terminal as a case study in what it looked like when Louchheim was explicitly involved.

In 1957, the *New York Times* published the first images of what would become the TWA Terminal, along with a short descriptive text.[15] "The structure is symbolically designed to appear like some huge bird with wings spread in flight," Edward Hudson, a *New York Times* reporter who covered topics from construction to child crime to Korean visitors learning English, wrote. "The designer, Eero Saarinen, describes his handiwork in terms reminiscent of Frank Lloyd Wright. No part of this building, he says, could be a part of any other building." Hudson continued, describing Eero's description of two purposes—one to "make the passenger's transition from taxicab to airplane as painless as possible," the other "to capture and express the dynamic quality of an airline, and the spirit of flight itself."[16] This is the first published description of the building as a "bird" and the avian metaphors only proliferate from there. The message, throughout the publications that do everything from questioning the building's progress and celebrating its completion to assessing its failures and successes as a work of public architecture, remains focused and precise: the TWA Terminal is a marvel of modern engineering that represents a bird in flight.

The completion and opening date for the TWA Terminal was announced in that article as 1960—three years away. The terminal finally

AVIATION: UNUSUAL TERMINAL FOR IDLEWILD

By EDWARD HUDSON

TRANS WORLD AIR-LINES proudly announced last week the bold new design for its future terminal at Idlewild Airport. The structure is symbolically designed to appear like some huge bird with wings spread in flight. It is not unlikely that there were some misgivings about spending $12,-000,000 on so unusual a plan. Now the decision is made and T. W. A. is pinning hopes on the design's winning public acceptance.

The designer, Eero Saarinen, describes his handiwork in terms reminiscent of Frank Lloyd Wright. No part of this building, he says, could be a part of any other building.

He adds that he had two purposes in mind. One was to make the passenger's transition from taxicab to airplane as painless as possible. The other was to capture and express the dynamic quality of an airline, and the spirit of flight itself.

Startling Effect

The result is a design that is radical in appearance and one that seems to have a startling effect on those who view it for the first time. If it can do this in model size, no doubt it will have a striking effect when fully completed in 1960 and situated squarely in view of passengers approaching the terminal area along the main entrance roadway.

The design is decidedly different from other structures so far built or planned for the Idlewild passenger complex known as Terminal City. T. W. A. says, however, that the design will harmonize with the rest of the passenger project, scheduled

to be completed in 1960. And the Port of New York Authority, which holds a checkrein on airline planning, has given its approval.

The other structures are modern enough and probably, as the architects say, functional. But they involve less complex geometric shapes. The International Arrival Building, which will open Dec. 6, is long and low and straight except for the lobby arch and control tower at mid-point. Of the two previously announced terminal designs, Eastern Air Lines' is entirely conventional in outward appearance while Pan American World Airways', though not conventional, is oval-shaped and simple.

T. W. A.'s terminal, to be 500 feet long, will be covered its center by a thin concrete shell 300 feet wide and fifty feet high, whose convolutions will give the building its birdlike look. The shell is formed by four merging vaulted domes supported at four points. Two lateral domes extend outward and upward like wings. Glass sheaths the open expanses. And glass skylights fill in spaces between the domes. The front dome forms a visor-like marquee over the main entrance.

Despite the bold and daring architecture, the interior layout and planning is more conservative. Perhaps this is because more technical limitations exist in terminal planning than in architecture. Whatever the reason, T. W. A.'s terminal is not so revolutionary inside, with the possible exception of moving sidewalks that will carry passengers part way to and from

the planes. In regard to interior layout, Pan American's terminal design, with its parasol roof and oval shape seems to be more radical.

T. W. A. has not spared efforts to incorporate convenience and luxury into its new "crossroads" terminal, which will serve both its overseas and domestic passengers and will be the line's public showcase. T. W. A. officials are said to be studying the problem that Pan American may have already solved with its parasol roof, that of getting to and from planes in inclement weather. Under study, it was said, are various bridge devices that would span between plane exits and passenger loading buildings.

Passengers arriving at the new structure will enter one wing at street level through electronic doors and deposit their baggage at a long counter immediately inside. The opposite wing will hold a self-service baggage check-out counter. The main passenger area in the center will contain an information desk, two flight information boards, various shops, a restaurant, bar, and at the rear a semi-circular lounge from which the airport activities may be viewed through a 200-foot-wide window.

Moving sidewalks, as well as stationary ones, will be enclosed in two passageways about 125 feet long leading to two one-story buildings containing rooms from which passengers will board planes. These passageways will be covered with glass and illuminated at night by lighting at leg-level. There will be loading positions for fourteen jet planes. Part of the terminal may be completed and in use by mid-1960.

BIRDLIKE TERMINAL—Model of Trans World Airline's passenger building for International Airport at Idlewild was designed by Eero Saarinen.

Fig. 26. Oblique view of the TWA Terminal, the view that Eero Saarinen "got sick of," showing its raptor-like form. Location: New York, NY. © Wayne Andrews/Esto.

opened only in August 1962, almost a year after Eero died suddenly of a brain tumor in September 1961. The rest of Hudson's article focused on the relative tameness of the interior compared to the exterior, and highlighted the excitement of "moving walkways," that would help people move through the five-hundred-foot-long terminal.[17]

The picture shows the building from an unusual angle in that it is one that almost no person would see given the jet paths and distance. It is a photograph of the model—which looks more like a crouching beetle than a bird about to take flight. Yet, the rhetoric was clearly about birds, as the caption read "Birdlike Terminal—Model of Trans World Airline's Passenger building for International Airport at Idlewild was designed by Eero Saarinen."[18]

Between Louchheim's article being published in 1953 and Hudson's description of the TWA Terminal in 1957, Eero Saarinen's name had appeared thirty-six times in the *New York Times*, enough so that he was a familiar name to keen readers of the arts section, though he was not always a central element to the article (he was often mentioned in passing; or as part of a jury; or, once, as half of a wedding announcement).[19] And, of course, he had appeared on the cover of *Time*. It took five more years for the project to be completed, but the message and its clarity resonated through every printed investigation of the structure. In the years before his death, Louchheim worked with members of the press to keep them interested and on their toes; she also used the terminal as a point of negotiation and interest-gauging, promising the best pictures or the best access to various editors, particularly Cranston Jones at *Time*, Douglas Haskell at *Architectural Forum*, and James Hornbeck at *Architectural Record*. TWA, even before its completion, was already one of the most controlled buildings, and as such it offers us a compelling case study.

While Saarinen would publicly disavow any connection with birds, it will become clear through my analysis that it was Louchheim who introduced the idea of the building being seen through the metaphor of soaring wings, and that she maintained that singular idea through a number of publications. Because of her facility with writing, she would have understood how important an easily and immediately understandable hook the building would need, and how important metaphors could be to gently encourage an architecture-naive audience to accept this surprising structure. Correspondence with Cranston Jones, Ada Louise Huxtable, and a few other assorted interlocutors whose requests crossed her desk, demonstrates Louchheim's skill.

In October 1958, the *New York Times* published another story about the TWA Terminal. The dek read "Original Plans for Futuristic Unit at Idlewild Found to Be Too Expensive," and the article opened with the report that "Trans World Airlines may abandon the design of the $12,000,000 passenger terminal it had planned to build at New York International Airport, Idlewild, Queens." The building, however, stayed on message—and was referred to as a "futuristic, bird-like structure," and then, again repeating the motif, "Its contours were planned to resemble a giant bird with soaring wings."[20]

A few months later, Louchheim was in the midst of her own negotiations with Cranston Jones, corresponding about a museum exhibition, *Form Givers at Mid-Century*, and declined to give him photographs of the TWA project, though she couched that decision in incompetence. I hypothesize that this is because she had other plans for publishing the structure, and knew that it wasn't quite ready to be publicly assessed by the sophisticated audience a museum show would draw. On January 13, 1959, Aline wrote to Jones, giving a report on the firm's currently available photographs; the list opened with the St. Louis Arch, the GM Center, MIT Chapel and Auditorium, Milwaukee Museum, and the David S. Ingalls Hockey Rink at Yale. At the end of the letter and on a separate page she introduced TWA: "Material is in a mess and will be put in order and follow shortly" which I see as a polite way of giving Jones the exact same brush-off that Eero had given Davis, but in a much more self-effacing way.[21] Aline adopted responsibility for TWA's being "in a mess" and implied it just needed to be put in order. Louchheim's absorption of responsibility in this simple and single sentence speaks volumes concerning the role that she played as Head of Information Services, and the way in which her professionalism—and moments of performative lack of professionalism— was profoundly directed by her ability to personally throw herself on her sword and blame herself for any of the office's misdirection or delays.

That page, however, was a hit with Jones's team and in his response on January 16, he included a "much piqued (with curiosity) note from the MMA [Metropolitan Museum of Art] who by chance got page 2 of your note to me." He continued: "The office must be in a fine dither now, with the MoMA's 'Four Buildings' fast approaching, and 'Form Givers' (will Eero ever forgive us snitching that?) no smaller than a small cloud on the horizon."[22] Jones was organizing an exhibition called *Form Givers at Mid-Century*, which appeared at the Metropolitan Museum of Art in 1959, and which would include a "Saarinen Section."[23] He proposed including General Motors, MIT, Milwaukee, Yale, "And T.W.A. when you have it organized"—though it was clearly already organized enough to be in the Modern's *Four Buildings* exhibition. The project was—appropriately—becoming an elusive bird rather than a gracefully landing one, and when Jones sent a separate note on the same day to Gyorgy Kepes and Saarinen about the show, and said—"Saarinen Office advises all is chaos, and material will follow shortly."[24] Here the blame for the chaos falls on Aline as "Saarinen Office"—it is not the architect's fault, nor particularly her fault, but the advice of the disembodied Office. Here, another level of Aline's takeover is complete, as architect and wife, designer and storyteller, have merged into one unified being known as the Saarinen Office.

In February 1959, Ada Louise Huxtable, who had worked as an assistant curator in the Architecture and Design Department at the Museum of Modern Art and would become the nation's first full-time architecture critic in 1963, offered her critique of the Modern's *Four Buildings* show, which was actually titled *Architecture and Imagery*, and curated by Wilder Green.[25] The exhibition showed four structures: Jørn Utzon's Sydney Opera House; Guillaume Gillet's Notre Dame de Royan (in Royan, France); Harrison and Abramowitz's First Presbyterian Church (Stamford, Connecticut); and Saarinen's TWA Terminal. In the exhibition checklist, Saarinen's project was listed last.[26] In Huxtable's review in the *New York Times*, however, it was listed first—no accident, as nothing Huxtable ever did was an accident—and she and Aline had a mutually admiring relationship, as indicated by their letters. In early 1959 the project was still referred to as a "proposed" airport terminal, though construction began only three months later. Huxtable placed the four buildings in direct opposition to Miesian boxes (though without naming Mies directly), and offered that they were "examples of a significant new direction in architectural design."[27] She wrote that "they must be evaluated seriously."[28] Buildings that made use of the new possibilities in concrete, she argued, could be "belligerently personal in an impersonal world."[29] Huxtable praised Jørn Utzon's "billowing sails" at the Sydney Opera House, a project that Utzon had won through a competition on which Saarinen was a jury member; and then moved on to TWA.[30] "Saarinen's T.W.A. terminal is an outstandingly sensitive exercise in the creation of a special form, physically and psychologically suited to the purpose of the building."[31] Later, Huxtable described the form as "bird-like"—a direct nod to the *New York Times* language, an indication that the connection between structure and bird was being repeated by the Saarinen office.[32] Huxtable was clearly placing Saarinen in a different camp than the other three structures, pointing to its sensitivity and lightness and memorability, its true poetic grandeur and also, as was always her focus and wont, its creation of a space in which humans would have a novel experience.

The exhibition at MoMA was announced with a press release that directly quoted material provided by the Saarinen office, otherwise known as Louchheim. "The T.W.A. project, according to the architect, was planned to be distinctive and memorable while related to the numerous surrounding buildings and as a structure in which the architecture itself would express the excitement of travel and movement," the release, drafted by Elizabeth Shaw, publicity director of the Museum of Modern Art, proclaimed.[33] This release was sent to all the major art- and architecture-related news departments, and as such it is no accident that the language began to appear in multiple outlets. But the machinations of a press release and a large museum department was no real match for the machinations of Aline's small and ultrapersonal office that she was building at Bloomfield Hills.

Louchheim resigned her position as associate art critic for the *New York Times* in December 1959, cutting the last cord with her old career and allowing her to focus fully on working with the Saarinen office to publish TWA. The announcement appeared in the *Times*, and the few lines of the story covered the basics: she had resigned "to work on a book and other writing projects."[34] What the article does not mention is that the majority of her writing projects would, for a few years, be almost exclusively on behalf of Eero and would often take the form of letters. By January 1960, once construction had been underway for a few months, Aline was already working on having TWA published as far and wide as possible.

Corresponding with Allene Tallmey, features editor at *Vogue* magazine (a harbinger of TWA's appearance in multiple outlets, not just architectural publications, three years later), Aline delivered the "promised material for the additional spread on Eero."[35] She included a drawing of Dulles International Airport marked "substitute rendering," with the all-caps admonition "DO NOT USE THIS ONE, PLEASE!"—and then, in a remarkable turn away from supporting something, "This is fresher material than T.W.A."[36] TWA was by then still completely fresh, being not yet finished and not yet opened and not yet published everywhere, and

yet Louchheim understood that *Vogue* both then and now had a remarkable focus on being the first to publish something. Being able to offer
Dulles, and offering a "press release draft" and a "substitute rendering"
was a way of sidling up to Tallmey and offering something that, she could
intuit though it was never explicated, wasn't being offered to anyone else.
However, even though TWA might not have been seen as "fresh," it was
of course included, with a "Statement and photograph of model."[37] She
asked later, "May we see copy or proof on the buildings text? I think in
this kind of copy we don't have to worry about engineer, etc. credits but
we would like to check so we don't get into any trouble."[38] And then she
signed it "Love, Aline," a far more intimate and evocative sign-off than
had become her professional habit. Her request to see the text under
guise of checking credits is an example of her slickness and familiarity
with the tropes and practices of magazine publishing, where of course a
subject should never have approval over the text but often finds a method
that does not explicitly cross ethical lines.

In August 1960, the *New York Times Magazine* published an article—this
time glowing—about TWA's progress. Headlined "Bones for a 'Bird,'" the
article opened with the line "To achieve the smooth, serene contours of a
soaring bird—in solid concrete—workmen are in the final stages of building a vastly complex mold of wood and steel."[39] Then, once again reiter-
ating this idea of flight-turned-architecture, the article continued. "The
'soaring bird' will be the new passenger terminal for Trans World Airlines
at New York International Airport." The building "is the design of Eero
Saarinen and the construction is being done by Grove, Shepherd, Wilson
& Kruge." The photograph used here was *not* of the oblique model that
had been published in the earlier article, but rather of a straight-on look
at the building itself, showing the wings of the structure more clearly.[40]

The second image was of what looked to be a pile of haphazardly at-
tached timbers, and the caption indicated an awareness of this confusing mess: "On Purpose—not the result of a twister hitting a barn, these
timbers are part of the form for a buttress that will help support the arch-
ing 6,000 ton roof."[41] The playfulness became a signature of Huxtable's
work, although this article was not bylined. The article appeared in the
New York Times Magazine, an offshoot of the paper and which featured,
in that same issue, articles like a critique of the "current vogue for 'Vic-
toriana'";[42] a profile of former Princess Suga-no-miya, who was "Japan's
most publicized radio personality";[43] and a story on Chancellor Adenauer's "Rx For Vitality."[44] The *New York Times Magazine* was a place—as

it still is—for glossy full-page advertisements for fashion and household brands (then it was Bruxton shirts and Colgate toothpaste; now it is Bottega Veneta and Samsung). The appearance of architecture, and particularly of an article focused on construction, was novel for the *Magazine* pages, and it also announced architecture's gradual ascent into the mainstream, as well as the "look what they did there!" focus of the reading. Playful and smart without being deeply invested in understanding the architecture, the article still showed a gentler, softer way of looking at design—a playful approach that Eero himself, who was deeply playful with Aline but not generally in his correspondence or approach to architecture, would not have engaged in. And so, although there is no masthead and also no record of direct communication about this particular publication, its placement in the *Magazine*—which was the place for glossy photographs and general-interest articles (e.g., the "It's Princess Time" story about Japan's celebrity royalty)—demonstrates a shift in who was supposed to talk about architecture, and who was supposed to be interested in it.

Photography was central, both in the pages of the *Magazine* and to Louchheim's press strategies. Without good photography, even the best building could fall conceptually flat once physically flattened into two dimensions. The Saarinens, like many architects before and after them, were well aware of the potential pitfalls of bad photography, and were open to the huge gains to be made with good photography. In July 1960, photographer George Jones wrote directly to Aline about the photography of TWA, referring to a phone call from a member of Saarinen's New York office, in which they'd discussed a number of photographs he had taken during construction of TWA.[45] He sent file prints under separate cover, and then noted, with some displeasure, that while he understood that some of the pictures would be published by *Forum*, he wasn't sure which ones.[46] A handwritten note accompanied this letter and superseded it, updating the recipient with the news that *Forum* had returned the unused photos, which were now available for purchase and use by the Saarinen office.[47] He had taken these photographs, he wrote, for the Grove, Shepherd, Wilson & Kruge contracting company.[48]

Louchheim responded on August 1, thanking Jones for his photographs. "They are magnificent," she wrote. "Unfortunately, we did not receive them in time for use in the project we had in mind but we would like to purchase some of these for our own files."[49] She discussed details and then closed with, "We would, of course, want to know your price scale and whether you are interested in doing other architectural photography."[50] On the top she wrote a handwritten note, "To Pat for info," which can be read two ways—one, this goes to Pat (Burley) for her information, and two, this letter is to go to Pat Burley as part of the Information Services department.[51] Both readings work, and both readings help us to understand the way in which Aline professionally filed and adjusted and placed people and their work while maintaining this double response, both personal and professional.

Jones responded a few days later, agreeing to her keeping the photographs until she could return the ones she would not use, and then outlined his pricing, as well as his plans to return to TWA and keep taking in-progress photos.[52] His last paragraph contained the type of flattery necessary to close a client, saying how impressed he continued to be with how much had changed each time he visited Idlewild, and how many important elements of the building there were to capture. The only downside? He simply didn't have enough time to take all the photographs he believed could be taken. But then a-ha! A solution! Jones proposed the Saarinen office paying him a contract for the remaining construction period.[53]

In October, Jones followed up, having received no response. He recapped their correspondence, and then complained that he hadn't heard back. He closed with a paragraph describing the very good photographs he had taken of the concrete being poured onto the roof, and implied that he was sure this would be of great interest to Louchheim (and, by extension, Saarinen).[54] A week later Pat Burley responded, on Aline's behalf. "Mrs. Saarinen is in Europe and will not return until the end of the month," she wrote. "Please accept my apologies ... it is difficult to determine which of the prints we will use in future publications; therefore, I hesitate to order enlargements at this time."[55] However, the office was "certainly interested in having a record of all of the photographs that you have taken of T.W.A. and would like to order contact prints or proof sheets for our files," she said, and asked for a price schedule. I read this as a polite brush-off.

The project attracted a large amount of attention. In September 1959, Wolf von Eckardt, head of public relations at the AIA—a newly formed department that was finding its legs after years, as Andrew Shanken has argued, of complete disavowal of publicity efforts by AIA on behalf of architects—wrote to Saarinen, describing an article about contemporary architecture that he had written, and asking for permission to illustrate the piece with a photograph of a model of TWA.[56] The desire for a photograph of the model for a book indicates a level of interest in the project that far superseded usual publication requests, which demanded photography of finished projects, but were willing to accept a sketch or drawing.

Photography of the building would prove to be an ongoing issue. The Saarinens did not directly hire anyone to take photographs of TWA in its early stages (though later Aline would suggest—successfully—that they get Ezra Stoller on board) but were not immune to the helpful suggestions of people who wrote to them.[57] The architect Robert Damora of New Canaan, Connecticut, who had encountered (and photographed) both Eliel and Eero Saarinen's work in the late 1940s, for instance, wrote to Eero in 1960: "I went through your T.W.A. terminal yesterday and I was disturbed that published photographs of this structure had given me a distorted impression of the architecture involved."[58] Damora was a photographer interested in promoting a nuanced and supportive understanding of modern architecture, and saw this as an opportunity to participate in correcting the record on this building, which, as we have seen, caused some confusion to those who saw the existing images. "I wonder whether you feel, as I do, that your work is superficially and perhaps erroneously photographed?" The observation was not merely critical, but also meant to be helpful: "If so, would you try me in a series of T.W.A. photographs?"[59] The next sentence describes "your curvilinear structure and space" that is "past a height of clarity and beauty never to be seen again."[60] And the next paragraph moves in to close: "Would T.W.A. be interested in paying for such photographs taken now and at several succeeding stages of construction up to and including the finished building?" Damora offered that the photographs "might best represent both of you [the architect and the contractor] in advertising, public-relations, and architectural publication releases."[61] Damora's understanding of the value of photography in terms of "public-relations" is an indicator of his understanding of the way in which images and newspaper and magazine articles could work together to advance an architect's agenda; his history as a photographer before becoming an architect speaks to his familiarity with the media.[62]

Eero added his usual blocky marginalia directly onto the letter, and passed it along: "ALINE," underlined—appears in large capitals on the upper right of the letter, and then in smaller caps, "HE IS TERRIBLY GOOD—."[63] Aline responded also in handwriting—"EERO—we have wonderful [double underlined] pictures by George Jones." She softened her rejection, though. "But we can use this man later. Return this later, please," she wrote. A note from Eero responded to Damora. "I am afraid that T.W.A. is not interested in the kind of photographic program which you outline," he wrote, once again passing the buck—this time to "TWA" as an abstract entity when in fact the decision was very clearly made by Aline.[64] However, he kept the lines open, as per Aline's instructions: "It would probably be a good idea if you would send a schedule of your rates to Mrs[.] Patricia Burley, who is working with Aline in our Information Department."[65]

Louchheim's press correspondence about TWA showed her control of the message, as well as the project's place in the larger ecosystem of architectural publishing. One further example of the "bird" metaphor and a series of letters between Louchheim and Douglas Haskell offers clarity on the way in which the two colleagues began to formulate new rules for architectural publishing.

On Thursday, December 8, 1960, the *New York Times* again wrote about TWA, though in an entirely different tone. The caption of a photograph of a model read: "IMAGINATIVE DESIGN . . . Eero Saarinen is the designer." Whereas in the 1958 article Saarinen was mentioned only at the end, here he takes center stage. The title? "T.W.A.'s Terminal Standing on Own," which we can also read metaphorically. "Work on the bird-like structure, designed by Eero Saarinen, was begun on June 4, 1959," the article said.[66] Once again, the "bird in flight" idea was quoted—and it was called a "futuristic terminal," directly borrowing the language from the earlier article or, more likely, from a consistent press message being created by Aline.[67]

She was also developing ways to ensure that her favored colleagues got the best stories. In July 1961, Douglas Haskell, editor of *Architectural Forum*, wrote a long letter to Eero Saarinen: "FORUM would like to explore the possibility of doing a special feature on the T.W.A. terminal building at Idlewild, with a thoroughness comparable to that which was given in the current July story on the Chase Manhattan Bank," he began.[68] "Question number two relates to arrangements which might be made which would give FORUM the incentive to go all out," Haskell wrote.[69] "The recent habit amongst corporations and architects of issuing releases on important buildings in the same detail to all publications has meant that any additional information which might be dug out through the initiative of a magazine like this would go out to everybody."[70] To "do an outstanding job we would like to be assured that, beyond the routine releases which would inevitably go out to all publications, there would be a pledge that both the architect's office and the owner would work exclusively on a more comprehensive story with FORUM."[71] This is the first mention of exclusivity in the surviving Saarinen documents, and it is clear from Haskell's complex mode of description that it is an unfamiliar concept. Today, the necessity for a visual (and often informational) exclusive is absolutely standard and assumed—and yet it is clear from this correspondence that in 1961, the concept was so new and fragile that Haskell needed to delve far into details about why it would be so satisfactory. "FORUM goes to the most highly influential building audience in America composed of the experts in corporate, institutional, and public building enterprise."[72] He then mentioned the circulation numbers, 62,000, a number that would be very respectable today, and adding that he is "not speaking of free circulation to architects who do not subscribe."[73] Shanken has observed that these pitches are similar to ones made in the early 1940s, when magazines were similarly concerned with their own solvency. The difference between the early 1940s and the early 1960s is that, this time, Louchheim was involved, and Haskell had an available and professional interlocutor. The next paragraph is short and to the point. "It seems to us that our suggestion is a very fair and workable one. It would mean that you and we would come to a conclusion and then go to T.W.A. with it." He closed the letter with, "With all best to you and Aline," and it is at first surprising that this is the first mention of her—given how closely Haskell worked with Louchheim—but on closer reflection, makes sense.

Louchheim's not being directly included is surprising because of her relationship with Haskell, but a note from R. (presumably Eero's secretary, Ruth), writes—"Eero, Aline has copy," in handwriting on the top left. So, Aline was included but not explicitly mentioned. However, she had been kept in the loop, in the form of an office memo sent July 19, the day of the phone call, from Eero and to Aline, Pat, and John Dinkeloo, then a young partner in the firm.[74] The memo jumped right in, with no opening salutation. "The FORUM is interested in making a large article on T.W.A. similar to the one they made on Chase Manhattan," Eero wrote.[75]

> If FORUM does this, then they would insist on the same kind of an arrangement as they had with Chase Manhattan. This arrangement is that all the ordinary information (photos and information about the building) is available to all the magazines, but that the FORUM had the inside track on special and more information. I made no promises. I said that we would have a meeting here to clarify dates and policy and let him know.[76]

Haskell was changing his mind about exclusivity after an earlier snafu, which he described in a letter written February 10, 1961. Here, Haskell outlined his requests for exclusivity. "May I suggest that in the future with your finished jobs—since they all, in the end, command your love—you simply work out a date for a general release to architectural magazines."[77] It is clear that Haskell had a good memory for perceived exclusivity slights, for this came after a year of tension between himself and Louchheim over exclusivity and competition.

In 1960, the year before, the Saarinen office and *Forum* had butted heads over *Architectural Record* publishing photography of ES&A's own office. In that instance, despite having given some of the material to *Record*, Louchheim made a concerted argument for having still saved some exclusive material for *Forum*. She wrote Haskell a long explanatory letter outlining what she had saved explicitly for *Forum*—"the series of candid camera shots of Eero and the designers at work on models"—and expressing surprise and dismay that "you would be so distressed that another magazine should publish a particular job with a limited point of view."[78] Her willingness to insult *Record* by saying it had a "limited point of view" was a sign of loyalty to *Forum*, one that would prove fruitful. Haskell forgave her, and yet stood firmly by *Forum*'s principles: "I guess we are the only publication in the field which regularly draws a sharp distinction, in publishing any article, whether it was written especially for FORUM or whether it was reproduced from some other publication."[79] His use of "I guess" indicates that this was all relatively new to these publications; and his willingness to overlook her disloyalty in giving material to *Record* demonstrates a clear personal affinity for Louchheim. This discussion shows the way in which they were collaborating in a new field that was saturated with promising projects and ambitious architects who wanted to see themselves in magazine pages.

Haskell, Louchheim, and Saarinen were working out a new type of publication relationship on the fly. Haskell wanted assurances that the projects he undertook to publish wouldn't blindside him by appearing elsewhere. Louchheim wanted the projects to have as wide a range of good publicity as possible. Saarinen, who was ambitious, surely wanted to be published everywhere. Present here is a working-out of what would become standard in most firms, and a honing of the rules of exclusivity that today govern architectural publication.

This pickle felt eternal. "Both Eero and Peter Blake indicate that you were upset by the fact that we had allowed *Architectural Record* to publish the Yale Colleges and Peter worried that you would be even more upset that Record will be publishing Dulles International Airport," Louchheim wrote to Haskell in 1960.[80] She made a distinction between "when a client sets a release date for publicity (and is anxious for publicity)" versus when not, and said that when not, "we have conscientiously reserved this material in the hope that *Forum* would follow through on the portfolio section about which you spoke so very many months ago." She added that "we have also turned down requests from the two other architectural magazines who wished to do portfolio sections on Eero's total work." We see here power dynamics—Louchheim playing up her loyalty to *Forum* while simultaneously doing the same to Hornbeck at *Record*. She ended her letter to Haskell by saying, "It was our impression that your reinvention in *Forum* was to do the kind of job that no other magazine would be in a position to do—that is, to focus on the genesis of architectural ideas in this office, pointing up the similarity of approach which leads to totally different results since each problem has been so conscientiously and carefully studied in its own terms."[81]

This other magazine must be *Record*, which is mentioned by Haskell in his letter a day later, "It is simply a problem that we have to meet—that Record now makes such a system of picking up such full material from clients, including statements from the architects which are published as if they had been written especially for Record."[82] We know, however, that Louchheim *did* give involved access to *Record* for the 1962 campus planning article, and that only a few days *before* this beseeching letter to Haskell she had written to Thomas Creighton of *Progressive Architecture* stating that "on most jobs we have stopped giving any kind of exclusive because we think it is a childish system."[83] This disdain for the "childish system" is nowhere apparent in her response to *Forum*, nor in her communications with Hornbeck at *Record*.

They were still unable to work things out completely; just a year later, as we saw earlier, Haskell had to write Louchheim again about this issue of exclusivity. Here his suggestion, that "you simply work out a date for a general release to architectural magazines" remains relevant.[84] The next and final page of the letter reads, "As you know, Eero is in my mind the most valiantly independent architect now working in the United States to his own convictions, undeterred by the fashions subscribed to by others; I hope to do nothing that will keep him from having every chance."[85]

It is incongruous that he suggests to Louchheim that she just have one release date for everything, having just a year earlier sent her an angry letter about how when there's a single release date then everyone gets the same material. What this indicates, however, is not that Haskell, who was supremely gifted and organized, is disorganized and can't figure out what's going on; what it indicates is that even publishers and editors were working out how best to work with architectural firms to gain material, thus giving us insight into the free-for-all context into which Louchheim was able to enter and invent a job for herself—and, decades later, for hundreds of architectural publicists. Because Haskell was wavering back and forth; because Hornbeck was sending beseeching requests for access to work, there was enough of a sense of inconsistency and experimentation that Aline was able to mobilize her skills as social butterfly and keenly attuned art and architecture critic.

In the July 1963 issue of *Forum*, Haskell wrote an editor's letter that addressed these shifting norms. It opened with a bold-type sentence reading **"Is anyone covering this beat?"** and went into an exegesis of publishing rivalry. "Once in a while a relatively small magazine like FORUM can scoop the entire daily press of New York on stories such as the one about the outrageous tax penalties imposed on the Seagram Building," Haskell wrote. "The reason, unhappily is simply this: with very few exceptions, U.S. newspapers are doing a terrible job in their coverage of architecture and building."[86] This lack of good newspaper coverage meant that anyone who was interested in architecture would have been drawn to one of the top specialty architectural publications. Louchheim's early work for the *New York Times* was instrumental in drawing some attention to architecture, but it was the magazines that were able to promote the work of architects without architects needing to advertise. Commissioning patrons, from families looking for private residences (in the model of Wright's patrons the Kaufmanns, or Philip Johnson's patron Dominique de Menil) to city-changing planners like Robert Moses, who was involved with both the New York City Planning Commission and the New York State Power Authority, among other positions, while Saarinen was designing the TWA Terminal, had access to these periodicals. They may not have been able to visit every single building, but architectural work was being disseminated through publication and photography, which gave commissioning patrons easy access to a huge pool of talent, and made architects feel that they were in the mix of things without necessarily needing to go to Philip Johnson's garden parties.

Returning to solely the realm of architecture for a moment, it is useful to note that Reyner Banham in 1986 observed that the International Style "must be the first architectural movement in the history of art based almost exclusively on photographic evidence rather than on the ancient and preciously unavoidable techniques of personal insertion and measured drawing ... the power of the photograph comes from the fact that like the works of engineering they represented they were understood to be the product of the scientific application of natural laws ... the photographs repressed a truth as apparently objective and modern as that of the functional structures they portrayed."[87] Architectural historian Claire Zimmerman puts the rise of photography into context: "Photographs evidently threatened the integrity of architecture in a way that construction technique and modern consciousness did not," she writes.[88] Her pragmatic approach lines up with my hypothesis that the increased availability of accurate representation was important for both patrons and designers. "Photographs provided a format for the dissemination of information about buildings that was demonstrably more effective than lithographic drawings."[89]

This emphasis on photography as communication was being concurrently developed by photograph-heavy publications like *Life*, *Look*, and *National Geographic*. The first photograph appeared on the cover of *National Geographic Magazine* in 1959, seventy years after the travel magazine was first published.[90] In 1961, the magazine featured a work of architecture on the cover: the Eisenhower-occupied White House.[91] Architecture and photography were thus publicly linked; architecture, in the form of the presidential residence, became a form of representation of the outgoing presidential couple. *Life* magazine, founded in 1883 as a humor magazine, emphasized photography between 1936 and 1972. It was the "first all-photographic American news magazine," and published now-renowned photographers like Henri Cartier-Bresson, Alfred Eisenstaedt, and Dorothea Lange.[92] The appetite for photojournalism was high; and with the appetite for intriguing images came an appetite for photographs of buildings—particularly spectacular buildings like Saarinen's bird-like TWA.

Returning to a central narrative of the publication of TWA, Haskell and Louchheim's history of smoothing things out meant that it did not take a long time to come to an agreement. On August 7, 1961, Eero responded to Haskell, with a cordial and friendly opening, "Dear Doug," once again personalizing the professional relationship, and continuing, "We are all for such a story and are now pulling together the first things as suggested in your letter."[93] And then, having reached his maximum comfort with organizing press-related activities, he wrote, "Aline will be in charge here: therefore, either write to her or write to me." By first directing Haskell towards Aline and then implicating himself and his own correspondence as part of what falls under Louchheim being in charge, Saarinen fully expressed a singular working persona, made up of the characters of both Louchheim and Saarinen. Beyond referring to each other off the stage of a letter, as was explored in the correspondence with Davis, this level of collaboration showed how the couple could act virtually interchangeably.

Saarinen did not need to write this letter directly to Haskell. More likely, it was a calculated maneuver—one that is often practiced today, where direct communication with an architect rather than the architect's public relations person is a way of ensuring excellent editorial care and attention—to bring Haskell into the inner sanctum. On the top, in handwriting, are a few addenda. First, just above the date, is written "To Aline + Pat for info," again this doubling of "information" as code for "message" and also the ownership of Aline and Pat of the Information Services department.[94] However, it seems that the Saarinen office was happy to keep the exclusivity deal, as a letter dated February 19, 1962, from Chester Kerr, Director of Yale University Press (which was to publish a Saarinen monograph), to Aline suggests that he was happy with the planned publication.[95] Once again, everyone was working out how exactly, in this age of photography becoming more disseminated, to maintain exclusivity. A monograph is a different project from a magazine, but neither Kerr nor Haskell would have wanted to be scooped by the other.

Haskell was not the only person working out exclusivity issues, nor the only person with whom Louchheim was corresponding. Louchheim's friend James Hornbeck at *Architectural Record* may have caught wind of this exclusivity plan, for on March 5, 1962, he wrote to Louchheim, "We feel that the T.W.A. terminal is a very important building which will deserve big treatment in the architectural press when it is finished," he opened.[96] "In accordance with our policy in such matters, it seems logical to us that material on the finished building should be made available to all architectural magazines at the same time, so that each of us will have an equal opportunity."[97] He closed by asking "how publicity on the finished building will be handled, and when we should plan to publish our feature on it?"[98] This subtle competitiveness, couched in terms like "it seems logical" is a way of removing himself from the equation and rendering moot any competition with *Forum*. There were not a large enough number of magazines that "all architecture magazines at the same time" could have referred to more than three or four publications; the implication here is a subtle slap on the wrist for not having made these images available to all. Nevertheless, Louchheim's agreement with Haskell prevailed; her loyalty paid off in a number of publications, most notably a posthumous story about Saarinen that ran in the April 1962 issue of *Architectural Forum*.

The article was titled "Eero Saarinen: A Complete Architect," a glowing headline. Written by Walter McQuade, a staff critic for *The Nation* who would go on to write multiple books about architecture and receive a gold medal for criticism in 1974, and who had written about MIT, it was a lengthy article that opened with a reminiscence from one of Saarinen's colleagues, and aimed to give an overview of the recently deceased architect's career.[99] Louchheim appeared in the first paragraph, described as "his wife Aline," another example of the type of professional disavowal that I have illuminated elsewhere, a personal cover that allowed her to do her work.[100]

McQuade called Saarinen "the most famous young architect in America, perhaps the world."[101] The article was written after Saarinen's death, so we can trust with great certainty that Louchheim was instrumental to its development. McQuade referred to Dulles as "sinewy, majestic"; to the Yale colleges as "rich, rough"; and to the CBS building as "toughly intellectual." It is the kind of precise but metaphorical architectural description that sounds very much like Louchheim—an indication that her ideas had crossed the barrier between subject and observer. McQuade described Saarinen's lack of pretentiousness and his drawing habits, "He was one designer who did most of his sketching on ugly, yellow, lined legal pads, not crisp tracing paper," he wrote. The next sentence introduced Louchheim, a connective junction. It is likely the information about those yellow legal pads came directly from Louchheim. "Aline Saarinen remembers when he was coming to New York to court her nine years ago, taking her out to exquisite dinners at the best restaurants," McQuade wrote.[102] We read earlier a thorough accounting of their courtship, and I see here yet another emphasis on the personal so as to deflect from the professional influence Louchheim had over Saarinen's career. She could have given McQuade a number of quotable remarks about their early relationship; she could have told him about her work as an art critic for the New York Times, or discussed the ways in which she worked with Saarinen on his chapel drawings and speeches, or clarified how instrumental she was in organizing publicity for the office. The fact that the early description here is entirely about "exquisite dinners" is a way of becoming invisible so that she can be more effective. McQuade then interviewed his contemporaries, like Philip Johnson and Elia Kazan, and began to point out how savvy Saarinen was.[103] McQuade pointed out that "Saarinen recognized that the sure way to get good employees was to get interesting jobs, and he developed into a forceful client's man to do it."[104] Then the author returned to Louchheim, and ran a long quotation from her about Saarinen's working method, this time explicitly emphasizing her own contributions: "We had dinner usually about 7:30, then coffee and some talk, and then we would go to the workroom." "There was a break about 10:30 or 11 for a drink, and perhaps a look at the news, then long, wonderful conversations, discussions, and yellow-pad drawings over night caps."[105] We can see now where the yellow pad information on the first page came from. I read here Louchheim's inserting herself into the history of Saarinen's productive creativity. For while she began the description by talking about familial patterns, she wove her way through into a more professionalized role, that of Saarinen's late-night interlocutor who was there while Saarinen was actively drawing.

Moving to the personal, McQuade published one of Saarinen's lists, this one "a half-serious master-appraisal sheet for a future wife."[106] We know from our earlier reading of Saarinen's letter to his psychiatrist about his ambitions that this list was in fact more than half-serious. He continued: "Mrs. Saarinen, a well-known and very smartly dressed art critic, sometimes read her day's production of prose to her husband in the evening; typically, he would sit drawing a chart with a rising and falling line of interest as she read from page to page, then present it to her."[107] This could be read, at first, as an easy critique of Louchheim's work—that she wrote work that was then judged, that she sometimes lost interest. But it appears more likely that McQuade was taking Louchheim seriously as a writer by indicating the way in which Saarinen took her work seriously, listening to it every night with keen editorial pencil in hand. It is a way of reminding the readers of *Forum* that Louchheim's writing was independent—something that she would have relied on as she was embarking on a book project about Saarinen's work. McQuade closed with this line: "The firm is too busy just now completing old jobs and beginning new ones."[108] I attribute this sentiment entirely to Louchheim, who very quickly responded to Saarinen's death by pushing ahead and taking care of the office at large—by ensuring that projects were finished—and by stewarding his reputation even after death.

The first *Forum* mention of TWA came in 1958, with a description of "T.W.A.'s graceful air terminal," and furthermore—"a birdlike structure was developed by Eero Saarinen," already using the idea of the bird as expressive metaphor.[109] Two years later in 1960, *Architectural Forum* was consistent with the bird imagery, publishing that "the concrete bird stands free," reporting that "the formwork is stripped from Eero Saarinen's great shell for T.W.A. at Idlewild."[110] This consistency of voice and message is understandable now that it has been clarified how powerfully Louchheim had Haskell's ear.

Articles on the TWA project had been planned for multiple 1962 publications, but Eero's sudden death in September 1961 shifted the landscape. After his death, the TWA Terminal became the capstone of this career. Many critics—like McQuade—were supportive. Some, like Huxtable, did not let her friendship with Louchheim influence her critical

Fig. 28. Interior shot of TWA Terminal, complete with travelers, as described in *Architectural Forum*, "catching the excitement of the trip." Note the surprisingly intimate scale of the interior of the building as compared with its exterior monumentality. Location: New York, NY. © Ezra Stoller/Esto.

take on the building.[111] The project was completed to much attention eight months after Saarinen's death, and on May 18, 1962, the *New York Times* reported on the ceremonial opening of the terminal.

Featuring two photographs, one taken from the interior and picturing a sweeping expanse of glass that overlooked the runways, the caption (there was no long text story) read: "NEW TERMINAL AT IDLEWILD: The nearly completed Trans World Airlines terminal at New York International Airport was opened yesterday for inspection by reporters. The massive structure, designed by the late Eero Saarinen, is being built at a cost of $15,000,000." A second photograph, also taken from inside,

NEW TERMINAL AT IDLEWILD: The nearly completed Trans World Airlines terminal at New York International Airport was opened yesterday for inspection by reporters. The massive structure, designed by the late Eero Saarinen, is being built at a cost of $15,000,000. The waiting area, with glass wall looking out over airfield, is shown here.

The New York Times
A FEELING OF MOVEMENT: The glass and concrete building suggests a giant bird in flight. Passengers will leave and board planes through telescopic passageways linking terminal with arriving and departing aircraft. Main concourse is shown in photograph.

Fig. 29. Untitled article, *New York Times*, May 18, 1962. © 1962, The New York Times Company. All rights reserved. Used under license.

shows people thronging the swooping staircases, the caption for which repeats the bird metaphor: "The glass and concrete building suggests a giant bird in flight."[112] The opening for "inspection by reporters" is a precursor to the practice of the contemporary "press preview" where a coterie of national journalists were flown in to see a newly completed building before it formally opened to the public, although as is clear from the *Forum* discussion between Haskell, Saarinen, and Louchheim, much of the press contracts and contacts had been worked out far in advance of the public viewing.

Saarinen's TWA Terminal appeared elsewhere in print, including in a seven-page spread in the July 1962 issue of *Contract Interiors*, written by none other than Edgar Kaufmann Jr., son of Edgar Kaufmann, the department store magnate to whom Louchheim had written in the mid-1950s to propose Eero for a job.[113] Aline's original effort may not have succeeded, but it is possible to trace an early seed that was cultivated through her careful correspondence into an interest that blossomed almost a decade later in the form of a glowing review of Saarinen's TWA building.

On July 7, 1960, Ada Louise Huxtable wrote a letter to Louchheim. It was a continuation of a conversation about the State Department program. The important part for us is a postscript, asking for a single good photo of the TWA Terminal so that she could include it in a forthcoming piece for *Art in America*. She signed it "Ada Louise." Huxtable felt (or at least expressed) an overt debt to Louchheim.[114] Six months earlier, she had written to Louchheim: "I have never had the opportunity to tell you properly how deeply I have appreciated your recommendation to the *Times*, and how much it has meant to me. Needless to say, any subject you want is yours, anytime." She closed with, "And gentlemen still prefer blondes!"[115] In February, Aline responded: "I don't think gentlemen prefer blonds when there is an attractive brunette nearby." And yet, Huxtable's photography request was coolly professional. Their friendly relationship could have been influenced by their unusual positions; Louchheim also no doubt saw the value in having Huxtable in her corner.

In 1957, reporter Edward Hudson wrote about an "unusual terminal for Idlewild" in the news pages of the *New York Times*.[116] The first paragraph is evocative and narrative: "The new structure is symbolically designed to appear like some huge bird with wings spread in flight." Compare this with the formulaically factually descriptive opening paragraphs we have read about the Kresge Auditorium. Hudson's sentence is steeped in the kind of language that Louchheim used, while the clarity of the bird image transforms what could have been seen as bizarre architecture harkening a complex new age of air travel into a legible idea. Hudson paraphrases Saarinen's two interests—one, "to make the passenger's transition from taxicab to airplane as painless as possible," and two, "to capture and express the dynamic quality of an airline, and the spirit of flight itself." The messaging—part of which, as Jayne Merkel observed, came from TWA president Ralph Dawson, who wanted "a building that captured 'the spirit of flight'"—is central, clear, easy to follow, and is repeated throughout the press coverage of the terminal.[117] In 1959, Ada Louise Huxtable called the TWA model "an exercise in the creation of a special form, physically and psychologically suited to the purpose of the building," which, while not directly mentioning the bird connection, supports the message that this structure represents exactly what it's programmatically meant to be.[118] Her support of the building was probably influenced by her friendship with Aline as well as her professional acumen.

Fig. 30. Straight-on night shot of TWA Terminal, in color and illuminated by its own interior lighting, showing the clarity of Saarinen's form (and perhaps shades of an inverted grapefruit). Location: New York, NY. © Ezra Stoller/Esto.

A document containing a large amount of information about Eero Saarinen & Associates, which was presumably put together about 1960 as a brief primer about the firm and its current projects for a potential new client, has been preserved intact. It begins with a "General Description of Firm" and moves on to describe the awards and honors received, biographical information about the partners, and a financial statement. It concludes with two lists of projects—one a "past record of performance," and one titled "some buildings in progress."[119] The past record is spare and factual. For instance, the "Auditorium and Chapel" at MIT is described as "an auditorium seating 1200, covered by a dome of thin shell concrete construction and a small brick chapel." The General Motors project is equally blandly described—"a $70,000,000 320-acre project, involving complete planning and design of 17 major structures and subsidiary buildings, for General Motors' most advanced research." The

Fig. 31. Travelers chatting inside the main atrium of the TWA Terminal, opened 1962. Location: New York, NY. © Ezra Stoller/Esto.

Ingalls Rink, which I have positioned as a "transitional" structure in this voyage from factually based disorder to Aline-produced poetic order, is here described as "an arena of dramatic form and structure seating 3000," the most expressive description on this page. "Some buildings in progress," then, describes TWA as "a thin shell vault for a new terminal, which expresses the drama of flight and excitement of travel."[120] The words used were evocative, full of visceral adjectives and active nouns that invited the reader to imagine the perfect home for a new age of air travel.

The word "excitement" appeared in 1962, in an *Architectural Forum* article about TWA. The headline read: "I want to catch the excitement of the trip."[121] The article addresses the substantial amount of precompletion publicity. "To thousands of architects and travelers, that design was famous long before it rose laboriously to spread its concrete wings," the article opened. "Now that [it] is finished and in operation, T.W.A. looks, from the air, more like a giant horseshoe crab than a bird in flight."[122] Yes, the author, who is anonymous, is saying that it does not look like a bird, but similarly to how Saarinen being seen in counterpoint to Mies meant that he was nevertheless being seen in relation to Mies, even this disavowal of how it looks is proof of how thoroughly embedded into even the most critical eye the idea of "TWA = bird in flight" had become. The article quickly became positive and ended by describing the project as a "truly fantastic work."[123]

In her biography, Merkel outlines the design process, which she reports went through various drawings and models and introduces the apocryphal breakfast grapefruit story, here cited as Kevin Roche's remembrance: "Eero was eating breakfast one morning and using the rind of his grapefruit to describe the terminal shell. He pushed down on its center to mimic the depression that he desired, and the grapefruit bulged. This was the seed for the bulges in the shell."[124] Why did TWA not remain "the grapefruit building"? Probably because Louchheim would have known that referring to an air terminal as "the bulging grapefruit" was far less compelling than referring to it as a "soaring bird." Merkel also recounts how many of the construction drawings were made through a process of "translating" the models into drawings—first by photographing them, and then producing drawings based on those photographs. Here we see again the power of the study model—a sense of working out through one medium an issue (how to turn a bulging grapefruit into a soaring and exciting bird-like structure) and then refining that through translation into other media. The drawings are not one-to-one representatives of the models. Rather, what we are seeing with this TWA process—and which was new for Saarinen's practice—is the introduction of iterative design processes happening through what *appears* to be repetition, but is in fact creation. This multifaceted process, borrowing insights and possibilities from multiple worlds—"wire-framed rough cardboard," photographs, and construction drawings—is similar to the multiple worlds that came together to represent what became a singular vision about TWA.[125] We can see in the photographs that were selected for release—and Louchheim corresponded heavily with photographers about TWA—the same type of translation and ultimately *creative* act that I argue Louchheim was engaged in. Translation in architecture—switching from one mode and medium to another—has often been seen as simply variations on a theme: an elevation shows something different from a section, but they are both inherently representative of the same building. I argue that in fact an elevation and a section are different *buildings* in that buildings don't exist simply as structures, but as multivalent ideas. So a model of TWA and a photograph of a model of TWA and the photograph that Louchheim chose to send to an editor all need to coalesce together to produce what has come to be seen in the popular imagination as "the TWA Terminal." Kresge, for instance, does not have such a confluence or congealing of meaning and idea. TWA does, even now.

Merkel refers to the TWA process as a type of architectural media spectacle.[126] Even as Louchheim disavowed how carefully she was controlling things—writing to Cranston Jones, for instance, that the TWA material was "chaos,"—it is clear that the fact that she even could hold back on releasing images because they were "chaotic" shows both how powerful a project it was, and how close to her chest she held the cards. Not a single other project is treated this way and delayed by Louchheim. She is, even when annoyed, remarkably helpful in providing images even for people she doesn't quite want to help (the orthodontist and amateur architecture enthusiast Dr. Otopalik—who requested and received images based on an upcoming presentation to "a group of college graduates"—comes to mind).[127] And yet when Jones requests TWA images for a major Saarinen story, she claimed she could not send them because everything was in chaos. She even responded to Dr. Otopalik first with a letter providing tear sheets and then actual photographs, and then wrote to him, "Please help me with my stupidity—what is Orthodontics?"[128] Louchheim was not stupid. Her epistolary performances of incompetence were just that: performances.

In the introduction to *Eero Saarinen: Shaping the Future*, a multi-authored catalogue that accompanied a touring exhibition dedicated to Saarinen's work in 2006, the historian Eeva-Liisa Pelkonen writes, "Saarinen's clients also profited from the fact that the architect was completely conversant with modern media, garnering extensive press coverage and presaging the contemporary phenomenon of the celebrity architect who designs signature buildings and furniture."[129] And while his interventions in Louchheim's profile of him do indicate a pre-Louchheim skill, the firm's comfort with the media increased once Louchheim became involved. Pelkonen gives her credit, but as with everyone else, stops at a naming and a definition. "Eero's second wife, Aline B. Saarinen . . . became his close professional confidant and public relations advisor."[130] This is the last mention of Louchheim's contributions in this text. A few paragraphs later, Pelkonen cites Louchheim's 1953 *New York Times* profile, but without mentioning that it was written by Louchheim. This is another example of what we have seen happen before—where a historian is aware of Louchheim, mentions her, describes her, and then moves on as though her contributions are as irrelevant as they are, as was Louchheim's intention, invisible.

This survey of publications about TWA clarifies how instrumental Louchheim was in working out issues of exclusivity, photography, and textual consistency on behalf of the office. The repetition of certain motifs, particularly the metaphor of the bird, when linked to Louchheim's early interventions, demonstrate the depth of her involvement. Part of the challenge has been that much of her work happened through allusions and elisions, and I have read between the lines in an attempt to produce connections and find patterns. A project of this scope and public profile was at the time unusual for the office, and Louchheim's care with the project and ability to shepherd the office through its completion while maintaining creatively useful relationships with writers like McQuade and editors like Haskell demonstrate her unwavering commitment to the reputation of the Saarinen office.

I close this chapter by analyzing a short letter that I find very useful in terms of understanding how involved Louchheim was in developing public relations practices for the office. It is a letter from Louchheim to William A. Hewitt of Deere & Company, and it is the clearest explication of her practices that I have found in the available archives. Linking what she wrote in this letter with what we have previously explored demonstrates some of the substance behind my readings. She wrote this letter after Saarinen's death, and so in my reading I include not only her professional overtures but also an analysis of her reckoning with her shift from intimate living partner to posthumous reputation protector.

"Let me explain, in my longwinded way, how I have managed our public relations, the thinking behind our procedures and then, my thoughts about Deere & Company's building," she wrote. She then outlined four "target moments for publicity." First was the "decision to build or award an architectural commission"—evident in the way in which the TWA project was announced in the *New York Times* in 1958 before construction had even begun. Second was "acceptance of design or award of contract or start of construction." Third was "construction," where Louchheim said that "local press coverage is assured," while "architectural press is interested occasionally," evident in the publications in the *New York Times* about the TWA timbers and the concrete being poured, which appeared in 1959. The fourth stage was "completion or dedication," when "local, specialist, architectural press coverage are assured," and "national and international coverage become available through effort and organization." Stage four, Louchheim wrote, "represents the big moment towards which all of our public relations efforts are directed.... It is imperative not to jeopardize the important Stage 4 coverage."

The second page of the letter was far more evocative. Louchheim began the salutation again, marking a shift from professional correspondence to personal. "Dear Bill," she wrote. "When Eero was courting me, he told me I was used to living in 'rabbit' time and that I must learn architecture involves 'elephant' time. I know your elephant has had a particularly long gestation period, but it will be a beautiful baby." She was referring to the John Deere World Headquarters, which opened in 1964.

She signed the letter, "Affectionately, EERO SAARINEN AND ASSOCIATES," and then in the space, a handwritten "Aline," and then below that a typed "Aline B. Saarinen, (Mrs. Eero.)"[131] This list of sign-offs is an opportunity to track the way in which Louchheim was coming to terms with Eero's absence and also with her multiple identities. She would become the editor of a book on Saarinen, the author of her own book, and a newscaster. And yet she still identified herself first as EERO SAARINEN AND ASSOCIATES and also, and I have seen this in no other correspondence, as "Mrs. Eero."[132]

This chapter has shown, through a variety of case studies, the ways in which Louchheim interpreted Saarinen's work on his behalf, and worked diligently and creatively in her correspondence with editors and writers to always promote the Saarinen office's interests. While it is likely that the wide publication of the TWA Terminal was in some part due to its status as a public airplane terminal at a moment when air travel was becoming commonplace, and perhaps in part to the untimely death of its architect, it is the consistency of message and metaphor (particularly in terms of the "bird" idea) that sets this project apart. In my introduction, I discussed the general rise of publicity in the United States. This project, with its remarkable forms and surprising construction, garnered a remarkable amount of attention and a wide variety of interpretations. The 1960s became an architectural time of great change, with aggressive formalism beginning to sweep America, a new freedom after the modernist postwar style of the 1950s.[133] Saarinen's work was poised to usher in this new frontier of architecture, expressed by designers like Paul Rudolph, whose 1960 Lower Manhattan Expressway received a considerable amount of attention even though it was never built; Louis Kahn, whose 1965 Exeter Library was a powerful study in abstraction and shapes; or Alison and

Fig. 32. View from inside the TWA Terminal towards the tarmac, the gridded wall of windows reminiscent of MIT's Kresge Auditorium, but clearly the next evolution of Saarinen's approach. Location: New York, NY. © Ezra Stoller/Esto.

Peter Smithson, who in the 1960s introduced theoretically dense propositions from the United Kingdom.

By the time Saarinen died, architecture had entered a new era. Ada Louise Huxtable's beginning her position as the first full-time architecture critic in America in 1963 coincided with there being four full-time architecture-focused magazines in circulation: *Architecture, Architectural Record, Architectural Forum,* and *Progressive Architecture.*[134] Witold Rybczynski has called the '60s the "glory days of modernism" in which "a crusading spirit fueled interest in reading and writing about the new movement."[135]

Rybczynski argued that "a reduction in intellectual content in the glossies was largely the result of an increased reliance on photography, especially color photography." This tracks with what I have illuminated in this chapter in terms of Louchheim's interest in carefully maintaining publication rights and image exclusivity. However, in the late 1950s and early 1960s, we catch our subjects at the perfect time: one in which architecture publications were thriving; public interest was at an all-time high; and publicity wasn't so recognized that Louchheim couldn't subtly and efficiently do her behind-the-scenes work.

CHAPTER SEVEN

On the Loss
of a Client
and Friend

Lives end not when we're ready, but when it's time. The week before an early draft of this book was due, a client of mine died. Lewis W. Butler had been my favorite client, which is something we're not supposed to say or admit, but was true. I'd started working with him in 2016, after I came back to the Bay Area from Sedona. He was a society architect who couldn't publicly name at least half of the people he worked for, a polymath, a tremendous reader, and art collector. His firm, Butler Armsden, produced work that was absolutely varied—we almost thought of him as having a design studio inside his firm because some of the work was so experimental and cool and some of it was so staid. Every so often we had an early morning coffee meeting and I loved our conversations, which were almost never about what we thought they should be about. Lewis and his right hand/COO, Chandra Campbell, were an extraordinary team. They managed hundreds of ideas and issues and problems and questions, without ever seeming to break a sweat.

Lewis loved dirt biking and reading books, gossiping about his daughter's cool friends, and volunteering to teach middle school kids about architecture. He was tall and had a shock of white hair and had gone to Andover, and so we bonded over the East Coast. He said that the only island he'd ever like to be stuck on was the island of Manhattan. When I moved from the Bay back to New York in 2018, he said that sounded great, and he looked forward to visiting me. He understood that my being in the epicenter of all media was good for him; I'd done the regional Bay Area thing as long as I could, and he knew it was time to move on. I hoped that, from New York, I'd be able to get him better publications. There were a few projects that I'd had high hopes for that had ultimately gone for the *San Francisco Chronicle*, even as I almost got him into the *New York Times*.

The last time I saw him, we had coffee and talked about Bari Weiss, the embattled *New York Times* opinion-page editor who had recently resigned. He'd met her at a party, with his daughter, and of course he was the kind of person who went to parties with his daughter. We talked about what life in New York was like, and how my divorce was going, and his art collection, and a lunch I'd gone to at the Century Club for Bjarke Ingels. At some point, he asked why it was that we were meeting, and I said something about just checking in on what we were doing, and he said, airily, "Oh I always know that you're doing what you're supposed to be doing." He trusted me and my firm to just get on with it.

A few months later, on a phone call about one of his projects, where I coached him on what to say and what not to say, he mentioned that he was exhausted, that he was having trouble sleeping, that he had anxiety all night. The next thing I knew he was starting a round of treatment for esophageal cancer. He seemed in good spirits, and I trusted he would be okay. When COVID-19 came to San Francisco, he wrote to me about putting on his Hazmat suit to go for his daily treatment. Still, I didn't think much of it. A few months later, I asked if he was willing to talk to a *Dwell* writer for a piece I wanted to put together and he responded that he couldn't really talk to anyone because of the damage to his throat, and right around then is when, completely independently, I decided that I really needed to stop doing this kind of work.

I ended up talking to his colleague Chandra, and telling her I wanted to step away but that my colleague would be happy to jump in. On the phone, I learned how dire things were: that his treatment hadn't worked, that he was going to be trying a round of experimental immunotherapy. I wrote him a few emails, sent him a package of books. I emailed him again and he responded that he was in the ER, so I sent him some flowers, and I stopped hearing back from him so much, but I knew that meant he was probably just getting sicker. I decided to leave him alone as much as possible; I didn't want to add a burden.

A few weeks later, I was on a hike in the woods and thought of him. Later that night, I wrote to him that I'd thought of him on my hike. I told him about how things were going in New York, that my divorce seemed to be finally over, that I hoped he was doing okay. He wrote back almost immediately, as was his wont, with a gentle kindness. A day later, Chandra emailed me with a special request. The second treatment hadn't worked, she said. Would I be willing, even though I was busy, to draft an obituary for her to have on hand? Of course I was. I spent the next few days thinking of Lewis, in that in-between moment of knowing a person is alive and knowing that they're going to die. I wrote him an email saying I wish we could have had more time to shoot the shit and talk about whether or not to call something "funky," an argument that we'd had once. (I'd told him it would be misunderstood if he used it.) I didn't talk about how unfair it was, even though we both knew that it was. Chandra had said it was a matter of weeks if not days, not months.

I drafted the obituary and sent it to Chandra, after first sending it to my most trusted first reader, my Yale collaborator and colleague Marianela. And I went for a walk in Central Park, and felt the urge to take a picture and send it to him. It was a picture of a bunch of grasses and then tall towers rising in the background—a little bit of nature, and a little bit of the city. "Just thought of you and wanted to send this picture of the only island you'll ever love," I wrote to him. I waffled on sending it, but decided to. I've never quite known what to do around the dying, but Lewis's death wasn't my first. It just felt a little complicated because we were colleagues.

The next day, Chandra sent an email saying that Lewis had died that morning. I stored the news for later, for when I felt like I had time to handle it. I called Marianela to give her the news, and started crying once I got on the phone with her. For the next few days, I cried off and on, every few hours. He had just been a colleague, I tried to tell myself. It wasn't like I was in his inner circle. We hadn't really been close friends, not in the way that I'm friends with so many other people. But he'd meant something to me as my client, and as a friend. The intimacy that we'd had had been based on a shared love of a field, architecture, that not many people love as much as we did. I found an interview with him from three years before he died in which he talked about wanting to keep doing architecture for years. I felt—still feel—so deeply disturbed that he didn't know how short his time was.

Lewis wasn't my Eero, of course. But his death, and the way that it impacted me, reminded me of how intimate and special these relationships can be, even when they're not romantic. Of how powerful a partnership between an architect and a writer can be—of how meaningful and creative and deep that connection can become. Lewis and I understood each other because we both loved to talk about angles and planes and materials and wood. We didn't have to talk about our personal lives to bond, didn't have to throw our traumas at each other. We just both liked the same thing, and liked to talk about it. I shepherded his career in the public arena for four years, and he respected me for it. I respected him for his talent and his intellectual vibrancy. It was a relationship unlike any other, and losing him as an interlocutor was a tragedy unlike any other. I had never thought that I could love a client, but I did love Lewis.

CHAPTER EIGHT

"I Really Am Not Interested in That Project"

Eero Saarinen died on September 1, 1961. The story could stop there, with the death of this singular, remarkable man, with the end of the architecture firm he founded. But because our story is about Louchheim, it doesn't stop there. Parts of it, yes; of course Eero could no longer stroll into the model shop and discuss the arches of TWA with his partner Kevin Roche; of course he would no longer be sitting face-to-face with Louchheim in their makeshift garage office. And yet while it is somewhat cliché to talk about someone's "spirit" living on after they die, it is true that Saarinen's work and aesthetic and ethos did live on, through the ministrations and words of Louchheim and the rest of the office.

In this chapter I will outline the ways in which Louchheim addressed the death of her husband and colleague, and trace the shift in her career after his death to show how thoroughly her words became part of what we have considered now to be a Saarinen canon. The chapter's title comes from a letter that she sent to an interested editor who was hoping to commission her to write a book about Saarinen. Her refusal came before his death; afterwards, she turned her attentions towards ensuring that the office continued; that the TWA Terminal was complete; that Saarinen's professional reputation was as protected as possible; and that her own career as a writer and public intellectual on the topic of architecture was secure.

His death was quick, and came with barely the faintest warning. After two weeks of slurred speech and unusual affect, a brain tumor was discovered. He was operated on, and died.[1] And yet, his work continued. We will read now the various ways in which Louchheim continued her project of narrating Eero's work on his behalf, and finished the fourth stage of her "benign takeover," ending their collaboration with a literal co-option of his words, in the publication of her book *Eero Saarinen on His Work*, in 1962.[2]

The condolences poured in, just as Louchheim sent cables to various interested parties. The cables were each different according to the recipient groups. A group of six close associates received a simple all-caps cable, EERO PASSED AWAY THIS MORNING.[3] The notable recipients are Astrid Sampe, the Swedish textile designer whom Saarinen had been considering leaving his first wife Lily for until he met Louchheim, and Finnish-Swedish architect Cyril Mardall. A larger group received the note—"EERO PASSED AWAY THIS MORNING. PLEASE DO NOT SEND FLOWERS. A MEMORIAL GIFT MAY BE SENT TO YALE UNIVERSITY IN EERO'S NAME."[4] It was signed "ES&A," for Eero Saarinen & Associates, a pragmatic signature that was in contrast to the emotional directives in the cable not to send flowers but to possibly send a gift, implying that the recipients would feel moved to action of some sort. This more fulsome announcement was sent to a group of eighteen men, many of them clients. N. M. Martin of IBM was listed next to Edmund Cooke of Deere & Company, both corporate clients whose commissions for offices had encouraged Saarinen to begin to change the landscape of corporate America.[5] Eliot Noyes, the architect and industrial designer who had written about Saarinen's MIT chapel, received one, as did architect Louis Kahn, who would die sixteen years later in a bathroom at New York's Penn Station, after bringing his own brand of concrete formalism to America.

A third cable was sent to a larger group that included both architects and members of the press like Cranston Jones and Douglas Haskell, and was a more intimate note informing them about the imminent memorial service:

EERO SAARINEN PASSED AWAY THIS MORNING. A MEMORIAL SERVICE FOR FRIENDS WILL BE HELD AT A LATER DATE. PLEASE DO NOT SEND FLOWERS. A MEMORIAL GIFT MAY BE SENT TO YALE UNIVERSITY IN EERO'S NAME.

EERO SAARINEN & ASSOCIATES[6]

The list of names here reads like a who's who of 1950s architecture and publishing. Mr. and Mrs. Charles Eames (listed exactly that way) share a page with early Modern Movement architect Pietro Belluschi, California icon and urban planner William Wurster, architect and DC Metro designer Harry Weese, philanthropist John D. Rockefeller III, landscape architect and frequent collaborator Dan Kiley, historian and critic Edgar Kaufmann Jr., architect Gordon Bunshaft, high modernist designer and MoMA curator Philip Johnson, MoMA director Alfred Barr, modernist architect Mies van der Rohe, and mobile sculptor Alexander Calder. The range of personalities, from Johnson and Barr, who had worked together at the Museum of Modern Art on curating the International Style exhibition, to Alexander Calder, who lived in Connecticut and whose swooping mobiles and curved forms clearly found resonance in Saarinen's curves, shows the range of social and professional connections that the office—partially because of Louchheim—featured.

Two additional sets of cables were unusual. Oscar Niemeyer, the Brazilian architect who rethought Brasilia; and Le Corbusier, the Swiss-Italian architect whose formalism and ability with public relations had turned out to be influential or at least in the same league with Eero's work, received the note "Eero Saarinen died Friday."[7] Alvar Aalto, Finnish architect, received a more personal cable: "Heartbroken Eero died after short illness Aline Saarinen."[8] The insertion of her name here, putting herself into the ring just as she did when she signed letters to Eero, is relevant to our story of how she positioned herself both during his life and after his death. Here, she is both avowedly emotional—"heartbroken" in fact—and, as opposed to the explanatory and straightforward cable that she sent to Niemeyer and Le Corbusier, she did not give the exact date of death, but rather gave the details of how—"after short illness"—which is so much more evocative and personal.[9] The levels of distinction here speak once again to Louchheim's sophisticated approach to various modes of communication and intimacy. She calibrated her performance of closeness so as to maintain the ties that she thought were most useful for Saarinen's long-term reputation.

Many obituaries appeared. Orvil Dryfoos, publisher of the *New York Times*, sent a copy of the *New York Times International Edition* directly to Kevin Roche at the Saarinen office, with a note saying that he'd received a wire from Aline—who he understood to be quite busy—indicating her pleasure with the obituary that ran in the *New York Times*. He included the International Edition obituary, and closed with his sympathy to Roche, and all the associates.[10] Again, Louchheim is present and mobilized on the page though not directly involved in the communication. Dryfoos's comment that he received a wire from her speaks to the lack of privacy of her involvement in her husband's death—that everything was public and, to use a contemporary term, shareable because of her publicly accepted role as Eero's representative. It is intriguing to see her on this page as an absent actor who takes up two thirds of the topics, as well as to see her as someone about whom Dryfoos intimates he knows a lot, which he did by alluding to her busy-ness. But then Dryfoos sends his sympathy to Roche and to all the associates, but never directly to Louchheim. She has been fully professionalized. But there are clues here not only about how Louchheim was handling her husband and business partner's death, but how her role was perceived.

The obituary Dryfoos enclosed opened with this line: "The death of Eero Saarinen at the height of his powers ... is a loss for architecture, for the Nation as a whole, and indeed for the world."[11] The obituary acknowledged that he "occasionally took a wrong turn to an aesthetic impasse," but then acknowledged that "he stood in the forefront of the entire contemporary movement on the path to a new environment, a new civilization." The last paragraph closes by saying that he'd been considered for the Oakland Museum, which ended up being completed in 1968 by Kevin Roche and John Dinkeloo, and that had he done it, he "could have helped to show this part of the world that artistic commitment—as another poet said—is to strive, to see, to find, and not to yield."[12] I read "this part of the world" to mean California. A handwritten note at the bottom both strengthens and disavows the somewhat critical note of the obituary. "This is from the heart, Allan," is, I believe, based on handwriting, written by Allan Temko, who would go on to write a Saarinen biography in somewhat challenging collaboration with Louchheim.

The Associated Press obituary, which also ran in the *New York Times*, was longer, and listed the Chancery Building of the United States Embassy in London, the TWA Terminal, and the GM Center in the second paragraph. The obituary repeated stories that Louchheim had written about eight years earlier in her *New York Times* profile, such as one about Eero following in his father's footsteps, as an infant "crawling under the drafting table of the studio-house at Hvittrask, Finland."[13] The article quotes Eero recounting that "except for a brief excursion into sculpture it never occurred to me to do anything but follow my father's footsteps," another line lifted from Louchheim's 1953 reporting. The rest of the obituary tells the story of both his and Eliel's submission to the St. Louis Arch competition, and then essentially finishes with this: "His heritage and his own talents made him one of this country's best-known, most respected and sought-after architects. His work has adorned many sections of the United States."[14] Then comes a kind of coda, that feels tacked on:

"On Feb 8., 1954, Mr. Saarinen married Aline Bernstein Louchheim, at the time and until 1959 associate art editor of *The New York Times*."[15] Her presence here feels random, ad hoc, and yet her professional connection to the *New York Times* is both a way of explaining why he had become so famous in the sentences that came before, and at the same time a way of distancing her from the grief of being a widow who has lost not only her husband, but her professional identity. The omission of her professional role as Eero's Head of Information Services is striking. She has returned, or more accurately, has been returned *by others*, on his death, to her pre-marriage identity, for though she officially held her *New York Times* position until 1959, her attention and focus turned away from her regular reporting trips and towards the work that Eero was doing at Bloomfield Hills. I read in this closing both an acknowledgement of her power—her public affiliation with the *New York Times* is culturally important and an easy reference to skill and value—and also perhaps a gentle nudge back to her own and solo identity. We know that after she wrapped up Eero's remaining projects, she moved on to become her own creative person once again, publishing a book that had nothing to do with Eero's work, and hosting television programs that had nary a visible catenary curve. Our identities are so often created through our own letters, through our own writing. And yet here, her identity is being carved from the outside, bestowed back upon her through Eero's death.

A memorial service for friends (a loose category that included professional contacts) was scheduled to be held in Saarinen's intimate MIT chapel on Saturday, September 9, 1961.[16] That his memorial should be in the chapel was fitting; it was a religious work that he had created, a project that he and Louchheim had discussed from their very first letters, and one that he had always been drawn back to. It was also a significant turning point in both Saarinen's architectural career and Louchheim and Saarinen's collaboration. In a sense, it was the last truly pre-Louchheim building to be done, and as such, having his memorial there was a marker of his individuality, of his own work. Just as Eero's death returned Louchheim to her own independent and noncoupled person system, so too did his death return him to a state of conceptual and practical individuality.

Louchheim was, as she had written to Aalto, heartbroken. And yet she had to immediately turn her attention to holding the office together. It became her job to both soothe the grief of Saarinen's partners, and to assure stakeholders like TWA, the contractors, the builders, everyone working on Dulles and other projects, that the work could and would go forward.

She did not have the luxury of time, a break, a retreat. She had to immediately jump into organizing the memorial service, sending cables to luminaries like Niemeyer and Corbusier, while making sure everyone involved in ongoing projects understood that none would falter. The link between her own and Saarinen's identity was intense here; she had, as we have seen, already inserted herself into the workings of Saarinen's office. The combination of her role as widow and her role as Head of Information Services solidified her role as an individual in the continued existence of the firm after its founder's death.

She also worked with Douglas Haskell on developing an obituary for Saarinen, which would run in October 1961 in *Architectural Forum*. The draft in the archive is a compelling piece of evidence showing Haskell's ease in asking Louchheim for editorial commentary—again, a mode of intimacy between editor and subject that is often frowned upon but was allowed here because of the depth of friendship and personal relationship that the two had developed, as we saw in chapter 4. We can see the typed-up description that, presumably, Haskell authored, or at least, closely oversaw, and then Louchheim's handwritten suggestions, which begin, on the first page, with simple suggestions—replacing "At Idlewild" with "And at," for example, although later her edits become more provocative.[17]

Her changes are worth examining in full. Haskell wrote: "Eero and his associates increasingly asked themselves what each separate client might be trying to become: what his unique situation might be, his purpose, his image of himself, which the building must meet and express." Louchheim cut words and changed punctuation, ending with this sentence: "Eero and his associates increasingly asked themselves what each separate client's unique situation might be, his purpose, which the building must meet and express." Reading those two next to each other, though reading the second requires a work of magical thinking and then nonmagical retyping, it is clear that the second is far more evocative and to-the-point, where the first wavers around personality-focused ideas. Louchheim's editorial skill is evident here in her ability to see a sentence and then craft a new sentence through simple omission of words. In a sense, her structural ability with a sentence here mirrors the way in which Eero was able to see structures and planes and windows that needed to be removed, or reshifted, or rethought. We can see Louchheim at work here, doing the work that she did, which was so often one of paring down, literal editing, which helped to crystallize and solidify exactly what it was that Eero did.

Her edits above are a microcosm of her larger contribution: recasting Saarinen's reputation in a way that was both more viscerally evocative and also more generally historical. Her removal of "his image of himself" in her edit speaks to a sensitivity to how this document would be read, and to the value in subsuming Saarinen's "image of himself" into the broader issue of what "the building could meet and express." Ironically, it was her removal of a mention of Saarinen's "image" that protected his image; it is a complex dance of language and reference that we have seen earlier Louchheim was extremely skilled at.

Later in the galley, describing the Dulles airport project, she replaced "the result of the beautiful and exhaustive analysis that he was able to do" with "so beautifully researched." Louchheim was aware of the way in which specific words, like "exhaustive," would evoke particular feelings with readers. "Exhaustive," though meant as a compliment, feels exhausting, tiring. It also undermines the message of Eero's architecture, which is that it was his extensive research and thought that led to an exploration into and expression of a greater—and deeply personal—human sentiment. The statement that comes after this reads: "Architecture is not just to fulfill man's need for shelter," Eero had said, "but also to fulfill man's belief in the nobility of his existence on this earth."[18] This statement would not have worked so well had it immediately followed the recounting of "exhaustive" analysis. It would have felt tired and overworked. Instead, with Louchheim's edits, it felt like the next obvious step.

The condolence letters poured in. One, written by Silkey Smith, arrived too late, and was in fact written too late. This is a perfect example of the relative slowness (compared to now) of correspondence that could lead to heart-wrenchingly delayed communications. Smith's letter was addressed directly to Eero, and said how sorry he was to have heard that Eero had gone through brain surgery. Smith wrote as a fellow sufferer, and recounted his own experience having a brain tumor removed and what kept him going. The next paragraph asked Eero to tell Aline how much Smith admired her writing in the *Times*, pre-Eero. Perhaps exaggerating, he said she was the only critic who could distinguish the front and back of a painting.[19]

Of course, he overdid the statement—obviously there were arts writers at the *New York Times* who could tell the difference between the front and the back of a painting, but again, Louchheim is being used here as a way of filling time and filling space, of moving the conversation forward. Of course, Saarinen did not receive the letter, having died two days earlier, and so the letter would have gone directly to Louchheim, who, by this point, was used to reading letters in which she was described in the third person though still directly addressed. What did this mean, to read this sideways slippage? In a sense, it was good practice for the next few years of her life, in which, even though Eero was dead, she still had to represent him and operate as his proxy.

On November 30, 1961, Robert W. Craig, executive director of the Aspen Institute, wrote to Louchheim to invite her to be a special guest in an executive session. He described the institute, and asked her to contribute her unique point of view.[20] It took Louchheim only a few days to respond. "Due to my husband's death and accelerated work for him and the office, I have fallen very far behind on a book for which I am under contract to Random House. As soon as I can, I will have to return to that project and devote myself exclusively to it."[21] We see here three competing interests. One is to deal with the accelerated work for Eero at the office. A second is to return to her own book. A third is her potential desire to participate in Craig's invitation. She noted in handwriting on her copy of the letter that it be filed in "pub." for publicity, showing that she was aware of how her own projects and work could contribute, theoretically and practically, to the expansion of Eero's own public relations.

The same week, she dealt with another volley, this time entirely unrelated to Eero, from Ruth Glover, Director of Research and Public Information at the Lavanburg Foundation, asking Louchheim to suggest some experts who might be able to write something about design and social problems. This was to be for a book about the Douglass Houses—a public housing project—in New York City.[22] In handwriting on the letter itself, Louchheim wrote in thick pencil verging on crayon "Katherine ^ Bauer [sic] Wurster" and then in the official reply typed, "The obvious and best person for your editor would be Catherine Bauer Wurster, Mrs. William Wurster." And then, deflecting in the case of further queries, she added, "The obvious person to advise you on the possible editors would be Douglas Haskell of the Architectural Forum."[23] This deflecting paragraph demonstrates that she is not interested in continuing the conversation, and also once again affirms her very close relationship with editor Douglas Haskell, and his wider importance.

On December 8, Louchheim wrote two separate letters to two recipients, both asking for personal documents related to Saarinen. One request was sent to the School of Architecture in Barcelona, Spain. She wrote, "I am trying to collect some of his non-architectural drawings, because he enjoyed drawing very much and revealed in these drawings not only his talent but much of his many-faceted and charming personality." And then, "Would it be possible to have a photograph of the 'telephone doodle' which he sent for that exhibition? Or even to have the original?"[24] We see here shades of the private grief that Louchheim, who had to keep up the publicity and forward momentum of the office, was not allowed—or did not allow herself—to show publicly. The slippage occurs in her description of his "many-faceted and charming personality," a description that has a way of bringing him back to life. So rarely was Louchheim publicly comfortable with commenting on her husband's intimate personality—it would have detracted from the strength of her points about his architecture—that we must read carefully and closely in order to see these moments of personal grief and desire slip through. It was a day for such requests.

She also wrote to a Dr. Schweighofer in Germany, asking for a copy of handwriting analysis that the doctor had done for Eero in July. "I am a writer," she wrote. It had been a long time since Louchheim had identified herself as a writer as opposed to a helpmeet or organizer or information provider, and we see here that she is beginning to reorient towards her own identity. She closed by saying that they had moved offices: "After his death, his partners and associates and I followed his plan." This is noteworthy because it is described as Eero's plan, even though we know it was made in collaboration with Louchheim, and because she lists herself last.[25]

On October 12, she acknowledged receipt of a picture from Nick Thimmesch, a political columnist at *Time* magazine, saying, "You are an angel. That Zimmerman picture is one of the very nicest and I look forward to the others. Oh, dear." She signed it "Fondly, Aline."[26] We see again shades of a private feeling—here, the shade comes in the form of a simple reference, an "oh, dear." She doesn't tell us what the "oh, dear," is about, but it is evocative and powerful—classic Louchheim. She knew how to use words, how to be "scalpel"-like, as Eero had said when they first met, and here the extremely short letter begins and ends with the feelings-oriented words "angel," and "dear." Narratively the letter is just two lines, almost a poem of half of a stanza, but remember this was barely a month after Eero died. Louchheim was still processing his death and his work and his future work and her future work—and doing all of it publicly.

Other acknowledgements of condolences were also filed under "pub," such as the one to Karl Baur-Callwey, editor of *Baumeister*, thanking him for his "very nice, sensitive and understanding obituary in your magazine."[27] Another one was sent to G. E. Kidder Smith, who'd written to Eero with a very long PS to Louchheim, and which she found only after her department went through extant office materials in preparation for the move from Bloomfield Hills to New England. On the letter, Eero had written in red pencil "ANSWER WITH THANKS" with a triangle pointing to the first paragraph, about a book that featured Eero's London embassy. The PS was directly to Louchheim, and was asking for her to intervene with the *New York Times*, which had featured the book in the Magazine Section and therefore was unwilling to review the book in the Book Review section. "It would be wonderful if you could put in a discreet word here," Kidder Smith wrote, and then parenthetically, "(Giedion recently wrote me that he would love to do a review of it.)" We see here an example of how the elite were able to organize their own publicity—that there were behind-the-scenes requests that would have been unavailable to others. Kidder Smith was a well-known writer and photographer, and Giedion was presumably a reference to architectural historian Siegfried Giedion, whose *Space, Time and Architecture*, published in 1941, was the essential defining text of the Modern Movement in the postwar decades. Aline responded that she could not intervene, that the *Times* did have this policy (however much she might have disagreed with it), but the exchange shows a few things of note: the assumption that a letter to Eero would be also easily passed on to Louchheim; that Louchheim was seen as having a powerful position with the *Times* even though she had resigned her position as associate art critic two years earlier; and that the publicity networks still relied on a system of word-of-mouth referrals.[28]

The architectural publication archive of The Avery Index shows eleven obituaries for Eero Saarinen published in the architectural press, including *Architectural Record*, *Architectural Forum*, *Architecture d'aujourd'hui*, *Baukunst und Werkform*, *Casabella*, *Architectural Design*, *Arquitectura*, and *Baumeister*. The range is American, English, Italian, French, and German, showing—even though he did not work extensively (or at all) in these countries—the international impact of Eero's reputation and work.

Louchheim acknowledged Allan Temko's obituary in a telegram. "Very touched and comforted by your editorial." she wrote. "Have written to you today." "Sincerely, Aline."[29] Most interesting is the idea that this is a communication that is actually heralding another communication. Louchheim and Saarinen spent much time in their letters talking about how they were going to talk, and about their letters, and where they were in the drafts of their letters, and that they were about to write more, a proper letter, or arrange a phone call; here, Louchheim is slipping back into that pattern but with a much-less engaged interlocutor, though Temko seemed to have a sort of obsession with Saarinen that he finalized in his biography. Writing to him to tell him that she *had* written to him that day, not that she was *going* to write to him, puts Louchheim into an in-between space. Did she need to write the telegram? What was its purpose? Perhaps she wrote something entirely different and wanted to keep this telegram there as one form of communication. This would not have been unusual, as Louchheim was used to wearing so many different hats with so many different single interlocutors that it would have been understandable for her to write a telegraph thanking Temko personally, again, using emotional words like "touched and comforted," and then to write him a brusquer and more professional letter about the ideas that he was going to begin putting forward.

These archives have shown the multiple levels at which Louchheim treated Saarinen's death as a work event as well as a life event. Because of the intimacy of her working relationship with him, she was automatically assumed by others to be both responsible for all incoming and outgoing correspondence and needs; because of the professionalism with which she had developed the Information Services offices, she was also approached—as she had been by Haskell for his obituary—on a professional level. The way in which she continued to work as Saarinen's closest colleague during the time of his death and shortly after speaks to the strength of her work, then and now.

Saarinen's death profoundly affected her personally, which we see in traces. However, shortly before his death, the two were engaged in what some office correspondence and assorted letters show to be a battle of the wills. A look at correspondence between Louchheim and Saarinen before his death shows how their working relationship had evolved.

A few months before Eero died, Thomas Creighton, editor of *Progressive Architecture*, asked Louchheim if she would write a book about her husband. "A long time ago … I wrote you asking your advice about a book on Eero and his work … I think you never replied, which I can understand, with the busy life you and Eero are leading," he wrote. And then, "Don't you think that a book by you, double qualified as a critic and as a close observer, would be a worth-while thing? Could you plan to do it when your present writing tasks are completed?" He then went on: "I know that Eero—who writes that he is too busy to cooperate on the 'definitive' article that I wanted to do—would also be too busy to help much with a book project. But that is always going to be true, I am sure, and I think the summary and critique are essential."[30] Louchheim's busy-ness here is seen as temporary—"when your present writing tasks are completed"— and also as "tasks," something that anyone with training could do and that doesn't specifically require Louchheim. The idea that she has "tasks" that she will complete, whereas Eero is "too busy" and that his being too busy is "always going to be true" cleaves the two completely. He is seen here as the great creative individual agent and actor, almost impossible to wrangle, and of course Creighton treats his busy-ness with deference. Louchheim does not receive the same personal respect: "Don't you think" is a more manipulative way of beginning a sentence than "Do you think?" Creighton is almost bullying Louchheim here, which is perhaps why she responds so forcefully, both internally to Eero, and externally to Creighton.

On July 28, two days later, which shows some office delay, Louchheim passed Creighton's letter to Eero with a typed note of her own on top. "Eero. Here we go again! Obviously, I don't want to." Signed only "A." This is in such marked difference to Saarinen and Louchheim's earliest correspondence. Eero's response comes in a handwritten memo, all capitals that bleed between lines of a yellow ruled legal pad, a scrap of paper that is nonetheless cut perfectly at the bottom but is ripped at the top right corner and then taped to the original letter with a strip of brown masking tape. (It is, in a sense, a home-made "Post-it.") "Aline:" it says, "THIS IS A LETTER TO YOU SHOULD YOU NOT ANSWER IT YOURSELF[?]" and then in much smaller letters, "LOVE EERO." As a visual object, the letter is fascinating, three layers of correspondence—the bottom one typed and perfectly organized by Creighton, signed with a "Cordially" and then also hand signed, and appearing on official Reinhold Publishing Corporation letterhead. Louchheim's note to Eero, the second layer, comes on a piece of paper obviously designed to be exactly that size, and is typed, but not on letterhead. And then the third from Eero, yellow on top and taped so that it connects Louchheim's letter to Creighton's, is a metaphor for the way in which what he said was ultimately the most important, and also he is aggressively throwing the ball back into her court, but then diminishes that aggression by signing it "LOVE EERO."[31]

In Louchheim's response to Creighton, she demurred. "I am very flattered that you think I would be a good author for a book about Eero. However, I really am not interested in that project," she began. "On the one hand, I think the world would feel it was impossible for a wife to be objective (and I am somewhat inclined to agree) and on the other hand, I really like to expand my life by confining my writing to a larger world than my home. I am deeply involved with my present book but horrendously behind schedule and even giving up as much as possible of my work for Eero in order to get us moved and to complete my manuscript." She finished with the note: "I am turning your letter over to Eero, who will take it up from here." There are three moments of handwriting marginalia, one in pen saying "File"; one in pencil saying, in Louchheim's hand, "publ.", and then a bright-red pencil line under the last line and with an underlined "E" and an arrow pointing.[32] The date was July 31, 1961, a few months before Eero would die.

The language here is important. "I really like to expand my life by confining my writing," she wrote. The tension between expansion and confinement here is again scalpel-like, and also speaks to a different approach than she'd had seven years earlier, when she so aggressively positioned herself as his ideal coworker/helpmeet. That she wanted to expand her life shows that she was, perhaps, running out of steam as Eero's representative. The desire to file all of these issues under "publ." shows that she was starting to file even her own life into professional folders. I read between the lines here a personal frustration that bleeds into her precise language. "I really am not interested in that project" is much stronger than her later refusals imply—that she thinks it would be impossible for a wife to be objective is not directly an excuse but is far less overt and direct than her saying "I really am not interested in that project." That she tells Creighton later that she is "giving up as much as possible of my work for Eero" is also of note—the work is not "with" Eero, she does not describe it as "my collaboration with my husband," but "work for Eero."[33] It seems as though she is about to leave things in the hands of her assistant Pat Burley, and move on. Nevertheless, less than a year later, she was at work on the book *Eero Saarinen on His Work*.

The book was to be published by Yale University Press, and although she wrote it, Louchheim referred to herself as "editor," for example in a letter to an interlocutor, Mrs. Joseph, gently correcting some factual errors the latter had made. The book was drafted by January 1962. Presumably an editor, Mrs. James Gould Cozzens, wrote to Louchheim saying that she'd done a great job and that it would be an important book.

Fig. 33. Aline Saarinen, after Eero's 1961 death, holding a copy of the book *Eero Saarinen on His Work*, which she wrote despite some ambivalence about it. Box 2, folder 13, Aline and Eero Saarinen Papers, 1906–1977, Archives of American Art, Smithsonian Institution.

Importantly, she said how much she liked the subtitle as Louchheim had provided, another sure sign that it was in fact Louchheim's work that created and produced this book.[34]

The book was first published in 1962. It opened with a selection of statements Eero had made, edited by Louchheim, and was organized thematically. Notably, there are a few instances of Louchheim's citing Eero as having written a statement "to a journalist," when the journalist, as we know, is her. For instance, "What you newspaper and magazine writers, who work in rabbit time, don't understand is that the practice of architecture has to be measured in elephant time."[35] That snippet is described as having been written "to a journalist, February 14, 1953."[36] February 14 of course is Valentine's Day, though this was not explicitly noted. Saarinen wrote this observation to Louchheim in the context of a deeply personal, romantic, and evocative Valentine's Day card, very shortly after they had met and while she was still writing her *New York Times* profile.

Fig. 34. Aline Saarinen presumably lecturing about history as part of her post-Eero career, undated but about late 1960s. Box 3, folder 10, Aline and Eero Saarinen Papers 1906–1977, Archives of American Art, Smithsonian Institution.

The legend of her working in rabbit time whereas he worked in elephant time has been repeated throughout the decades, but there are multiple layers of knowledge production happening here, layers of knowledge that contemporary readers would not have possessed.

The Eero and Aline Saarinen papers were given to the Smithsonian in 1981, and it is extremely unlikely that they were passed around the office or around editorial departments before then. And so Louchheim in this book-writing process was fully embodying an embrace of the personal into the professional, and vice versa. Her willingness to co-opt this particular love letter indicates a general willingness to use what Eero wrote to her privately in order to amplify his own voice musing on his profession. There are two ways to read this: the redeployment of a remark that was made in a personal context in a professional one; or, that she retroactively read his personal correspondence as professional correspondence, an idea that I find much more engaging. We have read much about the interweaving of the personal and the professional, the way in which their early letters were half job applications and half love letters. This book, which I see as her final act of benign takeover, of merging her words with his practice, then becomes, through this lens, a revisionist history of their

relationship. We know that before he died they may not have been getting along very well (suggested by the brusque and professional memos
we have seen), and so it is possible that her enlistment of his love letters
into her professional project was more than just using the material she
had. It is possible that this was also a way for her, retroactively, to understand that perhaps everything that Eero did and said was ultimately in
service to his career. We discovered earlier how ambitious he was when
considering leaving Lily Swann in favor of someone who could make him
more famous. Were these little clues of Louchheim's disavowal of herself
as actor and calling herself instead "a journalist," a way of her reckoning
with her own relationship, with coming to terms with a past that ended
up not how she wanted it to? Reading deeply into this book is a way of
watching Louchheim not only do a professional job as representative of
her husband, but also a personal job of making sense of her past. Similar
to the way in which Saarinen used form and planes and light to explore
his deeply humanistic sense of the world and how it could be, Louchheim
used words. Is it any surprise, then, that her words are deeply revealing?

For the section "On Himself," Louchheim opened with the opening
paragraph of "a *New York Times* interview January 29, 1953." This was the
interview that she did with him, the interview during which they later
decided they fell in love, the interview during which, as we read, they
drove together and clasped hands over the gearshift and turned a corner. "A better name for architect is form-giver and until his death in 1950,
when I started to create my own form, I worked within the form of my
father,"—*New York Times*, April 26, 1953. The remark is from Louchheim's
story, but the text does not overtly signify that.

These moments are sprinkled throughout Louchheim's text. In a drawing that she included of the MIT chapel, there's a note—"do you think it is
getting too complicated?"—very likely a direct address to Louchheim, as
Saarinen never asked his partners these kinds of questions, whereas early
in their epistolary relationship, while the chapel was being designed and
when he *was* sending her pictures and drawings, he definitely at least per-
formed deference to her thoughts.

Later, Louchheim quoted Eero: "I am interested that you write you
think I will make my big contribution in concrete. It is a material which is
beginning to interest me more and more. It presents many challenges as
well as many opportunities. It seemed the inevitable material for the Milwaukee [Art Museum] building. I supposed someday it will even prove

to be competitive with steel for high-rise buildings." This was described as, "To a journalist, May 5, 1953."[37] The *New York Times* article came out in April, so we know that this is postpublication, part of their continuing and ongoing conversation, conversation that would not have happened were it not for Louchheim.

Furthermore, the book repeated Saarinen's claim that the TWA Terminal's relationship to a bird was "really coincidental." "That was the last thing we ever thought about," Louchheim quoted Eero saying, in a *Horizon* interview on June 19, 1959. But then: "Now, that doesn't mean that one doesn't have the right to see it that way or to explain it to laymen in those terms, especially because laymen are usually more literally than visually inclined."[38] We know that Louchheim was directly responsible for the "bird" narrative, and so this inclusion of a pseudoquotation, and the way it is framed, bears some interpretation. There is the overt statement first—that the bird image was "really coincidental" and "the last thing we ever thought." This helps to buttress Eero's image as someone who is far beyond simple metaphors, who wouldn't have done a building that looks like a bird. That was too simple and quick a metaphor, too much like the kind of thing a shallower thinker would have thought. And so Louchheim quotes Eero *really* disavowing it—"the last thing we ever thought about." But then we have a turnaround, this time focusing on the idea of the layman. As we know, Louchheim often referred to herself as a layperson, someone who had a keen interest in the arts and architecture but who was not a professional. This was a combination of keen tactics—pretending that she was sort of dense and didn't get things as a way of getting better access to architects and ideas—and also a larger cultural sense in the 1950s that women were still mostly supposed to work at home, that for a woman to be a true expert was an exception rather than a culturally understood rule. If we read here "Aline" instead of "laymen," we see a whole host of meaning opening up. Louchheim *was* more verbally than visually inclined, and that was a tremendous skill that helped not only Eero in the office but also the interpretation of his architecture. Louchheim is in conversation with Eero here, though posthumously, granting him the freedom to say that he didn't want anyone to think that TWA looked like a bird while at the same time then quickly pivoting to give credence to her own idea, though without overt credit.

Once published, her book received attention in a variety of periodicals. Reviews appeared in publications like *Domus*, *L'Oeil*, and, curiously,

The American Scholar, where reviewer Frank Getlein wrote thrillingly of Eero's work: "Thus the hump-backed roof and swelling walls of the [Ingalls] Yale University hockey rink, calling to mind, with no trace of historicism or animal metaphor, such northern things as Viking prows, stave churches and surfacing seabeasts."[39] Calling to mind my discussion about the way in which Louchheim began to develop a consistent narrative of Eero's work, is Getlein's description of the hockey rink, often referred to as "the Yale whale," zoologically specific to the point of calling it a humpback, and then disavowing the ease of that metaphor and saying this was of course emblematic of "no trace of animal metaphor."

Getlein says that "the [architect's] statements are expertly selected and reveal thought in progress as designs grew," though he does not acknowledge that Louchheim both selected and, as we know, edited the statements.[40] Remy Saisselin, writing in the *Journal of Aesthetics and Art Criticism*, wrote that the book was "very handsome" but "difficult to review" as "the architecture speaks for itself." Interestingly, he did not seem overly taken with the style, writing: "As for Saarinen's statements, letters, writings, reproduced here in the form of excerpts or comments it is hardly fair to discuss them since some of them are clearly out of context."[41] This critique of contextlessness comes with context: "The question we may ask ourselves is whether architects are to be edited as if they were writers of maxims," Saisselin says, and then continues, "The most interesting statements are the architect's own comments on specific works," comments which Louchheim was freer to edit than just about anything else. (She certainly would not have taken her editorial acumen to any of the other contributors' words with nearly the amount of freedom that she did Eero's.)[42]

John Jacobus, in the *Journal of the Society of Architectural Historians*, wrote of Louchheim's contribution and contrasted her book to Allan Temko's biography, which he called "much too tremulous." Jacobus described Louchheim's work as something she "prepared," rather than wrote, another intimation of her having held a job that was not a hundred percent editorially demarcated yet.[43] Rather than "edited," calling it "prepared" implies that Jacobus had some sense—or we can infer some sense retroactively—that all of Louchheim's life was a preparation for this book. Louchheim did more than edit lines and put various points together with various images. Her work, since 1953, was a preparation for this project—a continuous exploration into and attempt to understand Saarinen's work, his ethos, his forms, his ideals.

Jacobus claimed to understand why Temko's book failed and Louchheim's succeeded. His fundamental argument was that Eero's career is conceptually somewhat elusive, devoted to a certain monumentality and also featuring "designs that bravely tacked into the wind of entrenched modernism." Jacobus noted that Saarinen was "frequently scourged by professional critics," though that is a bit of an overreach. Jacobus did clearly delineate Louchheim's contributions: "Aline Saarinen's editing lets the reader see these qualities, and to grasp them slowly and, consequently, compassionately," he writes. "Of all the architects of the 1950s, Eero remains perhaps the greatest enigma—a much greater one, certainly, than Kahn—and yet his buildings, by themselves and on their own, are accessible to a large idea, and his ideas about architecture are not especially difficult."[44] Not especially difficult!? From the letters and sketches we have seen, Saarinen's ideas about architecture *were* difficult, to him. He struggled with where to place an arch, how to work with the curve of the Ingalls Rink. He felt and wondered deeply about what the best shape for a structure was, and how to best build it. Saarinen was not an easy architect; his ideas were not easy. Then why does Jacobus think he was? Formalism was superficial to Jacobus and he was perhaps searching for epistemological depth. "His remarks about his own works are disarmingly open and revealing," Jacobus writes, "indicating that he was quite content with an outwards, literal expression of the problem at hand."[45] Disarmingly open and revealing sounds ... like Louchheim! I have shown earlier that Eero's writing about architecture was often complicated and confusing, and that it was always and invariably, post-1954, marked by Louchheim's clarity, her "scalpel"-like precision, that helped Eero's work to be *perceived* in a certain way. Also, her having edited this book means that she did far more literary and narrative intervention than perhaps Jacobus realizes by calling her interventions "preparation" and "editing."

Jacobus is appalled by Temko's "journalistic flair," but we also see clues in his critique of Temko about how well Louchheim did her job. "There is less need for the biographer of Eero Saarinen to provide the kind of *explication du text* [sic] which is mandatory in the case of our more intellectual or philosophic designers," Jacobus writes.[46] But why should that have been? Why wasn't Saarinen seen as an intellectual or philosophic designer? He certainly felt that he was an intellectual; Saarinen traveled and gave lectures and papers, and we know from his letters that he deeply contemplated meaning, form, humanity. I contend that Saarinen was in fact deeply philosophical; his unwavering commitment to the idea that buildings could represent some ideal truth, or some ideal fact about a building or a company (as Jacobus points out he did with the GM project). History has shown that we place Saarinen into a philosophical camp rather than a resolutely formalist one. The comparisons between Saarinen and Kahn are often made, as they were made then, but Jacobus's dismissal of Temko seems personal, though he says it isn't. "This architect's buildings are rather too fragile as monumental statements to require much historical analysis let alone encourage it," Jacobus continued.[47] The St. Louis Arch had not yet been built, though it would end up being a monument that called for much historical analysis. And, of course, the TWA Terminal has become a monumental project, still hotly discussed (though now those debates take place on Facebook and often among the few remaining staff and freelance architecture journalists).

Jacobus shows his hand with a breathless sexism, veiled as a call for more "serious" work. "It is vitally necessary that the serious writer on Eero Saarinen single out the links that exist between his own work and that of his contemporaries and predecessors," he writes.[48] But why? That is one strain of architectural history, to place architects in context with their predecessors, and their contemporaries, and as we saw in chapters 1 and 3, it is something that Saarinen himself did, sending that list of architects he admired to Louchheim while she was reporting her article, or fretting about becoming dean of Yale's School of Architecture, something that he believed would historically situate him. Saarinen wanted to be famous in his own imagined future, and he also felt himself to be in conversation with surprising interlocutors, like Mies—whose angular insistence on "less is more" was in total counterpoint to Saarinen's enigmatic, swooping curves. But Jacobus is denying Saarinen's reality here by critiquing Temko so hard, and he also is blind about women. "All the more regrettable," he closes the section on the Saarinen books by saying, "that Allan Temko has contented himself by using these perceptive comments as the mere ornaments of a text that is more in accord with the editorial standards of *Vogue* and *Harper's Bazaar* than with serious architectural criticism."[49] So Jacobus's possibly unconscious contention is that the woman, Louchheim, who actually wrote for *Vogue*, put together an ideal book; while the man, Temko, put together an "insubstantial tirade," more in line with overtly female publications.[50]

Is it because Jacobus assumed that this was all Eero's words that Louchheim simply put together, whereas Temko had a responsibility to write his own words? Temko has at his disposal all the words available to him in the English language, that is, the language he happens to be writing in, and uses these words to create a descriptive discourse about the story of Saarinen's work, the making of monuments like the St. Louis Arch, which Temko called "a great structure that will stand as one of the chief works of the age."[51] Jacobus assumes that Louchheim, however, did not create discourse but rather neutrally presented the existing truth and story by "organizing" and "preparing" Saarinen's words. And this is part of how Louchheim was able to be so successful; she fostered the assumption among people who were not intimately working with her, like Creighton or Haskell, that she was representing precisely what Saarinen already said, that her contribution was to simply pass the information along, without adding discourse. Jacobus completely elides the editorial interventions that she made, not only in organizing the book, selecting the images and the statements, but in being there from the very beginning. The fact, as we have seen, that she uses letters sent to herself (and describes them as "to a journalist," obviously trying to hide the fact that they were sent to her, something that would have been missed by the majority of readers who weren't very knowledgeable about Saarinen), is a sign of her total takeover. The letters sent to her are her own intellectual property. And so I conclude by observing that Louchheim used chunks of existing text the same way that Temko used words—to create a particular discourse that represented and narrated the story of Saarinen that she wanted the world to see. Her selections are far from neutral; they are a deeply creative act on par with Temko's own writing, a repetition of an act she did for so much of Saarinen's working life.

Jacobus believed that he was praising a man, Eero Saarinen, for being a brilliantly legible architect. He was, in fact, unwittingly valorizing the work of a woman, Aline Louchheim, who was the prime actor and audience in the creation of the wisdom gathered in the book *Eero Saarinen on His Work*. It is but one more instance in a long line of instances I have demonstrated of Louchheim's contributions being at once intensely powerful and utterly invisible.

Epilogue

While I was writing the TWA chapter, the building was acquired by a large development company that announced plans to turn the structure into a luxury hotel, which opened in 2019. The hotel's visual branding is powerfully tied to Saarinen's visual mythology. The language is just as connective. The ad copy reads: "T.W.A. hotel, a 512 room hotel landing soon at JFK airport," and is presented over a straight-on computer-produced photorealistic rendering of the renovated structure. The project was widely covered; CNN, *USA Today*, Curbed, *Architectural Digest*, the *Wall Street Journal*, and ABC News are just some of the news outlets that have given the project ample column inches and glowing visual coverage.

And so, Saarinen was in the news again. His reputation was so carefully managed after his death that even six decades later, his work remains legible and exciting. Recently I flew into New York. I saw his terminal from overhead, rising as if a phoenix from the rubble of the construction site and scaffolding that currently surrounds it. The angle was oblique, the one Saarinen was sick of. And still, I saw the bird soar.

Today, I think about Aline's contributions to the field, and to the practice of publicity in architecture. I see traces of her work everywhere, in the way in which I email with my colleagues, in the way in which my colleagues email with me. Perhaps there is something to be said for the way in which we keep repeating professional and personal behaviors; just as Aline and Eero fell in love, so do we. While I was writing this book, I fell in love with a designer. Almost immediately, we started planning our collective future. I would be his Aline, and he would be my Eero. Had I not had these models, I imagine I would still have gravitated towards the kind of

Fig. 35. Aline Saarinen and Eero Saarinen together, and in love. Box 3, folder 23, Aline and Eero Saarinen Papers, 1906–1977, Archives of American Art, Smithsonian Institution.

role I told him I would love to do. But because I had these models, because I had their words and memos and letters floating through my mind, I was able to bring a deeper, more potent, more lasting energy to our conversations about how, exactly, our lives won't be split in two; how we will work together; how our creative lives and our personal lives will be forever intertwined. These are conversations which are ongoing, in between projects and renovations and ideas and disagreements and communions. A friend wrote recently that so much of what happens in the world happens because of love. And so I have tried, here, to write a book that works as a piece of history. But I have also tried to write a book that reminds us that so much of what we take as history—whether a sweeping *longue durée*, or a moment of modernist rupture—has happened because of two people, who loved each other.

Acknowledgments

Many years ago, during my first week of graduate school, a professor in the department of architecture suggested that I might see what Professor Margaretta M. Lovell happened to be teaching that semester, and further suggested that, no matter what it was, I enroll. And so it was that a few days later, I found myself in a fourth-floor seminar room, admiring a drawn floor plan and reading Charles Dickens. For three months, I was introduced to and immersed in Professor Lovell's world: one in which our jobs were to read, and read carefully; one in which we learned, through observation, the nuanced and critical development of an argument; one in which our work, no matter its contours, was addressed with a level of dedication and seriousness that I have yet to see replicated.

I have felt, every day, a profound gratitude that she became my advisor—first in graduate school, and now in life. Her clarity and confidence have seen me through personal and professional challenges; her high standards have set a bar I aim every day to meet; and her breadth of knowledge has continued to expand my understanding of the known—and knowable—world. She has taught me to be a sharper thinker, a deeper scholar, and a kinder (yet far more challenging) instructor, not to mention the countless administrative storms she has weathered on my behalf. I am forever in her debt.

It was through Professor Lovell that I was invited to join the Berkeley Americanist Group, my true intellectual home while I was at UC Berkeley. In particular, Elaine Yau, Caroline Riley, Sarah Gold McBride, Mia Crary, William Coleman, Kappy Mintie, Emma Silverman, Susan Eberhard, Elizabeth Bacon, and Mary Okin have read multiple drafts of chapters; offered constructive and encouraging critique and commentary; and been a constant source of engagement, thoughtfulness, and true collegiality. I hope to live up to the standards they have set.

Kathleen Moran taught me how to teach and has been a force for good academically, professionally, and personally since the day Andrew Shanken invited me to serve as teaching assistant (GSI) for their cotaught class. Speaking of, Professor Shanken has been an invaluable resource, and I continue to be astonished by his intellectual and personal generosity. David Henkin consistently pushed me to think more clearly and more capaciously about historical issues; and Richard Hutson proved an invaluable member of my committee. I am also grateful to C. Namwali Serpell for working with me early on in thinking through issues of narrative and language. Professor Christine Palmer in the American Studies Department has been a source of encouragement, perspective, and kindness; Michael Cohen has always shown up at the right place at the right time to provide commiseration and idealism.

Professor Thomas Farber instilled in me the drive to produce the best sentences I possibly could. His Tuesday afternoon nonfiction writing workshops sustained me, and his support has meant everything to the development of my career as a writer. Professor Vikram Chandra has taught me that good prose is not enough, and his generosity, open-mindedness, keen readings, and enthusiasm for plot have made me a better fiction and nonfiction writer. The late Professor Bharati Mukherjee had an incalculable impact on my life; her support of my writing life has been a constant lighthouse.

I met Athena Scott through a research and mentorship program the summer of 2015. She was an invaluable research assistant, and is an incredible force; she not only organized my thoughts and archives and went to Yale on my behalf to read hundreds of dusty documents, but also offered deeply insightful readings of my topic. I am thrilled that our paths have continued to intersect, and am forever grateful to her contributions. I am grateful also to Lauren Brooke Scott, who energetically and enthusiastically agreed to help me with image and text permissions and figures, and whose tenacity and dedication to this project got me over the finish line.

I am extraordinary grateful to Hal and Donald Louchheim for graciously granting permission for me to quote from the many letters that their mother, Aline Bernstein Louchheim Saarinen, wrote. I am so excited to see how her namesake does. A huge thanks as well to Abigail Jones, daughter of Cranston Jones, and Geoffrey Hornbeck, son of James

Hornbeck, and Matt Damora, son of Robert Damora, for allowing me to publish their fathers' work memos—I promise, they're very exciting! I am grateful as well to fellow Saarinen scholar Jayne Merkel for her support of and enthusiasm for this project.

Thanks as well to Erica Stoller and Caroline Hirsch at ESTO, who graciously and generously provided extraordinary photography of many of Eero Saarinen's projects, and to Marisa Bourgoin and Lindsey Bright at the Archives of American Art at the Smithsonian Institution for their heroic scanning efforts and fiscal generosity in providing many of the images in this book.

And while I will never know the identities of reviewers #1 and #2, without their keen, incisive, and supportive read of early versions of this book, it would both not exist and be a far paler imitation of itself. I am particularly grateful to reviewer #2, who suggested incorporating more of my own experiences and fully embracing the hybrid nature of this project. If you ever want to tell me who you are, I'd love to buy you a coffee. I am also extremely grateful to reviewer #3, whose necessary support brought this project to completion, and whose view of the book sustained me as I rewrote it.

I will forever be grateful for my good luck to have run into Michelle Komie at the Princeton University Press book stand at the Society for Architectural Historians conference, where I told her that I was working on something about the Saarinens and could I email her? Our first phone call about this project was intellectually enlivening and profoundly gratifying. I always dreamed of Princeton University Press as the ideal home for my work, and am so happy that this book has landed here. Kenneth Guay has been a wonderful guide through the ins and outs of publishing, and I feel so lucky that both Michelle and Kenneth worked as hard as they did to bring this project to completion through a pandemic, and more. Thanks as well to Aviva Arad for incredibly thorough copyediting; I am so grateful that this book will make its way into the world through your expert hands.

Thank you also to my many parents—Garry Hagberg, Catherine Wilson, Alexander Rueger, and Julia Rosenbaum—who have been invaluable intellectual role models and the best supporters a person could ask for. I am truly lucky to have landed on this earth as their daughter. Thanks particularly to Alex Rueger, who requested materials from the University of Alberta Library on my behalf, and who put up with my very loud and furious typing for the two months that we were Canadian roommates. It was his gentle yet daily encouragement that re-ignited my progress when it had briefly stalled. Thank you to my brother, David Rueger, whose combination of total pragmatism and intellectual verve I have always admired, and to Emily Crystal Yu for always being on the other end of the phone, and for being such a lively and lovable addition to our family.

Thank you to my friends, who mostly have no idea what I do all day, but who have occasionally asked me about my book and then convincingly said that it sounds interesting. I couldn't have made it through the last few years without any of you, but of particular note are Lauren Hoffman, Chani Lisbon, Jackie Shea, Erica Anderson, Jason Snell, Fletcher Foti, and Michael and Lynn Elliott-Harding. Thank you to Martin Pedersen, Philip Nobel, Elizabeth Kubany, Andrea Monfried, Stacee Gravelle Lawrence, Richard Cook, Ellie Stathaki, and Nick Compton for teaching me how to think and write about architecture for a public audience. Thank you to Marianela D'Aprile for intellectual, emotional, and political companionship, and for asking the right questions at every turn. I'm so glad you'll be home by the time this book comes out. WWDHD! Thank you to Amale Andraos for all the support, both personal and professional, and for modeling an ideal life. Thank you to Maddie Hanson, whose loving guidance and constant encouragement have helped me to see my life in a clearer—and more generous—perspective. Thank you to Elizabeth Clark, who has shown me how to take what comes at once incredibly deeply and incredibly lightly. Thank you to everyone in the rooms, everywhere, for always keeping me company.

And, of course: for the first time in my life, I feel that words aren't quite enough. Thank you, Paul Loebach. Thank you for bringing a cattle dog named Boo into my life; for agreeing, on our fourth date, to edit my response to my readers' reports; and for everything since then—for your extraordinary capacity to keep making things fun; for your dedication to my finishing this project (and to everything else I ever want to try); for your unswerving belief in *us*, and all that we can do together. Sometimes it seems like I wrote this book as a way of preparing myself for meeting you and being with you. Now that we are together, my life, as Aline wrote to Eero, no longer has to be split in two. I love you, and I can't wait to see what we do next.

Notes

Chapter 1: Women in the Design World, Then and Now

1. Alice T. Friedman, *Women and the Making of the Modern House* (New York: Abrams, 1998).
2. Despina Stratigakos, *Where Are the Women Architects?* (Princeton, NJ: Princeton University Press, 2016), 5.
3. Ibid., 3.
4. Annmarie Adams, "Women and the Making of the Modern House," *Journal of the Society of Architectural Historians* 57, no. 4 (December 1998): 474.
5. Ibid.
6. Mary Anne Hunting, "Edward Durell Stone: Perception and Criticism" (PhD diss., The City University of New York, 2007), 20.
7. Ibid.
8. Olgivanna Lloyd Wright, *Frank Lloyd Wright: His Life, His Work, His Words* (New York: Horizon Press, 1966).
9. Roger Friedman and Harold Zellman, *The Fellowship* (New York: Regan, 2006).
10. Ibid.
11. Wolfgang Saxon, "Olgivanna Lloyd Wright, Wife of the Architect, Is Dead at 85," *New York Times*, March 2, 1985, 29.
12. Ibid.
13. Katy Kelleher, "The Forgotten Story of Mrs Bauhaus," *Artsy*, September 7, 2018, https://www.artsy.net/article/artsy-editorial-forgotten-story-mrs-bauhaus.
14. Ibid.
15. Ibid.
16. Nancy Gruskin, "Designing Women: Writing about Eleanor Raymond," in *Singular Women: Writing the Artist*, ed. Kristen Frederickson and Sarah E. Webb (Berkeley: University of California Press, 2003), 152.
17. Ibid.
18. Ibid.
19. Ibid.
20. *Interview*, directed by Steve Buscemi (Sony Pictures Classics, 2007).
21. Eva Hagberg, *Dark Nostalgia* (New York: Monacelli Press, 2009).

Chapter 2: When Aline Met Eero

1. Aline and Eero Saarinen Papers, 1906–1977. Archives of American Art, Smithsonian Institution.
2. Ibid.
3. Eric Saarinen, "Forgiving My Dad," *Scandinavian Review*, Summer 2016, http://www .amscan.org/app/uploads/2016/08/SR_Summer_2016_Saarinen_article.pdf.
4. Ibid.
5. Eeva-Liisa Pelkonen and Donald Albrecht, introduction to *Eero Saarinen: Shaping the Future* (New Haven, CT: Yale University Press, 2006), 2.
6. "Domestic Interiors," *Architectural Forum* 67 (October 1937): 239–368.
7. Ibid.
8. Ibid.
9. "Art: The Maturing Modern," *Time*, July 2, 1956.
10. Ibid.
11. Avery Index of Architectural Periodicals, Columbia University.
12. Ibid.
13. Alden Whitman, "Aline Saarinen, Art Critic, Dies at 58," *New York Times*, July 15, 1972.
14. Andrew Jacobs, "Aline Saarinen," *The Encyclopedia of Jewish Women*, Jewish Women's Archive, https://jwa.org/encyclopedia/article/saarinen-aline-bernstein.
15. Mardges Bacon, *John McAndrew's Modernist Vision* (New York: Princeton Architectural Press, 2018), cited in Cathleen McGuigan, "Women of the Bauhaus: Aline Saarinen," *Architectural Record* (June 2019).
16. McGuigan, "Women of the Bauhaus."
17. Ibid.
18. Em Bowles Locker Alsop, "Aline Bernstein Saarinen, 1935," *Vassar Quarterly* 46, no. 5 (May 1, 1961), 27.
19. Ibid.
20. "J. J. Louchheims Have a Son," *New York Times*, June 6, 1937; "Son Born to Joseph Louch-heim," *New York Times*, June 1, 1939.
21. "The Art News Annual," *New York Times*, February 4, 1945.
22. Aline B. Louchheim, "Using the Abstract: Hartford Show Reveals How Industrial Firm Puts a Collection to Work," *New York Times*, December 21, 1947, 169.
23. Ibid.
24. Aline Saarinen, Lecture on "Style," Vassar College, 1966, box 5, folder 5, Eero and Aline Saarinen Papers, 1906–1977, Archives of American Art, Smithsonian Institution.
25. Aline B. Louchheim, "To Do or Not to Do; Being an Open Letter to the Director of California's Modern Institute," *New York Times*, January 4, 1948; "The Unseeing Eye; Gaps in Our Secondary School Teaching Make for Later Blindness to Art," *New York Times*, February 8, 1948; "The Label 'Modern'; Boston Institute Statement on Change of Name Leads to New Controversy," *New York Times*, March 28, 1948.
26. Aline B. Louchheim, "For a Modern Monument: An Audacious Design," *New York Times*, February 29, 1948, 8.
27. Ibid.
28. Ibid.
29. Ibid.

30. Josep Lluis Sert, Fernand Léger, and Siegfried Giedion, "Nine Points on Monumental-ity," in *Architecture Culture 1943-1968*, ed. Joan Ockman and Edward Eigen (New York: Rizzoli, 1993), 29–30.

31. Ibid.

32. Letter from Daniel Schwars to John McAndrew, October 27, 1952, box 15, folder 247, Eero Saarinen Collection (MS 593), Manuscripts and Archives, Yale University Library.

33. Memorandum from Daniel Schwars to Miss Duvitzky, November 28, 1952, box 15, folder 247, Eero Saarinen Collection (MS 593), Manuscripts and Archives, Yale University Library.

34. Alexandra Lange, "Love & Architecture," *Design Observer*, October 22, 2009, https://designobserver.com/feature/love--architecture/11517.

35. Jenny Xie, "Eero Saarinen's Love Letters to His Wife Are Utterly Adorable," Curbed, February 13, 2015, https://www.curbed.com/2015/2/13/9992378/valentines-day-eero-saarinen.

36. Amelia Taylor-Hochberg, "Eero Saarinen's Love Letters," Archinect, February 12, 2016; Cathleen McGuigan, "Aline Saarinen: '50s Wonder Woman," *Newsweek*, November 5, 2009.

37. Eero Saarinen to Dr. Bartelmeier, April 1952, box 2, folder 49, Aline and Eero Saarinen Papers, 1906–1977, Archives of American Art, Smithsonian Institution.

38. Ibid.

39. Eero Saarinen to Dr. Bartelmeier, January 12, 1953, box 2, folder 49, Aline and Eero Saarinen Papers, 1906–1977, Archives of American Art, Smithsonian Institution.

40. Aline B. Louchheim to Eero Saarinen, 1953, box 2, folder 15, Aline and Eero Saarinen Papers, 1906–1977, Archives of American Art, Smithsonian Institution.

41. Aline B. Louchheim to Eero Saarinen, 1953, box 2, folder 15, Aline and Eero Saarinen Papers, 1906–1977, Archives of American Art, Smithsonian Institution.

42. Ibid.

43. William H. Chafe, *The American Woman* (New York: Oxford University Press, 1972); or as cited in Joanne Meyerowitz, *Not June Cleaver: Women and Gender in Postwar America, 1945-1960* (Philadelphia: Temple University Press, 1994), 4.

44. Aline B. Louchheim to Eero Saarinen, 1953, box 4, folder 22, Eero and Aline Saarinen Papers, 1906–1977, Archives of American Art, Smithsonian Institution.

45. Ibid.

46. Eero Saarinen to Aline B. Louchheim, 1953, box 2, folder 26, Aline and Eero Saarinen Papers, 1906–1977, Archives of American Art, Smithsonian Institution.

47. Aline B. Louchheim to Eero Saarinen, February 11, 1953, box 2, folder 15, letter 2, Aline and Eero Saarinen Papers, 1906–1977, Archives of American Art, Smithsonian Institution.

48. Ibid.

49. Aline B. Louchheim to Eero Saarinen, February 11, 1953, box 2, folder 15, Aline and Eero Saarinen Papers, 1906–1977, Archives of American Art, Smithsonian Institution.

50. Thomas Augst, *The Clerk's Tale: Young Men and Moral Life in Nineteenth-Century America* (Chicago: University of Chicago Press, 2003).

51. Letter from Eero Saarinen to Dr. B, 1952–1953, box 2, folder 49, Aline and Eero Saarinen Papers, 1906–1977, Archives of American Art, Smithsonian Institution.

52. Aline B. Louchheim to Eero Saarinen, undated, box 2, folder 15, Aline and Eero Saarinen Papers, 1906–1977, Archives of American Art, Smithsonian Institution.

53. Aline B. Louchheim to Eero Saarinen, undated, box 2, folder 15, Aline and Eero Saarinen Papers, 1906–1977, Archives of American Art, Smithsonian Institution.

54. Ibid.

55. Ibid.

56. Ibid.

57. Daisy Alioto, "Elizabeth Gordon's International Style," Curbed, May 10, 2017, https://www.curbed.com/2017/5/10/15592658/elizabeth-gordon-house-beautiful-frank-lloyd-wright.

58. In the absence of clear dates, I have used context clues and references to earlier conversations in order to establish a working chronology of their letters.

59. Aline B. Louchheim to Eero Saarinen, undated, box 2, folder 15, Aline and Eero Saarinen Papers, 1906–1977, Archives of American Art, Smithsonian Institution.

60. Aline B. Louchheim to Eero Saarinen, undated, box 2, folder 15, Aline and Eero Saarinen Papers, 1906–1977, Archives of American Art, Smithsonian Institution.

61. Ibid.

62. Aline B. Louchheim to Eero Saarinen, undated, box 2, folder 15, Aline and Eero Saarinen Papers, 1906–1977, Archives of American Art, Smithsonian Institution.

63. Ibid.

64. Ibid.

65. Letter, Aline B. Louchheim to Eero Sarinen, box 2, folder 15, Aline and Eero Saarinen Papers, 1906–1977, Archives of American Art, Smithsonian Institution.

66. Ibid.

67. Aline B. Louchheim to Eero Saarinen, box 2, folder 15, Aline and Eero Saarinen Papers, 1906–1977, Archives of American Art, Smithsonian Institution.

68. Ibid.

69. Ibid.

70. Aline B. Louchheim to Eero Saarinen, undated, box 2, folder 15, Aline and Eero Saarinen Papers, 1906–1977, Archives of American Art, Smithsonian Institution.

71. Aline B. Louchheim to Eero Saarinen, undated, box 2, folder 15, Aline and Eero Saarinen Papers, 1906–1977, Archives of American Art, Smithsonian Institution.

72. Aline B. Louchheim to Eero Saarinen, undated, box 2, folder 15, Aline and Eero Saarinen Papers, 1906–1977, Archives of American Art, Smithsonian Institution.

73. Aline B. Louchheim to Eero Saarinen, undated, box 2, folder 15, Aline and Eero Saarinen Papers, 1906–1977, Archives of American Art, Smithsonian Institution.

74. Aline B. Louchheim to Eero Saarinen, undated, box 2, folder 15, Aline and Eero Saarinen Papers, 1906–1977, Archives of American Art, Smithsonian Institution.

75. Aline B. Louchheim, "Now Saarinen the Son," *New York Times*, April 26, 1953.

76. Pierluigi Serraino, "Case Study: Eero Saarinen," *Architectural Record*, May 1, 2016, https://www.architecturalrecord.com/articles/11666-case-study-eero-saarinen.

77. Eero Saarinen to Aline B. Louchheim, March 16, 1953, box 2, folder 26, Aline and Eero Saarinen Papers, 1906–1977, Archives of American Art, Smithsonian Institution.

78. Ibid.

79. Beatriz Colomina, *Privacy and Publicity* (Cambridge, MA: MIT Press, 1994).

80. Louchheim, "Now Saarinen the Son."

81. Eero Saarinen, Letters to Psychiatrist, 1953 and 1954, box 2, folder 49, Aline and Eero Saarinen Papers, 1906–1977, Archives of American Art, Smithsonian Institution.

82. Ibid.

83. Louchheim, "Now Saarinen the Son."

84. Ibid.

85. Ibid.

86. Ibid.

87. Eero Saarinen to Aline B. Louchheim, box 2, folder 15, Aline and Eero Saarinen Papers, 1906–1977, Archives of American Art, Smithsonian Institution.

88. Aline B. Louchheim to Eero Saarinen, undated, box 2, folder 15, Aline and Eero Saarinen Papers, 1906–1977, Archives of American Art, Smithsonian Institution.

89. Ibid.

90. Aline B. Louchheim to Eero Saarinen, April 29, 1953, box 2, folder 15, Aline and Eero Saarinen Papers, 1906–1977, Archives of American Art, Smithsonian Institution.

91. Ibid.

92. Ibid.

93. Ibid.

94. Ibid.

95. Ibid.

96. Ibid.

97. Ibid.

98. Aline B. Louchheim to Eero Saarinen, May 2, 1953, box 2, folder 16, Aline and Eero Saarinen Papers, 1906–1977, Archives of American Art, Smithsonian Institution.

99. Eero to Aline, box 2, Folder TK, Aline and Eero Saarinen Papers, 1906–1977, Archives of American Art, Smithsonian Institution.

100. Ibid.

101. Ibid.

102. Aline B. Louchheim to Eero Saarinen, May 2, 1953, box 2, folder 16, Aline and Eero Saarinen Papers, 1906–1977, Archives of American Art, Smithsonian Institution.

103. Ibid.

104. Kevin Roche, interview with author, January 16, 2016.

105. Aline B. Louchheim to Eero Saarinen, box 2, folder 16, Aline and Eero Saarinen Papers, 1906–1977, Archives of American Art, Smithsonian Institution.

106. Ibid.

107. Eero Saarinen to Aline B. Louchheim, box 2, folder TK; Aline B. Louchheim to Eero Saarinen, May 2, 1953, box 2, folder 16, Aline and Eero Saarinen Papers, 1906–1977, Archives of American Art, Smithsonian Institution.

108. Ibid.

109. Ibid.

110. Aline B. Louchheim to Eero Saarinen, May 13, 1953, box 2, folder 16, Aline and Eero Saarinen Papers, 1906–1977, Archives of American Art, Smithsonian Institution.

111. Aline B. Louchheim to Eero Saarinen, undated, box 2, folder 16, Aline and Eero Saarinen Papers, 1906–1977, Archives of American Art, Smithsonian Institution.

112. Ibid.

113. Aline B. Louchheim to Eero Saarinen, undated, box 2, folder 16, Aline and Eero Saarinen Papers, 1906–1977, Archives of American Art, Smithsonian Institution.

114. Aline B. Louchheim to Eero Saarinen, box 2, folder 16, Aline and Eero Saarinen Papers, 1906–1977, Archives of American Art, Smithsonian Institution.

115.   Ibid.

116.   Ibid.

117.   Aline B. Louchheim to Eero Saarinen, undated, box 2, folder 17, Aline and Eero Saarinen Papers, 1906–1977, Archives of American Art, Smithsonian Institution.

118.   Aline B. Louchheim to Eero Saarinen, undated, box 2, folder 17, Aline and Eero Saarinen Papers, 1906–1977, Archives of American Art, Smithsonian Institution.

119.   Ibid.

120.   Ibid.

121.   Aline B. Louchheim to Eero Saarinen, undated, box 2, folder 17, Aline and Eero Saarinen Papers, 1906–1977, Archives of American Art, Smithsonian Institution.

122.   Ibid.

123.   Aline B. Louchheim to Eero Saarinen, undated, box 2, folder 17, Aline and Eero Saarinen Papers, 1906–1977, Archives of American Art, Smithsonian Institution.

124.   Ibid.

125.   Eero Saarinen to Dr. B, undated, box 2, folder 49, Aline and Eero Saarinen Papers, 1906–1977, Archives of American Art, Smithsonian Institution.

126.   Aline B. Louchheim to Eero Saarinen, undated, box 2, folder 17, Aline and Eero Saarinen Papers, 1906–1977, Archives of American Art, Smithsonian Institution.

127.   Aline B. Louchheim to Eero Saarinen, undated, box 2, folder 17, Aline and Eero Saarinen Papers, 1906–1977, Archives of American Art, Smithsonian Institution.

128.   Aline B. Louchheim to Eero Saarinen, undated, box 2, folder 18, Aline and Eero Saarinen Papers, 1906–1977, Archives of American Art, Smithsonian Institution.

129.   Aline B. Louchheim to Eero Saarinen, undated, box 2, folder 18, Aline and Eero Saarinen Papers, 1906–1977, Archives of American Art, Smithsonian Institution.

130.   Aline B. Louchheim to Eero Saarinen, undated, box 2, folder 18, Aline and Eero Saarinen Papers, 1906–1977, Archives of American Art, Smithsonian Institution.

131.   Aline B. Louchheim to Eero Saarinen, undated, box 2, folder 18, Aline and Eero Saarinen Papers, 1906–1977, Archives of American Art, Smithsonian Institution.

132.   Ibid.

133.   Ibid.

134.   Aline B. Louchheim to Eero Saarinen, July 1953, box 2, folder 18, Aline and Eero Saarinen Papers, 1906–1977, Archives of American Art, Smithsonian Institution.

135.   Aline B. Louchheim to Eero Saarinen, undated, box 2, folder 18, Aline and Eero Saarinen Papers, 1906–1977, Archives of American Art, Smithsonian Institution.

136.   Aline B. Louchheim to Eero Saarinen, undated, box 2, folder 18, Aline and Eero Saarinen Papers, 1906–1977, Archives of American Art, Smithsonian Institution.

137.   Ibid.

138.   Scott Cutlip, *The Unseen Power: Public Relations: A History* (New York: Routledge, 1994), 10.

139.   Ibid., xiv.

140.   Edward L. Bernays, "Recent Trends in Public Relations Activities," *The Public Opinion Quarterly* 1, no. 1 (Jan., 1937): 147–51.

141.   Jacqui L'Etang and Magda Pieczka, *Public Relations: Critical Debates and Contemporary Practice* (New York: Routledge, 2006), 266.

142.   Ibid.

143. Ibid.

144. Ibid.

145. Ibid.

146. Aline B. Louchheim to Eero Saarinen, undated, box 2, folder 19, Aline and Eero Saarinen Papers, 1906–1977, Archives of American Art, Smithsonian Institution.

147. Ibid.

148. Ibid.

149. Ibid.

150. Frank Lloyd Wright, *An Autobiography* (London: Longman's, Green, 1932); M. M. Lovell note to author, August 17, 2018.

151. Eero Saarinen Biographical Data Sheet, undated, box 41, folder 78, Eero Saarinen Collection (MS 593), Manuscripts and Archives, Yale University Library.

152. Aline B. Louchheim to Eero Saarinen, undated, box 2, folder 19, Aline and Eero Saarinen Papers, 1906–1977, Archives of American Art, Smithsonian Institution.

153. Ibid.

154. Ibid.

155. Ibid.

156. Ibid.

157. Ibid.

158. Ibid.

159. Ibid.

160. Andrew Shanken, letter to author, October 2, 2018.

161. Ibid.

162. Ibid.

163. Ibid.

164. Eero Saarinen to Aline B. Louchheim, undated 1953, box 2, folder 26, Aline and Eero Saarinen Papers, 1906–1977, Archives of American Art, Smithsonian Institution.

165. Aline B. Louchheim to Eero Saarinen, undated, box 2, folder 21, Aline and Eero Saarinen Papers, 1906–1977, Archives of American Art, Smithsonian Institution.

166. Ibid.

167. Ibid.

168. Ibid.

169. Ibid.

170. Eero Saarinen to Aline B. Louchheim, May 22, 1953, box 2, folder 28, Aline and Eero Saarinen Papers, 1906–1977, Archives of American Art, Smithsonian Institution.

171. Aline B. Louchheim to Lester Markel, undated, box 2, folder 21, Aline and Eero Saarinen Papers, 1906–1977, Archives of American Art, Smithsonian Institution.

172. Ibid.

173. "Aline Louchheim Wed to Architect," *New York Times*, February 9, 1954.

174. Ibid.

175. Aline B. Louchheim to Eero Saarinen, "A Birthday Card," August 1954, box 2, folder 23, Aline and Eero Saarinen Papers, 1906–1977, Archives of American Art, Smithsonian Institution.

176. Ibid.

Chapter 4: Kresge and Ingalls

1. Michelle Miller, "AD Classics: Kresge Auditorium/Eero Saarinen and Associates," Arch-Daily, April 3, 2014, http://www.archdaily.com/492176/ad-classics-kresge-auditorium-eero-saarinen-and-associates.
2. Ibid.
3. Ibid.
4. Alastair Gordon, *Naked Airport: A Cultural History of the World's Most Revolutionary Structure* (New York: Metropolitan Books, 2004), 1.
5. Miller, "AD Classics."
6. Ibid.
7. Ibid.
8. Letter from Aline Saarinen to Eero Saarinen, undated 1953, box 2, folder 15, Aline and Eero Saarinen Papers, 1906–1977, Archives of American Art, Smithsonian Institution.
9. Letter from Eero Saarinen to Aline Saarinen, February 2, 1953, box 2, folder 26, Aline and Eero Saarinen Papers, 1906–1977, Archives of American Art, Smithsonian Institution.
10. "Buildings in the Round: MIT Completes Two of Today's Most Talked about Buildings: A Cylindrical Chapel and a Domed Auditorium," *Architectural Forum* 104 (January 1956): 116–21.
11. When written, this was a neutral observation. After the 2016 US presidential election, "people are talking about" has become a much more loaded phrase.
12. "Buildings in the Round," 117.
13. "Saarinen Challenges the Rectangle: Designs a Domed Auditorium and a Cylindrical Chapel for MIT's Laboratory Campus," *Architectural Forum* 98 (January 1953): 126–33.
14. Ibid.
15. Ibid.
16. Ibid., 127.
17. Ibid.
18. Ibid., 126–27.
19. Donald Albrecht and Eeva-Liisa Pelkonen, eds., *Eero Saarinen: Shaping the Future* (New Haven, CT: Yale University Press), 2006, 33.
20. "Buildings in the Round," 117.
21. Glenn Collins, "Edward A. Weeks, 91, an Editor of the Atlantic Monthly, Is Dead," *New York Times*, March 14, 1989, http://www.nytimes.com/1989/03/14/obituaries/edward-a-weeks-91-an-editor-of-the-atlantic-monthly-is-dead.html.
22. "The Mike Wallace Interview, Edward Weeks, August 24, 1958," https://hrc.contentdm.oclc.org/digital/collection/p15878coll90/id/70.
23. Edward Weeks, "The Opal on the Charles," *Architectural Record* 118 (July 1955): 131.
24. Ibid., 131–37.
25. Ibid., 131.
26. Ibid., 135.
27. Ibid.
28. Ibid., 137.
29. N. Keith Scott, "M.I.T. Auditorium, An English View," *Architectural Record* (July 1955): 138.

30. Eliot Noyes, "Kresge Auditorium, Massachusetts Institute of Technology, Cambridge, 1955, Eero Saarinen and Associates, (tied for fifteenth)," *Architectural Record* (November 1956): 200.

31. Ibid.

32. Ibid., 199–200.

33. Richard Knight, *Saarinen's Quest: A Memoir* (San Francisco: William Stout, 2008); Pierluigi Serraino, *Eero Saarinen, 1910–1961: A Structural Expressionist* (New York: Taschen, 2007); Jayne Merkel, *Eero Saarinen* (New York: Phaidon, 2005).

34. Knight, *Saarinen's Quest*, 21.

35. Ibid.

36. Ibid., 22.

37. Ibid.

38. Ibid.

39. Pierluigi Serraino, afterword to Knight, *Saarinen's Quest*, 152.

40. Ibid.

41. Ibid., 156.

42. Ibid., 157.

43. Scott Sullivan, "Saarinen's Plans for Rink Approved by Corporation," *Yale Daily News*, December 17, 1956, 1.

44. Ibid.

45. Ben Harris, "Speaking of Sports," *Yale Daily News*, March 5, 1957, 6.

46. Albert S. Pergam, "Construction Nearing Completion on Major Projects," *Yale Daily News*, September 11, 1958.

47. Neil M. Herring, "Controversial 'Turtle' Crosses the Finish Line," *Yale Daily News*, October 15, 1958, 1.

48. Ibid.

49. Merkel, *Eero Saarinen*, 124.

50. Ibid., 126.

51. Walter McQuade, "Yale's Viking Vessel," *Architectural Forum* 109 (December 1958): 106–11.

52. Ibid., 110.

53. "David S. Ingalls Hockey Rink, Yale University, New Haven, Conn.," *Architectural Record* (August 1957): 187–89.

54. Jonathan Barnes, "The New Collegiate Architecture at Yale," *Architectural Record* 131 (April 1962): 128.

55. "College Buildings," *Architectural Record* 131 (April 1962): 129.

56. James Hornbeck to Aline Saarinen, June 30, 1960, box 14, folder 226, Eero Saarinen Collection (MS 593), Manuscripts and Archives, Yale University Library.

57. James Hornbeck to Aline Saarinen, box 14, folder 226, Eero Saarinen Collection (MS 593), Manuscripts and Archives, Yale University Library.

58. Ibid.

59. Letter from Patricia Burley to James Hornbeck, July 25, 1960, box 14, folder 226, Eero Saarinen Collection (MS 593), Manuscripts and Archives, Yale University Library.

60. James Hornbeck to Aline Saarinen, September 14, 1960, box 14, folder 226, Eero Saarinen Collection (MS 593), Manuscripts and Archives, Yale University Library.

61. Letter from Wayne Andrews to Aline Saarinen, October 30, 1958, box 2, folder 40, Aline and Eero Saarinen Papers, 1906–1977, Archives of American Art, Smithsonian Institution.

62. Ibid.

63. Ibid.

Chapter 6: "Bones for a Bird"

1. Katherine Wisniewski, "92 Years of Architecture through Time Magazine Covers," Curbed, February 4, 2015, http://www.curbed.com/2015/2/4/9996152/time-magazine-architect-covers.

2. "Art: The Maturing Modern," *Time*, July 2, 1956, http://content.time.com/time/subscriber/article/0,33009,891296,00.html.

3. Ibid.

4. Ibid.

5. Ibid.

6. Ibid.

7. Ibid.

8. Ibid.

9. Letter from Eero Saarinen to Aline Saarinen, March 16th 1953, box 2, folder 26, Aline and Eero Saarinen Papers, 1906–1977, Archives of American Art, Smithsonian Institution.

10. Ibid.

11. Alice T. Friedman, "Eero Saarinen: Modern Architecture for the American Century," *Places Journal*, June 2010, https://placesjournal.org/article/modern-architecture-for-the-american-century/.

12. Ibid.

13. Ibid.

14. Aline Saarinen, ed., *Eero Saarinen: On His Work* (New Haven, CT: Yale University Press, 1962), 10, quoted in Friedman, "Eero Saarinen."

15. Edward Hudson, "Aviation: Unusual Terminal for Idlewild," *New York Times*, November 17, 1957, 405.

16. Ibid.

17. Ibid.

18. Ibid.

19. *New York Times* website, search term, "Eero Saarinen," https://www.nytimes.com/topic/person/eero-saarinen.

20. "T.W.A. Restudying Terminal Design," *New York Times*, October 11, 1958, 40.

21. Letter from Aline Saarinen to Cranston Jones, January 13, 1959, box 273, folder 905, Eero Saarinen Collection (MS 593), Manuscripts and Archives, Yale University Library.

22. Letter from Cranston Jones to Aline Saarinen, January 16, 1959, box 273, folder 905, Eero Saarinen Collection (MS 593), Manuscripts and Archives, Yale University Library.

23. Eeva-Liisa Pelkonen, "The Search for Communicative Form," in Albrecht and Pelkonen, *Eero Saarinen: Shaping the Future*, 93.

24. Letter from Cranston Jones to Gyorgy Kepes and Aline Saarinen, January 16, 1959, box 273, folder 905, Eero Saarinen Collection (MS 593), Manuscripts and Archives, Yale University Library.

25. Elizabeth Shaw, "Architecture and Imagery—Four New Buildings Press Release," Museum of Modern Art, February 11, 1959, http://www.moma.org/momaorg/shared /pdfs/docs/press_archives/2448/releases/MOMA_1959_0014.pdf?2010.

26. Elizabeth Shaw, "Four New Buildings—Architecture and Imagery," Museum of Modern Art, https://www.moma.org/documents/moma_master-checklist_326140.pdf.

27. Ada Louise Huxtable, "Four Model Buildings under Museum Review," *New York Times*, February 15, 1959, 369.

28. Ibid.

29. Ibid.

30. "The Competition," Sydney Opera House Trust, https://www.sydneyoperahouse.com /our-story/sydney-opera-house-history/the-competition.html.

31. Ibid.

32. Ibid.

33. Shaw, "Architecture and Imagery—Four New Buildings Press Release."

34. "Aline B. Saarinen Resigns," *New York Times*, December 1, 1959, 46.

35. Letter from Aline Saarinen to Allene Tallmey, January 25, 1960, box 273, folder 906, Eero Saarinen Collection (MS 593), Manuscripts and Archives, Yale University Library.

36. Ibid.

37. Ibid.

38. Ibid.

39. "Bones for a 'Bird,'" *New York Times Magazine*, August 21, 1960, 296, 298.

40. Ibid.

41. Ibid.

42. James Laver, "The Stuffy Age We Yearn for," *New York Times Magazine*, August 21, 1960, 28.

43. Robert Trumbull, "It's 'Princess Time,'" *New York Times Magazine*, August 21, 1960, 60.

44. Flora Lewis, "Adenauer's Rx For Vitality," *New York Times Magazine*, August 21, 1960, 23.

45. Letter from George Adams Jones to Aline Saarinen, July 20, 1960, box 273, folder 906, Eero Saarinen Collection (MS 593), Manuscripts and Archives, Yale University Library.

46. Ibid.

47. Ibid.

48. Ibid.

49. Letter from Aline B. Saarinen to George Adams Jones, August 1, 1960, box 273, folder 906, Eero Saarinen Collection (MS 593), Manuscripts and Archives, Yale University Library.

50. Ibid.

51. Ibid.

52. Letter from George Adams Jones to Aline B. Saarinen, August 12, 1960, box 273, folder 906, Eero Saarinen Collection (MS 593), Manuscripts and Archives, Yale University Library.

53. Ibid.

54. Letter from George Adams Jones to Aline B. Saarinen, October 19, 1960, box 273, folder 906, Eero Saarinen Collection (MS 593), Manuscripts and Archives, Yale University Library.

55. Letter from Patricia Burley to George Adams Jones, October 25, 1960, box 273, folder 906, Eero Saarinen Collection (MS 593), Manuscripts and Archives, Yale University Library.

56. Letter from Wolf von Eckardt to Eero Saarinen, September 10, 1959, box 273, folder 904, Eero Saarinen Collection (MS 593), Manuscripts and Archives, Yale University Library.

57. Memorandum from Aline Saarinen to Joe Lacy, Kevin Roche, John Dinkeloo, box 273, folder 908, Eero Saarinen Collection (MS 593), Manuscripts and Archives, Yale University Library.

58. Letter from Robert Damora to Eero Saarinen, December 7, 1960, box 273, folder 906, Eero Saarinen Collection (MS 593), Manuscripts and Archives, Yale University Library.

59. Ibid.

60. Ibid.

61. Ibid.

62. Email from Matt Damora to Eva Hagberg, August 2, 2021.

63. Letter from Robert Damora to Eero Saarinen, December 7, 1960, box 273, folder 906, Eero Saarinen Collection (MS 593), Manuscripts and Archives, Yale University Library.

64. Letter from Eero Saarinen to Robert Damora, December 22, 1960, box 273, folder 906, Eero Saarinen Collection (MS 593), Manuscripts and Archives, Yale University Library.

65. Ibid.

66. "T.W.A.'s Terminal Standing on Own," *New York Times*, December 8, 1960, 70.

67. Ibid.

68. Letter from Douglass Haskell to Eero Saarinen, July 20, 1961, box 273, folder 907, Eero Saarinen Collection (MS 593), Manuscripts and Archives, Yale University Library.

69. Ibid.

70. Ibid.

71. Ibid.

72. Ibid.

73. Ibid.

74. Memorandum from Eero Saarinen to Aline B. Saarinen, Pat Burley, John Dinkeloo, July 19, 1961, box 273, folder 907, Eero Saarinen Collection (MS 593), Manuscripts and Archives, Yale University Library.

75. Ibid.

76. Ibid.

77. Letter from Douglas Haskell to Aline B. Saarinen, February 10, 1961, box 14, folder 226, Eero Saarinen Collection (MS 593), Manuscripts and Archives, Yale University Library.

78. Letter from Aline B. Saarinen to Douglas Haskell, March 17, 1960, box 14, folder 226, Eero Saarinen Collection (MS 593), Manuscripts and Archives, Yale University Library.

79. Letter from Douglas Haskell to Aline B. Saarinen, March 18, 1960, box 4, folder 226, Eero Saarinen Collection (MS 593), Manuscripts and Archives, Yale University Library.

80. Letter from Aline Saarinen to Douglas Haskell, March 17, 1960, box 14, folder 226, Eero Saarinen Collection (MS 593), Manuscripts and Archives, Yale University Library.

81. Ibid.

82. Letter from Douglas Haskell to Aline Saarinen, March 18, 1960, box 14, folder 226, Eero Saarinen Collection (MS 593), Manuscripts and Archives, Yale University Library.

83. Letter from Aline Saarinen to Thomas H. Creighton, March 14, 1960, box 14, folder 227, Eero Saarinen Collection (MS 593), Manuscripts and Archives, Yale University Library.

84. Letter from Douglas Haskell to Aline Saarinen, February 10, 1961, box 14, folder 226, Eero Saarinen Collection (MS 593), Manuscripts and Archives, Yale University Library.

85.   Ibid.

86.   Douglas Haskell, "Editor's Letter," *Architectural Forum* (July 1963).

87.   Reyner Banham cited in Claire Zimmerman, *Photographic Architecture in the Twentieth Century* (Minneapolis: University of Minnesota Press, 2014), 1.

88.   Ibid., 2.

89.   Ibid., 3.

90.   "National Geographic Magazine: 50 Years of Covers," *National Geographic*, https://www.nationalgeographic.com/magazine/national-geographic-magazine-50-years-of-covers/.

91.   Ibid.

92.   Wikipedia, s.v. "Life Magazine Contributors," accessed August 2, 2018, https://en.wikipedia.org/wiki/Life_(magazine)#Contributors.

93.   Letter from Eero Saarinen to Douglas Haskell, August 7, 1961, box 273, folder 907, Eero Saarinen Collection (MS 593), Manuscripts and Archives, Yale University Library.

94.   Ibid.

95.   Letter from Chester Kerr to Aline B. Saarinen, February 19, 1962, box 15, folder 246, Eero Saarinen Collection (MS 593), Manuscripts and Archives, Yale University Library.

96.   Letter from James Hornbeck to Aline B. Saarinen, March 5, 1962, box 273, folder 908, Eero Saarinen Collection (MS 593), Manuscripts and Archives, Yale University Library.

97.   Ibid.

98.   Ibid.

99.   "Walter McQuade, 72, Architecture Critic," *New York Times*, December 29, 1994, http://www.nytimes.com/1994/12/29/obituaries/walter-mcquade-72-architecture-critic.html.

100. Ibid.

101. Walter McQuade, "Eero Saarinen: A Complete Architect," *Architectural Forum* 116 (April 1962): 102–19.

102. Ibid., 102.

103. Ibid., 103.

104. Ibid., 104.

105. Ibid., 105.

106. Ibid.

107. Ibid.

108. Ibid.

109. "T.W.A.'s Graceful Air Terminal," *Architectural Forum* (January 1958): 78–83.

110. "The Concrete Bird Stands Free," *Architectural Forum* 113 (December 1960): 114–15.

111. Letter from Ada Louise Huxtable to Aline B. Saarinen, January 9, 1960, box 14, folder 226, Eero Saarinen Collection (MS 593), Manuscripts and Archives, Yale University Library.

112. "New Terminal at Idlewild," *New York Times*, May 18, 1962, 33.

113. Edgar Kaufmann, Jr. "Inside Eero Saarinen's T.W.A. Building," *Contract Interiors* 121 (July 1962): 86–93.

114. Letter from Aline Saarinen to Ada Louise Huxtable, February 12, 1960, box 14, folder 226, Eero Saarinen Collection (MS 593), Manuscripts and Archives, Yale University Library.

115. Letter from Ada Louise Huxtable to Aline Saarinen, January 9, 1960, box 14, folder 226, Eero Saarinen Collection (MS 593), Manuscripts and Archives, Yale University Library.

116. Edward Hudson, "Aviation: Unusual New Terminal for Idlewild," *New York Times*, November 17, 1957, 405.

117. Alastair Gordon, *Naked Airport: A Cultural History of the World's Most Revolutionary Structure* (New York: Metropolitan, 2004), 154, cited in Merkel, *Eero Saarinen*, 205.

118. Ada Louise Huxtable, "Four Models under Museum Review," February 15, 1959, *New York Times*, 369.

119. Firm Description for Unnamed Client (possibly Lincoln Center?), undated, box 41, folder 81, Eero Saarinen Collection (MS 593), Manuscripts and Archives, Yale University Library.

120. Ibid.

121. "I Want to Catch the Excitement of the Trip," *Architectural Forum* 117 (July 1962): 72–75.

122. Ibid., 72.

123. Ibid.

124. Kevin Roche quoted in Hart Laubkeman, "Form Swallows Function," *Progressive Architecture* (May 1992): 108, cited in Merkel, *Eero Saarinen*, 209.

125. Merkel, *Eero Saarinen*, 209.

126. Ibid., 213.

127. Letter from Dr. H. Brown Otopalik to Eero Saarinen, January 15, 1959, box 41, folder 83, Eero Saarinen Collection (MS 593), Manuscripts and Archives, Yale University Library.

128. Letter from Aline Saarinen to Dr. H. Brown Otopalik, January 20, 1959, box 41, folder 83, Eero Saarinen Collection (MS 593), Manuscripts and Archives, Yale University Library.

129. Albrecht and Pelkonen, *Shaping the Future*.

130. Ibid., 3.

131. Letter from Aline Saarinen to William Hewitt, March 26, 1962, box 14, folder 227, Eero Saarinen Collection (MS 593), Manuscripts and Archives, Yale University Library.

132. Ibid.

133. Andrea Lo, "How the 1960s and 70s Inspired Radical Architecture," CNN, https://www.cnn.com/style/article/radical-architecture/index.html.

134. Witold Rybczynski, "The Glossies: The Decline of Architecture Magazines," *Slate*, November 15, 2006, http://www.slate.com/articles/arts/architecture/2006/11/the_glossies.html.

135. Ibid.

Chapter 8: I Really Am Not Interested In That Project

1. Eric Saarinen, "Forgiving My Dad," *Scandinavian Review*, Summer 2016, http://www.amscan.org/app/uploads/2016/08/SR_Summer_2016_Saarinen_article.pdf, 19.

2. Aline B. Saarinen, ed., *Eero Saarinen on His Work* (New Haven, CT: Yale University Press, 1962).

3. Cable from Aline Saarinen to Various, September 1, 1961, box 3, folder 14, Eero Saarinen Collection (MS 593), Manuscripts and Archives, Yale University Library.

4. Cable from Aline Saarinen to Various, September 1, 1961, box 3, folder 14, Eero Saarinen Collection (MS 593), Manuscripts and Archives, Yale University Library.

5. For a thorough accounting of this, see Alexandra Lange, "Tower Typewriter and Trademark: Architects, Designers and the Corporate Utopia, 1956–1964" (PhD diss., New York University, 2005).

6. Cable from Aline Saarinen to Various, September 1, 1961, box 3, folder 14, Eero Saarinen Collection (MS 593), Manuscripts and Archives, Yale University Library.

7. Cable from Aline Saarinen to Various, September 1, 1961, box 3, folder 14, Eero Saarinen Collection (MS 593), Manuscripts and Archives, Yale University Library.

8. Cable from Aline Saarinen to Oscar Niemeyer and Le Corbusier, September 1, 1961, box 3, folder 14, Eero Saarinen Collection (MS 593), Manuscripts and Archives, Yale University Library.

9. Cable from Aline Saarinen to Alvar Aalto, September 1, 1961, box 3, folder 14, Eero Saarinen Collection (MS 593), Manuscripts and Archives, Yale University Library.

10. Letter from Orville Dryfoos to Kevin Roche, September 5, 1961, box 1, folder 2, Eero Saarinen Collection (MS 593), Manuscripts and Archives, Yale University Library.

11. "Eero Saarinen, Architect, Dies; Renowned for His Versatility," *New York Times*, September 2, 1961.

12. Ibid.

13. Ibid.

14. Ibid.

15. Ibid.

16. Cable from Aline B. Louchheim, box 2, folder 16, Eero Saarinen Collection (MS 593), Manuscripts and Archives, Yale University Library.

17. Letter and document from Douglas Haskell, October 1961, box 1, folder 2, Eero Saarinen Collection (MS 593), Manuscripts and Archives, Yale University Library.

18. Ibid.

19. Letter from Silkey Smith to Eero Saarinen, September 3, 1961, box 5, folder 40, Eero Saarinen Collection (MS 593), Manuscripts and Archives, Yale University Library.

20. Robert Craig to Aline Saarinen, November 30, 1961, box 14, folder 227, Eero Saarinen Collection (MS 593), Manuscripts and Archives, Yale University Library.

21. Aline Saarinen to Robert W. Craig, December 12, 1961, box 14, folder 227, Eero Saarinen Collection (MS 593), Manuscripts and Archives, Yale University Library.

22. Ruth Glover to Aline Saarinen, box 14, folder 227, Eero Saarinen Collection (MS 593), Manuscripts and Archives, Yale University Library.

23. Aline Saarinen to Ruth Glover, December 12, 1961, box 2, folder 227, Eero Saarinen Collection (MS 593), Manuscripts and Archives, Yale University Library.

24. Aline Saarinen to Promocion Arquitectura, December 8, 1961, box 2, folder 227, Eero Saarinen Collection (MS 593), Manuscripts and Archives, Yale University Library.

25. Aline Saarinen to Dr. F. Schweighofer, December 8, 1961, box 2, folder 227, Eero Saarinen Collection (MS 593), Manuscripts and Archives, Yale University Library.

26. Aline Saarinen to Nick Thimmesch, October 12, 1961, box 2, folder 227, Eero Saarinen Collection (MS 593), Manuscripts and Archives, Yale University Library.

27. Aline Saarinen to Karl Bauer-Callwey, box 2, folder 227, Eero Saarinen Collection (MS 593), Manuscripts and Archives, Yale University Library.

28. G. E. Kidder Smith to Eero Saarinen, August 5, 1961; Aline Saarinen to G. E. Kidder Smith, October 28, 1961, box 2, folder 227, Eero Saarinen Collection (MS 593), Manuscripts and Archives, Yale University Library.

29. Aline Saarinen to Allan Temko, box 2, folder 227, Eero Saarinen Collection (MS 593), Manuscripts and Archives, Yale University Library.

30. Thomas H. Creighton to Aline Saarinen, July 26 ,1961, box 2, folder 227, Eero Saarinen Collection (MS 593), Manuscripts and Archives, Yale University Library.

31. Eero Saarinen to Aline Saarinen, box 14, folder 227, Eero Saarinen Collection (MS 593), Manuscripts and Archives, Yale University Library.

32. Aline Saarinen to Thomas Creighton, July 31, 1961, box 2, folder 227, Eero Saarinen Collection (MS 593), Manuscripts and Archives, Yale University Library.

33. Ibid.

34. Mrs. James Gould Cozzens to Aline Saarinen, January 25, 1962, box 14, folder 229, Eero Saarinen Collection (MS 593), Manuscripts and Archives, Yale University Library.

35. Saarinen, *Eero Saarinen on His Work*.

36. Ibid.

37. Ibid., 48.

38. Ibid.

39. Frank Getlein, "Plastic Form, Ennobling Shelter," *The American Scholar* 32, no. 1 (1962): 148.

40. Ibid.

41. Remy G. Saisselin, "Review," *The Journal of Aesthetics and Art Criticism* 23, no. 2 (1964): 286.

42. Ibid.

43. John Jacobus, "Review: Eero Saarinen on His Work," *Journal of the Society of Architectural Historians* 22 no. 4 (Dec. 1963): 237.

44. Ibid., 238.

45. Ibid.

46. Ibid.

47. Ibid.

48. Ibid.

49. Ibid.

50. Ibid.

51. Ibid.

Bibliography

Archival Sources, Institutional

Aline and Eero Saarinen Papers, 1906–1977. Archives of American Art, Smithsonian Institution.
Eero Saarinen Collection (MS 593). Manuscripts and Archives, Yale University Library.

Interviews

Gunnar Birkerts
Kevin Roche
Hal Louchheim
Beatriz Colomina
Margaretta M. Lovell
Andrew Shanken

Primary Sources

"Aline B. Saarinen Resigns." *New York Times*, December 1, 1959, 46.
"Aline Louchheim Wed to Architect." *New York Times*, February 9, 1954.
"Aline M. Bernstein Wed at Deal, NJ." *New York Times*, June 17, 1935.
Alioto, Daisy. "Elizabeth Gordon's International Style." Curbed, May 10, 2017. https://www.curbed.com/2017/5/10/15592658/elizabeth-gordon-house-beautiful-frank-lloyd-wright.
Alsop, Em Bowles Locker. "Aline Bernstein Saarinen, 1935." *Vassar Quarterly* 46, no. 5 (May 1, 1961), 27.
"The Art News Annual." *New York Times*, February 4, 1945.
"Art: The Maturing Modern." *Time*, July 2, 1956. http://content.time.com/time/subscriber/article/0,33009,891296,00.html.
Barnes, Jonathan. "The New Collegiate Architecture at Yale." *Architectural Record* 131 (April 1962): 128.
Bierut, Michael. "Rest in Peace, Herbert Muschamp." *Design Observer*, October 9, 2007. https://designobserver.com/feature/rest-in-peace-herbert-muschamp/6037.
"Bones for a 'Bird.'" *New York Times Magazine*, August 21, 1960, 296, 298.

"Buildings in the Round: MIT Completes Two of Today's Most Talked about Buildings: A Cylindrical Chapel and a Domed Auditorium." *Architectural Forum* 104 (Jan 1956): 116–21.

"College Buildings." *Architectural Record* 131 (April 1962): 129.

Collins, Glenn. "Edward A. Weeks, 91, an Editor of the Atlantic Monthly, Is Dead." *New York Times*, March 14, 1989.

"The Competition." Sydney Opera House Trust. https://www.sydneyoperahouse.com /our-story/sydney-opera-house-history/the-competition.html.

"The Concrete Bird Stands Free." *Architectural Forum* 113 (December 1960): 114–15.

"David S. Ingalls Hockey Rink, Yale University, New Haven, Conn." *Architectural Record* (August 1957): 187–89.

"Domestic Interiors." *Architectural Forum* 67 (October 1937): 239–368.

"Eero Saarinen, Architect, Dies; Renowned for His Versatility." *New York Times*, September 2, 1961.

Goldberger, Paul. "Green Monster." *The New Yorker*, May 2, 2005. http://www.newyorker .com/magazine/2005/05/02/green-monster.

——. "Shaping the Void," *The New Yorker*, September 12, 2011. https://www.newyorker .com/magazine/2011/09/12/shaping-the-void.

Hagberg, Eva. "Up Close and Personal." Master's thesis, University of California, Berkeley, 2014.

Harris, Ben. "Speaking of Sports." *Yale Daily News*, March 5, 1957, 6.

Haskell, Douglas. "Editor's Letter." *Architectural Forum* (July 1963).

Herring, Neil M. "Controversial 'Turtle' Crosses the Finish Line." *Yale Daily News*, October 15, 1958, 1.

Hudson, Edward. "Aviation: Unusual Terminal for Idlewild." *New York Times*, November 17, 1957, 405.

Huxtable, Ada Louise. "Four Model Buildings under Museum Review." *New York Times*, February 15, 1959, 369.

"I Want to Catch the Excitement of the Trip." *Architectural Forum* 117 (July 1962): 72–75.

"J. J. Louchheims Have a Son." *New York Times*, June 6, 1937.

Kaufmann, Edgar, Jr. "Inside Eero Saarinen's T.W.A. Building." *Contract Interiors* 121 (July 1962): 86–93.

Lange, Alexandra. "Tower Typewriter and Trademark: Architects, Designers and the Corporate Utopia, 1956–1964." PhD diss., New York University, 2005.

——. "Love & Architecture." *Design Observer*, October 22, 2009. https://designobserver .com/feature/love--architecture/11517.

Latson, Jennifer. "How Eero Saarinen Became One of America's Best-Known Architects." *Time*, August 20, 2015. https://time.com/3994195/eero-saarinen-105/.

Laubkeman, Hart. "Form Swallows Function." *Progressive Architecture* (May 1992): 108.

Laver, James. "The Stuffy Age We Yearn for." *New York Times Magazine*, August 21, 1960, 28.

Lewis, Flora. "Adenauer's Rx For Vitality." *New York Times Magazine*, August 21, 1960, 23.

Lo, Andrea. "How the 1960s and 70s Inspired Radical Architecture." CNN, https:// www.cnn.com/style/article/radical-architecture/index.html.

Louchheim, Aline B. "Using the Abstract: Hartford Show Reveals How Industrial Firm Puts a Collection to Work." *New York Times*, December 21, 1947, 169.

——. "To Do or Not to Do; Being an Open Letter to the Director of California's Modern Institute." *New York Times*, January 4, 1948.

——. "The Unseeing Eye; Gaps in Our Secondary School Teaching Make for Later Blindness to Art." *New York Times*, February 8, 1948.

——. "The Label 'Modern'; Boston Institute Statement on Change of Name Leads to New Controversy." *New York Times*, March 28, 1948.

——. "For a Modern Monument: An Audacious Design." *New York Times*, February 29, 1948, 8.

——. "Now Saarinen the Son." *New York Times*, April 26, 1953, 26.

McGuigan, Cathleen. "Aline Saarinen: '50s Wonder Woman." *Newsweek*, November 5, 2009.

McQuade, Walter. "Eero Saarinen: A Complete Architect." *Architectural Forum* 116 (April 1962): 102–19.

——. "Yale's Viking Vessel." *Architectural Forum* 109 (December 1958): 106–11.

"The Mike Wallace Interview, Edward Weeks." August 24, 1958. https://hrc.contentdm .oclc.org/digital/collection/p15878coll90/id/70.

Miller, Michelle. "AD Classics: Kresge Auditorium/Eero Saarinen and Associates." ArchDaily, April 3, 2014. http://www.archdaily.com/492176/ad-classics-kresge -auditorium-eero-saarinen-and-associates.

Moore, Rowan. "The Bilbao Effect: How Frank Gehry's Guggenheim Started a Global Craze." *The Guardian*, October 1, 2017. https://www.theguardian.com/artanddesign /2017/oct/01/bilbao-effect-frank-gehry-guggenheim-global-craze.

"National Geographic Magazine: 50 Years of Covers." *National Geographic*. https://www .nationalgeographic.com/magazine/national-geographic-magazine-50-years-of -covers/.

"New Terminal at Idlewild." *New York Times*, May 18, 1962, 33.

Noyes, Eliot. "Kresge Auditorium, Massachusetts Institute of Technology, Cambridge, 1955, Eero Saarinen and Associates, (tied for fifteenth)." *Architectural Record* (November 1956): 199–200.

Ouroussoff, Nicolai. "Herbert Muschamp, 59, Architecture Critic, Dies." *The New York Times*, October 3, 2007. https://www.nytimes.com/2007/10/03/arts/design /04muschamp.html.

Pergam, Albert S. "Construction Nearing Completion on Major Projects." *Yale Daily News*, September 11, 1958.

Rosenfield, Karissa. "How Santiago Calatrava Blurred the Lines between Architecture and Engineering to Make Buildings Move." ArchDaily, January 20, 2013. https:// www.archdaily.com/321403/how-santiago-calatrava-blurred-the-lines-between -architecture-and-engineering-to-make-buildings-move.

Rybczynski, Witold. "The Glossies: The Decline of Architecture Magazines." *Slate*, November 15, 2006. http://www.slate.com/articles/arts/architecture/2006/11/the _glossies.html.

"Saarinen Challenges the Rectangle: Designs a Domed Auditorium and a Cylindrical Chapel for MIT's Laboratory Campus." *Architectural Forum* 98 (January 1953): 126–33.

Saarinen, Eric. "Forgiving My Dad." *Scandinavian Review*, Summer 2016. http://www .amscan.org/app/uploads/2016/08/SR_Summer_2016_Saarinen_article.pdf.

Schumacher, Patrik. "Parametricism—A New Global Style for Architecture and Urban

Design." In "Digital Cities," special issue, *Architectural Design* 79, no. 4 (July/August 2009): 14–23.

Scott, N. Keith. "M.I.T. Auditorium, An English View." *Architectural Record* (July 1955): 138.

Shaw, Elizabeth. "Architecture and Imagery—Four New Buildings Press Release." Museum of Modern Art, February 11, 1959. http://www.moma.org/momaorg/shared /pdfs/docs/press_archives/2448/releases/MOMA_1959_0014.pdf?2010.

———. "Four New Buildings—Architecture and Imagery." Museum of Modern Art. https://www.moma.org/documents/moma_master-checklist_326140.pdf.

Sullivan, Scott. "Saarinen's Plans for Rink Approved by Corporation." *Yale Daily News*, December 17, 1956, 1.

Taylor-Hochberg, Amelia. "Eero Saarinen's Love Letters." Archinect, February 12, 2016. https://archinect.com/news/article/147962820/eero-saarinen-s-love-letters.

Trumbull, Robert. "It's 'Princess Time.'" *New York Times Magazine*, August 21, 1960, 60.

"T.W.A.'s Graceful Air Terminal." *Architectural Forum* (January 1958): 78–83.

"T.W.A. Restudying Terminal Design." *New York Times*, October 11, 1958, 40.

"T.W.A.'s Terminal Standing on Own." *New York Times*, December 8, 1960, 70.

"Walter McQuade, 72, Architecture Critic." *New York Times*, December 29, 1994. http:// www.nytimes.com/1994/12/29/obituaries/walter-mcquade-72-architecture-critic .html.

Weeks, Edward. "The Opal on the Charles." *Architectural Record* 118 (July 1955): 131–37.

Wisniewski, Katherine. "92 Years of Architecture through *Time* Magazine Covers." Curbed, February 4, 2015. http://www.curbed.com/2015/2/4/9996152/time -magazine-architect-covers.

Whitman, Alden. "Aline Saarinen, Art Critic, Dies at 58." *New York Times*, July 15, 1972.

Xie, Jenny. "Eero Saarinen's Love Letters to His Wife Are Utterly Adorable." Curbed, February 13, 2015. https://www.curbed.com/2015/2/13/9992378/valentines-day-eero -saarinen.

Secondary Sources

Adams, Annmarie. "Women and the Making of the Modern House." *Journal of the Society of Architectural Historians* 57, no. 4 (December 1998): 474–76.

Albrecht, Donald and Eeva-Liisa Pelkonen, eds. *Eero Saarinen: Shaping the Future*. New Haven, CT: Yale University Press, 2006.

Augst, Thomas. *The Clerk's Tale: Young Men and Moral Life in Nineteenth-Century America*. Chicago: University of Chicago Press, 2003.

Barthes, Roland. "From Work to Text." trans. Stephen Heath, 1971, http://faculty .georgetown.edu/irvinem/theory/Barthes-FromWorktoText.html.

Bergdoll, Barry. "Félix Duban, Early Photography, Architecture, and the Circulation of Images." *The Built Surface* 2 (2002): 13–25.

Bernays, Edward L. "Recent Trends in Public Relations Activities." *The Public Opinion Quarterly* 1, no. 1 (January 1937): 147–51.

Borden, Iain. "Imaging Architecture: The Uses of Photography in the Practice of Architectural History." *Journal of Architecture* 12, no. 1 (2007): 57–77.

Cayer, Aaron and Peggy Deamer, Sben Korsh, Eric Peterson, and Manuel Shvartzberg, eds. *Asymmetric Labors: The Economy of Architecture in Theory and Practice*. Brooklyn, NY: The Architecture Lobby, 2016.

Chafe, William H. *The American Woman*. New York: Oxford University Press, 1972.

Chatman, Seymour Benjamin. *Story and Discourse*. Ithaca, NY: Cornell University Press, 1980.

Chattopadhyay, Swati. "Architectural Representations, Changing Technologies, and Conceptual Extensions." *Journal of the Society of Architectural Historians* 71, no. 3 (September 2012): 270–72.

Colomina, Beatriz. *Privacy and Publicity*. Cambridge, MA: MIT Press, 1994.

———. "Collaborations: The Private Life of Modern Architecture." *Journal of the Society of Architectural Historians* 58, no. 3 (September 1999): 462–71.

Crysler, C. Greig. *Writing Spaces: Discourses of Architecture, Urbanism, and the Built Environment*. New York: Routledge, 2003.

Cuff, Dana. *Architecture: The Story of Practice*. Cambridge, MA: MIT Press, 1991.

Cutlip, Scott. *The Unseen Power: Public Relations: A History*. New York: Routledge, 1994.

Deamer, Peggy. *Architecture and Capitalism: 1845 to the Present*. New York: Routledge, 2013.

DeLong, David G. and Ford Peatross, eds. *Eero Saarinen: Buildings from the Balthazar Korab Archive*. New York: W. W. Norton, 2008.

Derrida, Jacques and Eisenman, Peter. *Chora L Works*. New York: Monacelli Press, 1997.

Dreller, Sarah. *"Architectural Forum, 1932–64*: A Time Inc. Experiment in American Architecture and Journalism." PhD diss., University of Illinois at Chicago, 2015.

Frederickson, Kristen and Sarah E. Webb, eds. *Singular Women: Writing the Artist*. Berkeley: University of California Press, 2003.

Friedman, Alice T. *Women and the Making of the Modern House*. New York: Harry N. Abrams, 1998.

———. "Eero Saarinen: Modern Architecture for the American Century." *Places Journal*, June 2010. https://placesjournal.org/article/modern-architecture-for-the-american -century/.

Friedman, Roger and Harold Zellman. *The Fellowship*. New York: Regan, 2006.

Getlein, Frank. "Plastic Form, Ennobling Shelter." *The American Scholar* 32, no. 1 (1962): 148–50.

Giedion, Siegfried. *Space, Time, and Architecture*. Cambridge, MA: MIT Press, 1941.

Goffman, Erving. *The Presentation of Self in Everyday Life*. New York: Anchor Books, 1959.

Gordon, Alastair. *Naked Airport; A Cultural History of the World's Most Revolutionary Structure*. New York: Metropolitan Books, 2004.

Gutman, Robert. *Architectural Practice: A Critical View*. New York: Princeton Architectural Press, 1988.

Hagberg, Eva. *Dark Nostalgia*. New York: Monacelli Press, 2009.

———. "Johnson and Oil!" *Art Lies* 68 (Spring/Summer 2011).

Hitchcock, Henry-Russell and Philip Johnson. *The International Style: Architecture since 1922*. New York: W. W. Norton, 1932.

Hunting, Mary Anne. "Edward Durell Stone: Perception and Criticism." PhD diss., The City University of New York, 2007.

Jacobus, John, "Review: Eero Saarinen on His Work." *Journal of the Society of Architectural Historians* 22, no. 4 (December 1963): 237–39.

Kanekar, Aarati. *Architecture's Pretexts*. New York: Routledge, 2015.

Kelleher, Katy. "The Forgotten Story of Mrs Bauhaus." *Artsy*, September 7, 2018. https://www.artsy.net/article/artsy-editorial-forgotten-story-mrs-bauhaus.

Knight, Richard. *Saarinen's Quest: A Memoir*. San Francisco: William Stout, 2008.

Koolhaas, Rem, Bruce Mau and Hans Werlemann, eds. *S,M,L,XL*. New York: Monacelli Press, 1997.

Lamme, Margot Opdyck and Karen Miller Russell. "Removing the Spin: Toward a New Theory of Public Relations History." *Journalism & Mass Communication Monographs* 11, no. 4 (December 2009): 283.

L'Etang, Jacquie and Magda Pieczka. *Public Relations: Critical Debates and Contemporary Practice*. New York: Routledge, 2006.

Levine, Neil. "The Template of Photography in Nineteenth-Century Architectural Representation." *Journal of the Society of Architectural Historians* 71, no. 3 (September 2012): 306–31.

Lloyd Wright, Olgivanna. *Frank Lloyd Wright: His Life, His Work, His Words*. New York: Horizon Press, 1966.

Loeffler, Jane. *The Architecture of Diplomacy*. New York: Princeton Architectural Press, 1998.

McCarthy, Molly A. *The Accidental Diarist: A History of the Daily Planner in America*. Chicago: University of Chicago Press, 2013.

McGuigan, Cathleen. "Women of the Bauhaus: Aline Saarinen." *Architectural Record*, June 2019.

Merkel, Jayne. *Eero Saarinen*. New York: Phaidon, 2005.

Meyerowitz, Joanne. *Not June Cleaver: Women and Gender in Postwar America, 1945–1960*. Philadelphia: Temple University Press, 1994.

Markus, Thomas A. and Deborah Cameron. *The Words between the Spaces*. New York: Routledge, 2002.

Nesbit, Molly. "What Was an Author?" in "Everyday Life," *Yale French Studies*, no. 73 (1987): 229–35.

Nobel, Philip. *Sixteen Acres: Architecture and the Outrageous Struggle for the Future of Ground Zero*. New York: Metropolitan Books, 2005.

Pevsner, Nikolaus. *Pioneers of the Modern Movement*. London: Faber & Faber, 1936.

Roman, Antonio. *Eero Saarinen: An Architecture of Multiplicity*. New York: Princeton Architectural Press, 2003.

———. *Eero Saarinen: Objects and Furniture Design*. Madrid: Ediciones Poligrafa, 2013.

Rosa, Joseph. *A Constructed View: The Architectural Photography of Julius Shulman*. New York: Rizzoli, 1994.

Roubert, Paul-Louis. *L'Image sans qualités: Les Beaux-Arts et la critique à l'épreuve de la photographie, 1839–1859*. Paris: Monum/Editions du patrimoine, 2006.

Saarinen, Aline B., ed. *Eero Saarinen: On His Work*. New Haven, CT: Yale University Press, 1962.

Saisselin, Remy G. "Review." *The Journal of Aesthetics and Art Criticism* 23, no. 2 (1964): 286.

Saunders, William, ed., *Reflections on Architectural Practice in the Nineties*. New York: Princeton Architectural Press, 1998.

Saxon, Wolfgang. "Olgivanna Lloyd Wright, Wife of the Architect, Is Dead at 85." *New York Times*, March 2, 1985, 29.

Schwarzer, Mitchell. "History and Theory in Architectural Periodicals: Assembling Oppositions." *Journal of the Society of Architectural Historians* 58, no. 3 (September 1999): 342–48.

Serraino, Pierluigi. *Eero Saarinen, 1910–1961: A Structural Expressionist*. New York: Taschen, 2007.

Sert, Josep Lluis, Fernand Léger, and Siegfried Giedion. "Nine Points on Monumentality." In *Architecture Culture 1943–1968*. Edited by Joan Ockman and Edward Eigen, 29–30. New York: Rizzoli, 1993.

Shanken, Andrew. *194X: Architecture, Planning, and Consumer Culture on the American Home Front*. Minneapolis: University of Minnesota Press, 2009.

———. "Breaking the Taboo: Architects and Advertising in Depression and War." *Journal of the Society of Architectural Historians* 69, no. 3 (September 2010): 406–29.

Stevens, Garry. *The Favored Circle: The Social Foundations of Architectural Distinction*. Cambridge, MA: MIT Press, 1998.

Stratigakos, Despina. *Where Are the Women Architects?* Princeton, NJ: Princeton University Press, 2016.

Urbach, Henry. "Closets, Clothes, Disclosure." *Assemblage* 30 (August 1996): 62–73.

Wright, Frank Lloyd. *An Autobiography*. London: Longman's, Green, 1932.

Zimmerman, Claire. *Photographic Architecture in the Twentieth Century*. Minneapolis: University of Minnesota Press, 2014.

Index

Credits

Photo Credits

© 1948 The New York Times Company. All rights reserved. Used under license (fig. 3)

© 1953, The New York Times Company. All rights reserved. Used under license (fig. 11)

© 1956 TIME USA LLC. All rights reserved. Used under license (fig. 23)

© 1957, The New York Times Company. All rights reserved. Used under license (fig. 25)

© 1960, The New York Times Company. All rights reserved. Used under license (figs. 27, 29)

Aline and Eero Saarinen Papers, 1906–1977, Archives of American Art, Smithsonian Institution (figs. 1, 2, 12, 13, 24, 33–35)

Aline and Eero Saarinen Papers, 1906–1977, Archives of American Art, Smithsonian Institution. Reproduced with permission from Hal Louchheim (fig. 14)

Eero and Aline Saarinen Papers, 1906–1977, Archives of American Art, Smithsonian Institution (figs. 5–7)

Eero and Aline Saarinen Papers, 1906–1977, Archives of American Art, Smithsonian Institution. Reproduced with permission from Hal Louchheim (figs. 8–10)

© Ezra Stoller/Esto (figs. 15–19, 28, 30–32)

© Wayne Andrews/ESTO (figs. 4, 20–22, 26)

Text Credits

Letter from Robert Damora to Eero Saarinen reproduced with the permission of Matt Damora.

Letters from Aline B. Louchheim Saarinen to Eero Saarinen reproduced with the permission of Hal and Donald Louchheim.

Letters from Cranston Jones to Aline Saarinen reproduced with the permission of Abigail Jones.

Letters from James A. Hornbeck to Aline Saarinen reproduced with the permission of Geoffrey Hornbeck.

New York Times excerpts reproduced with the permission of the New York Times.

Time excerpts reproduced with the permission of TIME LLC.

CPSIA information can be obtained
at www.ICGtesting.com
Printed in the USA
JSHW032022220322
24150JS00002B/104